Soups of Italy

Soups of Italy

Cooking over 130 Soups
the Italian Way

Norma Wasserman-Miller

Illustrations by the author

William Morrow and Company, Inc. / New York

for Arthur and Tanya

Copyright © 1998 by Norma Wasserman-Miller
Illustrations copyright ©1998 by Norma Wasserman-Miller

It is the policy of William Morrow and Company, Inc., and its imprints and affiliates, recognizing the importance of preserving what has been written, to print the books we publish on acid-free paper, and we exert our best efforts to that end.

Library of Congress Cataloging-in-Publication Data

Wasserman-Miller, Norma.
Soups of Italy : cooking over 130 soups the Italian way/
Norma Wasserman-Miller.
        p.   cm.
Includes index.
ISBN 0-688-15031-4
1. Soups—Italy. 2. Cookery, Italian. I. Title.
TX757.W36   1998
641.8'13'0945—dc21   97-28669
                                                CIP

Printed in the United States of America

First Edition

1   2   3   4   5   6   7   8   9   10

BOOK DESIGN BY RICHARD ORIOLO
www.williammorrow.com

Foreword

*P*erhaps it's all in a name. My affinity for Italy must have started at birth when my father named me after his favorite Bellini opera, *Norma.* But nothing could have prepared me for my first visit to Italy eighteen years later while I was a painting student at Boston University. From the subtle atmospheric tones of Venice to the vibrant primary colors of the south, the whole of Italy seemed like one big work of art to me. The impressions were lasting ones. Little did I realize at the time that less than ten years later I would be opening my first business, Formaggio, a cheese and sandwich shop in Harvard Square modeled after my collective memory of the Italian *salumeria* and *caffè*.

A few years later, in 1978, when I opened Formaggio Kitchen, Italian cooking was synonymous with southern Italy. This was interpreted as *alla napoletana,* which translated in culinary terms as a thick tomato sauce on everything—pizza, spaghetti, eggplant, veal—nothing was spared the ubiquitous tomato. All of this was to change in the eighties with the "discovery" of northern Italy. It seemed as if overnight everything *haute couture* and *haute cuisine* became northern Italian. I too was swept away and made my second home in Verona. Living there became the inspiration for my first book, *Risotto,* the dish that epitomizes northern Italian cooking, where tomatoes are used sparingly—if at all.

Not surprisingly, this growing appreciation of Italian cuisine brought a new-found interest in Italian products. Formaggio Kitchen became a mecca for the finest Italian cheeses, pasta, meats, and olive oils. Even my customers' culinary lexicon changed. Parmesan became *parmigiano-reggiano*, olive oil became *extra vergine,* dried mushrooms became *porcini*, and rice became *arborio*. The pesto was from Genoa, the *aceto balsamico* from Modena, and the best *olio d'oliva* came from Lucca. And with these "new" riches from the Old World, it began to look as though Italy did indeed have more than just a north and a south.

Today, cooking has come to embody more than just styles of cuisine: eating healthfully has come to the forefront. Not surprisingly, the low-cholesterol Mediterranean diet, with its emphasis on vegetables, fish, legumes, and olive oil has become immensely popular. At last the sun-drenched cooking of southern Italy has been given the respect it deserves— tomatoes have become *pomodori*.

From the northernmost to the southernmost region, soup is the dish that embraces the whole of Italy. There is no special cuisine when it comes to preparing soup, only good basic ingredients prepared simply and healthfully. Is it not the time for soup to become *minestra* or *zuppa*? Perhaps it *is* all in a name. . . .

Acknowledgments

The wish to write a book on Italian soups started years ago with my doing what I love to do most: spending time in Italy enjoying its food and people. That was the fun part. The work of giving *Soups of Italy* its final form is a testament to the generosity, in spirit and time, of the many who helped me along the way.

I thank my agent and friend, Kay McCauley, and Kathleen Hackett, whose enthusiasm saw this book through its initial stages. My gratitude to designer Richard Oriolo and to my fine project editor, Ann Cahn. I give special thanks to my editor, Jennifer Kaye, for both her invaluable contribution in giving this book its final character and for being a joy to work with.

There were so many wonderful chefs and cooking instructors, but the contributions of a few permeate this book. In particular, I thank Giampiero Gemignani, and his mother, Edema, who allowed me to practically move into their kitchen at Solferino. Giampiero graciously shared his seemingly inexhaustible knowledge of cooking. Few top restaurants in Italy respect soups as much as Cibreo in Florence, where Fabio Picchi shared his extraordinary soup-making tips. I also thank Fulvia Sesani, a master teacher of northern Italian cooking.

As naturally helpful and welcoming as Italians are, my Italian friends not only opened their homes to me but made introductions to some wonderful chefs that I might otherwise not have met. In particular, I thank Marcello and Antonia Pera, who made Lucca feel like my second home. And *grazie* to Marco Mancinelli, Franco Crispino, Valentina Olivastri, and Valeria del Riccio, who for a few wonderful months assisted me in so many ways. And for their astute comments, I thank Kitty Adam, Lyndsey Posner, and Ellen Reid.

Lastly and mostly to my dear husband, Arthur, who in his own words was "zuppaman."

Contents

Introduzione

A soup by any other name is a zuppa, minestra, brodo, or pancotto. So vast is the world of Italian soups that these are just a few of the names used for this one basic dish. Along with pasta and risotto, soups are the major contribution to the primo piatto, the first course of an Italian meal. When we think of an Italian soup, it is most likely a hearty bowl of minestrone that springs to mind—and for good reason. With its colorful mosaic of vegetables, minestrone embodies everything a soup should be—flavorful, nutritious, and satisfying; however, to think of an Italian soup as only minestrone would be like thinking of rice as just risotto and pasta as merely spaghetti.

From the delicate broth soups that prepare the palate for the course to follow to the hearty soups that are meals in themselves, soups in Italy are considered an essential part of at least one and often two meals of the day. Prepared from almost every type of ingredient, this extraordinary range of soups is as numerous and varied as the multitude of pasta and risotto dishes we have come to know, yet they have not been given nearly the same attention. How is it that we have overlooked this oldest and most basic of dishes, the one that embraces the heart and soul of Italian cooking with its honest simplicity and richness of tradition—the soups of Italy?

When I returned to the chefs who had been so generous in their help with my first book, *Risotto,* and told them of my interest in soups, I soon discovered, with just a few notable exceptions, that great Italian chefs do not show off their culinary skills by making a soup. The tradition of soup cookery is largely maintained by the unpretentious cooking of the family-owned *trattoria* or *osteria.* One noted chef lamented that while his clientele wanted caviar, for him the real caviar are the simple beans that go into a good soup.

The other common reaction was one of considerable nostalgia. To learn about the soups of Italy is to learn about a diversity of culinary styles, formed by Italy's history, geography, agricultural production, and local traditions. Soups in Italy are uniquely regional dishes. Order a *pasta e fagioli* in the Veneto and a savory, dense pasta and bean soup will be set before you; order a *pasta e fagioli* in Campania and a delicate aromatic soup will arrive. You may be able to find a similar *risotto alla milanese* throughout Italy, but you will need to go to Tuscany for your *pappa al pomodoro,* Liguria for your *burrida,* and Venice for your *risi e bisi.*

Besides the joy of exploring the wide range of Italy's soups, there was another strong motivation I had in writing this book. Like so many, I have become increasingly mindful of not only the intrinsic nutritious properties of our food, but how we cook it. For most of us this means eating less meat, less dairy, fewer refined foods, and less fat. We now place a far greater emphasis on vegetables, grains, and legumes—the very core of most Italian soups. The slow simmer of a soup retains a much higher degree of vitamins than frying, roasting, or boiling those same ingredients. In Italian soup cookery, meat and cheese are used almost entirely as flavorings, and fats are minimal. Even what is referred to as creamed soups are usually pureed, without the addition of cream.

As you discover the pleasures of preparing Italian soups, the ingredients in your kitchen will take on a new complexion. That extra leek, those few carrots, the odd bit of rice or pasta, and the unused greens will become the inspiration for assembling a great Italian soup. After becoming familiar with how easy it is to make *pancotto,* your stale bread will become a welcome leftover. Your vegetable soup may be a light *minestra di verdura* one day; with the simple addition of beans and pasta it could easily become the next day's main-course *minestrone.* When trying to come up with an idea for a main dish, a substantial fish, legume, or vegetable soup will likely come to mind.

We think that making a soup involves many hours in the kitchen, yet the actual preparation time for most recipes is under thirty minutes. Cooking times can vary from minutes to hours, but even the longest-cooking soup requires only an occasional check of the temperature. The vast majority of Italian soups are not only easy to prepare, but can also be made ahead of time, some tasting even better when allowed to sit. Almost every time I prepare a soup, I end up spending less time in the kitchen—not more.

Above all else, soup remains *una cucina di casa,* "a cuisine of the home." Indeed, it was the homes and kitchens of so many gracious Italian friends and professional cooks that inspired the recipes and techniques for this book. The numerous recipes I came across had a notable lack of measurements and a heavy reliance on the words *in stagione,* "in season." Perhaps this is what I love most about Italian soup cookery—a reliance on simple, good ingredients along with the inventiveness to effortlessly turn them into flavorful soups with character and individuality.

Using Soups of Italy

There is no "right" way of making any particular soup, but there are "right" methods that can be applied to all soups. For this reason, the preparation techniques are used as the basis for all the recipes. The ingredients and directions are organized into distinct groupings: *battuto, sapori, brodo*, and *condimenti*. The terms and techniques are described on pages 12–17.

Ingredients The ingredients are listed by the order they are added. The exceptions are those ingredients that need prior preparation, such as dried legumes or dried porcini mushrooms, which are listed first.

Servings Most recipes are for 4 servings. These yield approximately 5 to 6 cups and provide first-course servings for 4 or a possible main course for 2 to 3. Soups that call for many ingredients and could easily be served as a main dish are written for larger quantities. These recipes have two serving numbers, such as 4 to 6 or 6 to 8. The first number indicates servings appropriate for a main course; the second, for first-course servings.

Measurements Many ingredients have two measurements: volume and weight. These are never exact; vegetables may be cut more or less finely, herbs may be packed tightly or loosely. Fortunately, preparing a soup does not require great accuracy.

   Oil If you are increasing a recipe, the cooking fat does not have to increase in proportion to the other ingredients. The size of your pan may alter the amount.

   Salt When salt is added at the beginning of a recipe, rather than say "to taste," I give an approximate amount. As soup cooks its liquid reduces and salt gains in intensity. The amounts given are low by Italian standards; you may want to add more as the soup cooks.

Adapting for a Vegetarian Diet A small addition of pancetta or prosciutto is considered an essential flavor in the preparation of many Italian soups. Increasing some of the other flavorings or substituting vegetable broth for water will compensate.

La Storia

The History

A *dish born of little money and much imagination, soup represents the most basic food preparation of* la cucina povera, *"the poor kitchen." The key tool of the peasant's cooking was a pot suspended by a chain over the fire. Water was the magic ingredient that turned staples such as bread, grains, eggs, vegetables, and herbs into countless soups. For hundreds of years, this simple peasant-based cooking was to exist side by side with the sumptuous* cucina nobile, *"cuisine of nobility."*

In perhaps the oldest cookbook, De Re Coquinaria, *Marco Apicio, in his writings which date back to* A.D. 30, *described the Roman dish known as* polus. *Based on the earliest grains and legumes, such as* farro, *chickpeas, and fava beans, this por-*

ridgelike soup was enriched with raw onions, garlic, lard, cabbage or other leafy greens; when circumstances permitted, scraps from the noble dining table or pantry were added. This was certainly not a dish eaten by the likes of Apicio, a patrician, who, legend has it, upon realizing his fortune had so dwindled chose to kill himself rather than relinquish his life of luxury. Apocryphal or not, the fact that this story exists illustrates the abyss that existed between rich and poor.

During the Middle Ages, theories of medicine appeared in treatises proclaiming that refined food was intended only for those of wealth and power, while the poor should eat food more appropriate to their hard labor. Onion, cabbages, and other vegetables taken from the soil were left to the peasants; fruit plucked from trees was thought better suited to the ethereal life of the aristocrat. Giacomo Albini, a physician to the house of Savoy, not only predicted illness for those not eating food according to their social rank, but he specifically stated that the rich should avoid heavy soups!

The word *zuppa* is thought to derive from the Gothic *suppa,* which means "a slice of bread, soaking." The etymology of this term conjures up medieval times when slices of bread functioned as plates, soaking up the juices of the pieces of meat and other foods placed on top. When combined with garlic and cooked in water, they became the first humble soups. Not surprisingly, Italy's earliest types of soups came to be known as *acquacotta* (cooked water) and *pancotto* (cooked bread). These primitive soups were added to the peasant's repertoire of boiled beans and grains. For centuries, along with polentas and porridges, they were to remain the dietary staple of the common people.

It wasn't until after the discovery of America that soups took on the wider interpretation that we have come to associate with Italian cooking. With the introduction of potatoes, corn, zucchini, pumpkins, tomatoes, sweet peppers, and *fagioli* (kidney beans), soups such as *minestrone* began to make an appearance. Although the soups might have become enriched, the economic plight of the poor remained unchanged. The name *minestrone* derives from *minestra,* recalling a time when the clergy was called upon to administer—*ministrare*—soup from vast cauldrons to the poor.

The most important cookery book of the seventeenth century is *L'Arte del cucinare (The Art of Cooking),* written by Bartolomeo Stefani, chef to the Gonzaga court of Mantua. Its most historically significant chapter is considered to be the three pages he dedicated to *ricette per vitto ordinario,* "recipes for ordinary life." Stefani takes as an example two ordinary families, one of eight people, the other of six. Not only does he indicate the daily menu but he offers a shopping list of what to buy and how much it will cost. Soups made with artichokes, fennel, fruit, and almonds are described, and a *minestra di pasta in brodo* (pasta in broth) is recommended for the start of the afternoon meal. For the first time, cooking for the average family was recognized.

In 1790, a veritable encyclopedia on gastronomy, *L'Apicio moderno (The Modern Apicio),* was published in Rome. Its author, Francesco Leonardi, was a key figure in Italian culinary history and chef to such notables as Louis XV and Catherine II. The first of his six volumes is devoted to *zuppe e minestre,* replete with recipes he collected throughout Europe. He describes a *zuppa alla genovese,* a soup from Genoa prepared with green vegetables, prosciutto, and meat broth. When it's ready to be served, whisked fresh eggs are added to give it the consistency of *stracciatella,* the name of the popular Roman soup made from broth and eggs. When Leonardi described this refined minestrone as *un piatto da offrire a dei principi,* "a dish fit for princes," he elevated the humble soup to new heights. He also describes a *zuppa di riso alla veneziana,* a Venetian soup described as rice cooked in a broth made from *cappone* (capon) and flavored with Parmesan. It shares much in common with the rice soups and *risotti* so fundamental to the present-day cooking of northern Italy.

By the nineteenth century the transition from the dual cuisine of the rich and poor to a single popular cuisine was becoming well established. In 1854, Giovanni Vialardi, noted chef of Vittorio Emanuele II, coined the term *cucina borghese,* "cooking of the middle class," which he also refers to as *alla cittadina,* "in the style of the town." Perhaps not by chance, this progression to a classless cooking coincided with the unification of Italy in 1861. When we remember that up until this time Italy was a loose configuration of lands held together mostly by geography, we can begin to understand the rich variety of Italian soups. In name Italy may have politically become one country, but to this day it remains an intensely regional land with distinct traditions and preferences.

In 1891, in what is considered Italy's most definitive book on cooking, *La Scienza in cucina e l'arte di mangiar bene* (*Science in the Kitchen and the Art of Eating Well*), Pellegrino Artusi brings together the cooking and culture of the aristocrat and the common man. Cooking was no longer distinguished by social class, but by good taste and common sense for living wisely and healthfully. Soups finally take their rightful place as an important part of the Italian meal. Even today, this remains one of the most widely read cookbooks in Italy.

With Italy's growing wealth, mass production of foods, dietary concerns, and cookbooks, soups have been widely adapted and in many cases refined. Nevertheless, Italians are still a strongly regional people who have great respect for their past. To this day, soups still retain the essential character of *la cucina povera,* evoking Italy's diverse cultural heritage from centuries ago.

Types of Soup

The very same vegetables prepared as a light *minestra* can become a hearty *zuppa* simply by ladling it over slices of bread. Increase the amount of bread and break it into pieces, which turns your soup into *pancotto*. Puree those same vegetables and transform them into a delicate *crema,* or add beans and pasta for a substantial *minestrone*.

What follows are the names Italians most often use to describe their soups. As with most rules, there are exceptions and some of Italy's best-known soups, such as *pasta e fagioli* and *ribollita,* omit these names altogether.

Minestra   Ranging from the most delicate *minestra in brodo* (broth soups) to the densest bean and grain soups, *minestre* almost always contain pasta or rice.

Zuppa   These rustic *zuppe* are served with bread instead of pasta or rice. Either accompanied by or ladled over slices of stale country bread, these rustic soups are the most regional of the Italian soups.

Pancotto   True to its name, "cooked bread" is the main ingredient of *pancotti*. Their other ingredients are almost exclusively vegetarian, with the simple addition of water. Soups referred to as *acquacotta* are included in this humble group of bread soups.

Minestrone   These are the "big soups," both in their ingredients and cooking times. Composed of a rich variety of vegetables, *minestroni* are fortified with legumes, grains, pasta, or rice.

Crema   These smooth, mellow soups are most akin to our "cream of" soups; however, cream is seldom used. Instead their creamy texture is usually the result of having been pureed—*passato*, the other name used to describe them.

Il Fondamenti

The Essentials

Preparing Soups the Italian Way

*I*n Florence, I had the pleasure of accompanying Fabio Picchi for his morning round of shopping for his restaurant, Cibreo. Much to our delight, fresh porcini had just started to make their much anticipated appearance in the markets. To my novice eye, they all looked wonderful. Fabio, with the care of a doctor examining a patient, picked up each and every mushroom, explaining that for his soup he wanted not the most beautiful ones, but those that had the most flavor. Their texture, smell, and color told him what he needed to know.

The preparation always starts with the ingredients, and in Italy this invariably means creating a meal around the best available products. Whether it's the glossy skinned zucchini or the tender purple artichokes on display at the market, or simply going to the pantry for dried borlotti beans or a can of San Marzano tomatoes, the ingredients come first.

Looking is very much part of the Italian culture. Whether it's a beautiful building, an elegant shop front, a person's face, or the colorful display of fruit and produce, rarely do you see an Italian walk by without his head turning in some direction of interest. Approached this way, food shopping can become a joyful experience. In addition to buying the ingredients you need, buy the ingredients that give you pleasure. Then use your cookbook as a way of turning these naturally good products into delicious and healthy soups.

If I could convey one thing about preparing Italian soups, it would be the flexibility and fluidity. Rarely are all the ingredients prepped and then added. There is a rhythm of getting one ingredient ready, starting to cook it, then preparing the next and the next. One flavor is deepening as another is being readied. You can extend or interrupt the cooking to suit your own timing simply by monitoring the heat.

Even though this cookbook gives "exact" measurements, these should merely be taken as one of many ways of doing a recipe. As you cook, your taste will become your guide. And if you contend that you are not a cook, what you are really saying is that you haven't had enough experience cooking. As you try more of these recipes, don't be surprised when in time you put your measuring spoons away and go by your instincts and creativity. This is what the Italian way of cooking is all about.

Elementi/Elements: *Battuto, Sapori, Brodo,* and *Condimenti*

Italians have a love and respect for the food they prepare. Their cooking techniques are not complicated. On the contrary, it is their very simplicity that brings the most out of every ingredient. The following terms describe the basic elements used in the preparation of all Italian soups.

Battuto The *battuto* is an essential flavoring for almost every soup. Deriving from the verb *battere,* which means "to strike," the *battuto* is an aromatic combination of ingredients that are finely chopped. Known as *odori* (scents), the most common ingredients are: onions, carrots, celery, garlic, and parsley, often with the addition of pancetta or prosciutto.

    The *battuto* is either added *a crudo* (raw) or, more commonly, sautéed with a little olive oil, becoming a *soffritto* (sautéed). The sautéed *battuto* often becomes the base for flavoring the other ingredients.

Sapori From the verb *insaporire,* "to make tasty," *sapori* are the main ingredients that give the soup its dominant taste and character. Depending on the recipe, the *sapori* can be sautéed with the *battuto—col soffritto*—before being combined with the broth or can added directly to the broth raw—*a crudo.*

Brodo The liquid component of all soups is the *brodo.* It can be the simple addition of water that becomes infused with the flavors of the other ingredients, or it can be a prepared broth made from meat, vegetables, or fish. When the broth is not a key element, *dadi* (stock cubes) can usually be substituted. Also included in this category are those ingredients that are cooked with the water to create a broth for the other ingredients.

Condimenti The *condimenti* are the elements, such as pasta or rice, that are added as the last ingredients to the soup. Garnishes and accompaniments also fall into this category. These include fresh herbs, *crostini* (croutons), slices of bread, freshly grated cheese, or a fine olive oil.

Tecnice/Techniques

Making a soup can basically be divided into two parts: preparing its ingredients and cooking them. After having washed, peeled, or trimmed your ingredients, preparation involves how to cut them. As for cooking, once you have chosen the right pot, cooking with the correct heat becomes the basis for achieving the best results.

This section devotes a major portion to describing the preparation and cooking of the *battuto*. Not only does the *battuto* set the stage for your soup, but you can prepare the other ingredients as the *battuto* is sautéing. This gives you the double reward of a shorter cooking time along with an even more flavorful soup.

Chopping and Cutting The size and shape of your ingredients not only determine their final appearance and texture but how quickly they cook. The following terms are used in this book:

> *minced* —very finely chopped
> *finely chopped* —a slightly larger texture than a minced *battuto*
> *coarsely chopped* —chopped random shapes, about ¼ to ½ inch
> *diced* —relatively uniform pieces, about ⅓ to ¼ inch
> *roughly chopped* —cut into random larger pieces

Battuto The ingredients of a *battuto* are minced or finely chopped in order for its flavors to disperse quickly. When there are several ingredients, it is quickest and easiest to chop them in a food processor. When there are only one or two ingredients, traditional chopping methods using a knife or *mezzaluna* are more effective.

Using a food processor Chopping several ingredients in a food processor usually works better than doing one at a time. The ingredients that are listed as "minced together" can all be added together and pulsed until the desired texture is reached. Before adding, the ingredients should be cut into pieces small enough to be broken down without catching on the blade; this holds true particularly for pancetta or prosciutto. Onions should be quartered, carrots and celery cut into short strips, and meat cut into small pieces.

Using a knife To chop vegetables and herbs finely you will need a heavy, well-sharpened chef's knife. Hold the tip of the knife down with one hand to keep the knife in one spot and, with your other hand on the handle, move the blade backward and forward over the ingredients with quick chopping movements. For the greatest efficiency, don't lift the knife too high from the cutting board.

Using a mezzaluna Hold the handles gently. Without lifting the blade from the chopping board, rock it back and forth from the extreme right to left while gradually moving it forward, then reverse the direction. Gather the scattered ingredients together before starting again and repeat the process until the right texture is reached.

Sapori Depending on the individual recipe, these main ingredients may be cut in a variety of ways. The more finely an ingredient is cut, the more quickly it will cook and its flavor blend into the soup; the larger it's cut, the more noticeable its flavor and texture. If you intend to puree the soup, only the size and not the shape matters. Vegetables used to thicken the soup, such as potatoes, should be chopped small enough to ensure they fully break down.

Using a knife To slice or chop hard vegetables, such as carrots, you will need a plain sharp knife, with a blade no smaller than 4 inches. For softer vegetables, such as leafy greens, tomatoes, or onions, a finely serrated knife is easier than a plain knife.

Using a food processor A food processor can be used for almost all ingredients. To maintain a uniform size it is best to add the individual elements in small batches. To better control their size, using short pulses works best. For slicing ingredients, such as mushrooms or onions, the thinnest slicing blade (2mm) will perform this task quickly. For harder vegetables, depending on the recipe, either the 2mm or the 4mm can be used.

Condimenti Using scissors is easiest for cutting small quantities of herbs; a food processor can be used for larger quantities. For broad-leafed herbs, such as basil, roll the leaves over themselves and cut into thin strips with a serrated knife. For chopping, see the three cutting methods under *battuto*. For grating cheeses, see page 24.

Cooking The basics of cooking a soup involve either sautéing or simmering your ingredients. Whichever method of cooking you use, they both depend on varying amounts of heat.

The terms used in this book are:

- **gentle sauté** Over low heat, the ingredients are rendered soft, without coloring; onions turn translucent, pancetta releases its fat, carrots and celery become tender, and garlic turns a pale golden color but never browns.
- **sauté** Varying from medium-low to moderate heat, the elements cook slightly faster than in a gentle sauté, with their color deepening. Onions turn pale golden and pancetta lightly browns. Your ingredients should never sizzle or fry.
- **sweat** Somewhere between sautéing and steaming, sweating involves cooking the ingredients in their own juices or in very little liquid to allow their flavors to intensify. After the ingredients have been sautéed, the pot is usually covered to allow the vapor to gently continue the cooking process without the risk of browning or burning. Using a heavy-bottomed pot and keeping the heat low are essential.
- **gentle simmer** The bubbles softly rise to the surface.
- **simmer** The temperature is maintained at a steady, slow boil.
- **lively simmer** This is a medium, not a rolling boil.

Battuto It is almost impossible to sauté the *battuto* for too long; it only becomes more flavorful. The secret is to keep the sauté gentle, which allows the vegetables to *fare appassire,* "to wither," and slowly release their flavors. This is particularly important when garlic is present, which should never be allowed to brown. To achieve the most flavorful *battuto* and extend its cooking time until your next ingredients are ready to be added:

1. Evenly spread the *battuto* and stir occasionally with a wooden spoon to ensure uniform cooking. If using a larger pot, you may need to add more oil.
2. If the *battuto* starts sticking to the bottom or to brown, add a little hot water or broth. To prolong the cooking, cover the pot and sweat the ingredients, adding a small amount of liquid if needed.

3. When onions or pancetta need a longer sautéing, they are added before the other ingredients.

Sapori The *sapori* may be added *a crudo*—without sautéing—but is more commonly stirred into the *battuto,* becoming infused with its flavors. In order to seal in the flavors, the heat for *sapori* is usually higher than for the *battuto.* More stirring is required at first until the ingredients start to release their liquid. Washed vegetables should be well drained so they sauté instead of steam; if you are sweating your *sapori,* draining is unnecessary.

Brodo Whether you are using homemade broth or just water, the temperature at which you add your *brodo* can make a difference. If you are cooking ingredients to create the broth or to thicken your soup, the *brodo* is added cold. To maintain the flavors and textures of your ingredients, the *brodo* is added hot. No temperature indicated in the recipe assumes room temperature.

> gentle simmer Many of the denser soups, such as minestrone and legume soups, are best cooked at a slow, gentle simmer in an earthenware or heavy-bottomed pot. Using a heat diffuser helps to maintain a constant slow simmer, or leaving the cover off or ajar allows the steam to escape, but you will need to replace the evaporated liquid.
>
> simmer The quicker-cooking soups are cooked at a simmer. The ideal simmer cooks steadily without ever coming to a boil. When the pot is covered, the temperature rises and can easily turn to a boil, so it is necessary to adjust the heat as the soup cooks. Or simmer with the cover off or ajar. When rice or pasta is added, the soup is brought to a lively simmer.
>
> boil Often the broth or water is brought to a boil before it is added to the other ingredients. When cooking your soup, avoid a rolling boil, which has no place in Italian soup cookery.

Fornimento/Equipment

Most soups demand only a few basic essentials: a knife for chopping the ingredients, a pot to cook them in, a spoon for stirring, and a ladle for serving. In addition to these basics, there are pieces of equipment that make preparing soups easier and quicker.

Soup Pots In Italy the pot most often used is a heavy saucepan or casserole dish. A heavy-bottomed pot not only helps keep the ingredients from sticking, but it allows for a slower and safer cooking as you ready the next ingredients to be added. Typically any heavy-bottomed pot such as Le Creuset, stainless steel, or anodized aluminum are fine choices; aluminum pans are best avoided as they react with certain foods, such as tomatoes and leafy greens.

It is helpful to have a variety of sizes on hand, and having two pots of similar sizes makes straining from one pot to another easy. Most recipes in this book can be prepared using a 3- to 4-quart pot. Stocks and large quantities require 8- to 10-quart pots. In addition, I find that a glazed earthenware pot that can be placed directly on the heat is indispensable for cooking dried legumes or for soups that require slow, gentle heat; it can also be placed in the oven. Choose pots with good-fitting lids. If the lid does not fit tightly, place foil under it.

Flame Tamer I use these often. They diffuse the heat, allowing for both a gentle and consistent cooking temperature, the best way to cook your legumes and longer-cooking soups.

Food Processor There are cooks who find these indispensable and those who think them unnecessary; I am of the former group.

Miniature food processors are inexpensive and can be used for chopping small amounts of vegetables and herbs. Since their blade is not as sharp as the larger processors, these are better for chopping, not mincing.

Cheese Grater There are a number of types. The simplest is a half cylinder that can be held directly over the soup. I quite like the ones readily found in Italy: the grater sits over a small drawer, allowing for easy grating and a container to catch the gratings.

Knives A good selection of well-sharpened knives is a must. For vegetables, a 3½- to 4-inch blade, both straight-edged and serrated, is indispensable. If you are not using a food processor or a *mezzaluna* to finely chop your *battuto,* a large, heavy-weighted chef's knife is essential.

Ladles At least one or two are needed for transferring or serving your soup. The best ladles are made from a single piece of stainless steel.

Whisk A good balloon whisk is particularly helpful for egg mixtures.

Wooden Spoons These simple tools are a must. Not only do you avoid what I find to be an irritating clanking noise, but they can be left sitting on top of your pot without turning hot. Also, they are gentle when it comes to stirring legumes, grains, pasta, and vegetables.

Pureeing Equipment Many soups call for a partial or complete pureeing, which may yield from a coarse-textured to a velvety smooth soup. The following methods can be used on their own or in combination:

Food Mill An invaluable tool for pureeing, a food mill is a hand-cranked blade that forces the food through a perforated disk, removing skin, seeds, and fiber. The mill has legs designed to fit over a pot or bowl to catch the food. Buy the largest one you can find; the small ones are limited in what they fit on and are almost impossible to manage. Look for the type made by Mouli, which has interchangeable blades.

Blender This is best for pureeing thinner soups and where larger quantities are involved. If adding very hot soup, warm the glass goblet before filling it to avoid cracking. Never fill more than three-quarters full as the liquid rises substantially when it purees, and hold the lid down so it is not forced off by the rising steam and ingredients. Alternatively, strain the soup first, adding only the solid ingredients with enough liquid for them to puree. If the blender does not puree the soup as fine as you would like, put it through a strainer.

Food Processors These are more effective when it comes to pureeing thicker soups and firmer ingredients. To avoid the problem of the soup leaking through the center cavity, it is best to add the solid ingredients with just a small amount of the cooking liquid or in small batches.

Handheld Immersion Blenders These are put directly into the pot. Unless you're using a professional model, these are best used only for very soft ingredients. To avoid a lot of spattering, remember not to lift out the blender as it is being swirled around your soup.

Strainer Although this is the most time-consuming way to puree your soup, using a fine-mesh strainer will give the most liquid puree. A metal strainer can be used, but a hair or nylon strainer is advisable, particularly where acidic ingredients are involved. To push the ingredients through the strainer it is best to use a small ladle and a repetitive up-and-down motion. Don't push too hard on the strainer to avoid damaging it.

Serving Bowls I alternate between two types: for hearty soups such as minestrone, bread soups, or the rustic *zuppe,* I like deep earthenware bowls. These are particularly appropriate if oil or Parmesan are to be stirred in. For the lighter *minestre,* especially for broth or pureed soups, I prefer wide shallow soup bowls. Whichever type you use, if serving your soup hot, it is always a good idea to warm the bowls just before serving.

Soup Tureen Known in Italy as *zuppiere,* soup tureens have the dual benefit of allowing the soup to be served at the table, ensuring that a hot soup will indeed be hot. Though perhaps less attractive, a covered casserole brought to the table will do the same, and so will your soup pot.

Ingredienti Fondamentali/
Fundamental Ingredients

Spezi/Spices One of Italy's top chefs, Giampiero Gemignani, having just returned from helping to set up the kitchen at Circo in New York, demonstrated for me the American way of using salt versus the Italian way. At first his hand barely moved as the grains of salt were gingerly dispensed; then his wrist robustly waved and the grains flowed liberally. He explained that Italians may seem to use more, but they use it wisely. Almost every recipe calls for the addition of spices. Knowing how to use them correctly will make a noticeable difference to your soup.

Sale (salt) The salt found in an Italian kitchen is *sale di mare,* sea salt. Used in two forms—*sale grosso* (coarse salt) and *sale fine* (fine salt)—its natural flavor subtly brings out the tastes of other ingredients without imparting the salty taste associated with refined table salt. Coarse grains are used at the beginning and during the cooking process and the fine grains as a seasoning, after the soup has finished cooking. Whichever stage of the cooking process you add any salt, do so judiciously. As soup cooks its liquid reduces, but the amount of salt does not; in fact, its flavor intensifies. Always take into account the saltiness of your broth, stock cubes, or the grated cheese you may be adding.

Kosher salt, which is free from additives and iodine, makes a fine substitute for the coarse-grained sea salt, though it should never be added at the end of cooking. Considered slightly less good than *sale di mare,* kosher salt is a far better cooking salt than refined.

Pepe nero (black pepper) Almost every recipe calls for freshly ground pepper. There's a reason for this: once pepper is ground much of its aroma and liveliness rapidly dissipates. Pepper is almost always added at the end of cooking; if added too early, its taste may become bitter. Tellicherry has the most well-rounded flavor.

Peperoncini (chili peppers) Not to be confused with the very hot Mexican or Indian chilies, Italian *peperoncini* are small dried red peppers with a mildly sweetish, medium-hot flavor. They should be used as a flavoring rather than a way of making a dish hot. Cooked whole and then discarded, they impart the mildest flavor; crushing them releases their full flavor.

You can buy them already crushed, but these are usually a combination of peppers from several countries and tend to be hotter. I like to buy them in their whole form, imported from Italy, so I know what I am getting and have the option of using them whole or crushed. Whole peppers can easily be crushed using a mortar and pestle. Chili peppers will keep for years in an airtight jar, stored in a cool, dark place. If they become cloudy or turn a dark red, discard.

Noce Moscata (nutmeg) Whenever possible, it is always best to grate the whole nutmeg.

Le Erbe Aromatiche/Aromatic Herbs

Nearly every Italian home has a variety of fresh herbs growing in the garden or in pots on the kitchen windowsill. A small but important part of almost every soup, herbs can be sautéed as part of the *battuto,* where their flavor melds into the other tastes, or added raw at the end of cooking for far greater impact. When substituting dried herbs, use about one half to one third the amount.

Allori (bay leaves) Used both fresh and dried, bay leaves are added whole and removed before serving. The fresh leaves impart a sweeter, more delicate taste than dried. When purchasing dried, look for Italian *alloro,* which is less pungent than the Pacific variety. Store dried leaves in a tightly closed container not exposed to light.

Basilico (basil) Fresh basil is one of the most widely used herbs in Italian cooking. Nothing can replace its rich peppery aromatic scent and flavor. Use only the leaves, not the flowers. Dried basil is never an appropriate substitute.

Maggiorana (marjoram) Most commonly used in Liguria, it is almost always used fresh.

Origano (oregano) Also known as wild marjoram, oregano is part of the same family. Its taste is similar but stronger than marjoram. This is one of the few herbs more often used in its dry form, but be careful not to use too much.

Prezzemolo (parsley) A mainstay of Italian cooking, parsley in Italy always refers to the flat-leafed variety, also known as Italian parsley. Its full flavor and soft texture is far superior to the curly variety. Wash in several changes of cold water and pat dry before chopping. Keep in mind that what looks like a lot will reduce dramatically once finely chopped. An average bunch yields about ¼ cup; a small bunch, about 2 tablespoons.

Rosmarino (rosemary) Along with parsley, rosemary is the most widely used herb. Fresh leaves are soft enough to chop, but if you blanch dried leaves for a few seconds they can then be used in the same quantities and ways as the fresh leaves. Rosemary's distinctive flavor can overwhelm if too much is added; sprigs, sautéed and removed, can be used to impart just a hint of flavor. To keep the leaves from dispersing during a lengthy cooking, wrap with clear thread or place in muslin.

Salvia (sage) Its flavor is unique in certain soups, particularly in Tuscany. If it's possible, sage should always be fresh unless imported from Italy. Dried sage has a different taste from fresh Italian or American sage and should be used sparingly.

Timo (thyme) Having a pungent taste with sweet undertones, thyme has a flavor that lingers and should be used carefully. It releases its flavor slowly and is best added at the beginning of cooking. If purchasing dried, avoid buying ground thyme.

Aglio/Garlic No Italian kitchen is complete without garlic. Throughout Italy, garlic is used much like salt, enhancing all the flavors of the other ingredients. In soup cookery it is most commonly added to the *battuto,* but a quick rubbing of garlic clove on bread can bring a simple *zuppa* to life.

Garlic can impart a mild or pungent taste in your soup depending not only on the quantity, but how and when you add it. For the mildest flavor, the whole clove is gently sautéed and then removed. The finer garlic is chopped, the more pronounced its flavor. Garlic mellows as it cooks; added raw, as in a pesto sauce, it has the greatest intensity.

Peeled garlic cloves can be used whole, crushed, or chopped, but are best not squeezed through a garlic press. When sautéing garlic, always do so over gentle heat.

Watch carefully so the garlic never darkens beyond a deep golden color; otherwise its flavor becomes bitter. If this happens, it should be discarded.

Buying and Storing Choose bulbs that are firm to the touch and free of blemishes; the plumper bulbs do not dry out as quickly. Green shoots indicate the garlic is no longer fresh. Store in a cool dry place that allows the air to circulate and do not refrigerate.

Preserving Peel, place in a jar, cover with extra-virgin olive oil, and refrigerate. For greater convenience, chop 20 or so peeled cloves in a food processor before placing in the jar and you will always have garlic readily available.

Formaggi di Grana/Grating Cheeses Probably no other country uses cheese in the multitude of ways as does Italy. The name used to denote hard grating cheeses—*grana*—is a central ingredient in the preparation of so many dishes, particularly the *primi piatti*. With the exception of soups prepared with fish, the majority of Italian soups call for the addition of these golden granules, which seem to complement almost every ingredient.

Parmigiano-Reggiano Though many cheeses may be referred to as Parmesan, the authentic article must be produced in designated areas, most notably Reggio-Emilia and Parma, and its hard golden rind branded with the words PARMIGIANO-REGGIANO. Aged for at least eighteen months, Parmesan has a distinctive taste and texture.

Buying and Storing If possible, purchase your Parmesan freshly cut from the wheel and with the rind still on; it will stay fresh longer and the rind can be a wonderful addition to many of your soups. Try to avoid buying it already grated; Parmesan is at its most aromatic when grated at the time of serving.

Tightly wrap in greaseproof paper and then in foil and store on the bottom shelf of the refrigerator. Properly stored, it can keep for months.

Grana Padano After Parmigiano-Reggiano, the best known grating and cooking cheese is *grana padano*. Although this cheese is less aged than Parmesan, its milder flavor still makes a fine substitute in almost all the recipes.

Pecorino (Romano) Made from the milk of *pecora* (sheep), *pecorino* is to southern Italy what Parmesan is to the north. Whether it is produced in Sardinia, Sicily, or another region, the grating variety of *pecorino* is generically referred to as *pecorino romano*, with many carrying the region of origin as part of its name, such as in pecorino Romano Sardo. Its sharper, saltier taste is called for in numerous soups.

Grassi/Cooking Fats From sautéing ingredients to adding *un filo*—a fine thread—of oil to the finished soup, almost every soup uses some form of fat. In northern Italy, butter and pancetta are commonly used, while olive oil is the clear choice in central and southern Italy. Although regional preferences still abound, there is a trend to replace the less healthy animal-based fats with olive oil. Its high nutritional value and digestibility have made olive oil increasingly popular throughout the whole of Italy.

There are numerous recipes where the addition of an animal-based fat is thought indispensable. In the earliest known recipes this usually meant using *lardo* or *strutto*, which are 100 percent fat. With changing tastes and dietary considerations, pancetta, which is made up of at least half meat, has become the animal fat of choice.

Olio d'Oliva (olive oil) This less flavorful and lighter oil is used primarily in combination with butter or for soups where a stronger flavor is less desirable.

Olio d'Oliva Extra Vergine (extra-virgin olive oil) When it comes to soup cookery extra-virgin olive oil is almost always the oil of choice. It has the best flavor and the best resistance to heat, making it preferable for the gentle sauté called for in so many recipes. Italian kitchens stock two types of extra-virgin olive oil, a basic one for cooking and an estate-bottled oil to add after the soup has finished its cooking.

Extra-Virgin Olive Oil When Italians say *extra vergine* they are referring to cold-pressed oil. However, outside of Italy this definition refers to oils with an acidity level of less than 1 percent. In modern factories, chemically refined oils can be de-acidified using alkali solutions, making these oils extra-virgin in name only. To further confuse the issue, oils imported from Italy are not necessarily Italian, but often a blend of oils from other countries. This is not to say they are unsuitable, but tasting is always your best guide.

Estate-Bottled Oils When oil is added as a condiment, its taste becomes as important as any other of the soup's ingredients. Italians sample their oils with the expertise of a wine taster, and various regions create oils of distinct differences. The green and grassy olive oil produced in the Chianti region of Tuscany is known for its peppery aftertaste, while the oil cultivated in nearby Lucca has a deep golden color and is renowned for its mellow, rich flavor. The Umbrian hillsides yield a more delicate oil, with Liguria producing the mildest olive oil, while those of Puglia and Sicily are gutsy and full of flavor.

Buying and Storing Buying a fine estate-bottled olive oil guarantees its quality and character. Older does not equal better; the keenest flavors fade with time and exposure to air and heat turns oil rancid. Oil is best stored in a cooler, darker spot in your kitchen and used within a year.

Burro (butter) Mainly used in northern Italy, butter is one of the most important animal fats. All butter used in Italian cookery is unsalted.

Pancetta (bacon) Used extensively in Italian cooking, particularly as part of the *battuto,* pancetta is often called the Italian version of bacon. Made from *pancia,* the belly of a pig, pancetta are layers of lean meat and fat, either smoked or unsmoked. It comes in two forms: *pancetta stessa,* a flat slab still attached to its rind to which only salt has been added, and more commonly *pancetta arrotolata,* seasoned with salt, pepper, and spices and then rolled and tied in a casing.

Cured When pancetta is listed as an ingredient in the recipes, with just a few exceptions, it is the cured, nonsmoked variety that is called for. If it is unavailable, there is no entirely satisfactory substitute. Salt pork or smoked bacon, briefly blanched, can be used; however, they lack pancetta's special flavor and, once blanched, do not sauté as well. These are best substituted when a recipe calls for simmering, as in flavoring legumes. I prefer to substitute prosciutto, augmented with prosciutto fat or olive oil.

Smoked Pancetta (*panacetta affumicata*) is closest to the choicest smoked bacon. Its taste can be best duplicated using a good-quality slab bacon rather than pre-sliced.

Buying and Storing Look for pancetta that has an equal proportion of meat to fat. The meat should be a rosy to red color, never brown, and the fat white, never yellowish. Have it sliced into ¼-inch pieces. Increasingly available are the small packets of precubed pancetta; unopened, these have a very long shelf life and are very convenient.

Pancetta will last, well wrapped, in the refrigerator for about a week or frozen for several months. As it is used in small quantities, it is best to freeze it in 1- to 2-ounce packages.

Prosciutto (ham) Prosciutto is the name given to ham: *prosciutto crudo* is uncooked and *prosciutto cotto* is cooked ham. It is the uncooked variety, cured in salt, that we think of as prosciutto. The two best known are *prosciutto di Parma*, which has a unique sweetness, and *San Daniele*, which is slightly saltier and more akin to our domestic prosciutto.

If possible, ask for the end piece of prosciutto. Not only can you probably pay less for it, but it has the right proportion of meat to fat for your *battuto* and its skin can be used to flavor your legumes or soup.

Grani/Grains Whether in the form of kernels or ground and made into bread or pasta, grains are used to fortify a vast variety of Italian soups.

Farro (spelt or emmer wheat) These nutty-tasting and firm grains may be part of the same family as wheat, but gastronomically *farro* is considered a distinct variety. Cultivated in central Italy, the best quality of *farro* is stone ground in relatively small quantities. If it is unavailable, substitute the smaller spelt grain that comes from the same variety of wheat. As a second choice, use barley in smaller quantities. *Farro* requires a soaking of 4 hours to overnight.

Orzo (barley) The barley used in soup cookery is *orzo perlato,* pearled barley. Although it can be added unsoaked, most Italians prefer to presoak barley for 4 hours to overnight for the fluffiest kernel. Rinse well under cold water until the water runs clear.

Pane (bread) A good hard-crusted homemade or country bread is essential in

many *zuppe*. Ideally, it should be a few days old with the center still slightly pliable. This allows for proper absorption of the broth without disintegrating into the soup. If your bread is not stale, the same effect can be achieved by drying it out in the oven. Unless you are serving the bread strictly as an accompaniment, airy French baguettes are best avoided.

Pasta The choice of pasta depends on the soup. The more robust *minestre* usually call for *pasta corta,* a short pasta such as *ditalini* or a flat pasta such as fettuccine or spaghetti broken into small pieces. Clear broth soups add the smaller *pastina* (small pasta) or fine noodles, such as *capelli d'angelo* (angel's hair). Pasta should always be cooked just until it becomes *al dente*, with some resistance to the bite. This is particularly true for soups, as the pasta continues to cook after the soup has been taken off the heat.

Always distinguish between using dried or fresh. Dried pasta swells and will be about twice as much in volume once cooked, while fresh pasta maintains almost the same volume. As a general guideline, an ounce of fresh pasta calls for about ⅔ ounce of dried pasta. When flat egg pasta is called for, I must admit to having become addicted to using the imported, though expensive, Cipriani pasta. It seems to combine the best qualities of both dried and fresh pasta with a wonderful texture and a fineness that allows it to cook very quickly.

Riso (rice) Two types of rice are used in Italian soup cookery: risotto and long-grain. Their difference lies mainly in the amount of starch molecules known as amlopectins. The long-grain variety contains less, while risotto rice contains more, yielding a creamier result.

Once you have added rice to the simmering soup, stir with a wooden spoon to prevent sticking. Cook until *al dente*, tender but still with a little firmness; the rice will continue to cook after your soup has been taken off the heat. If you are adding precooked rice, make sure it has been stored properly; cooked rice is very susceptible to bacteria.

Long-Grain Rice Carolina, patna, or basmati produces a fluffy rice when cooked. They all generally absorb 1 to 2 times their volume of liquid.

Risotto Rice *Arborio, Vialone Nano, and Carnaroli* give body and a denser texture to your soup. A risotto rice absorbs 2 to 4 times its volume. Vialone Nano has smaller, stubbier grains and remains the most distinct of the *risotti* rice; it also absorbs slightly less liquid than Arborio or Carnaroli. Should you prefer your soup to have a less dense texture, rinsing or soaking your risotto rice prior to cooking will reduce its starch content.

Legumi/Legumes Either as the main ingredient or added as a complementary ingredient, legumes are indispensable to a wide variety of soups throughout Italy. The following are the legumes used most often in Italian soup cookery:

Borlotti (rose coca, cranberry, or Roman beans) These medium-sized beans are mottled with deep crimson streaks, and when cooked, their skins turn rosy-brown and they develop a creamy texture with a delicate, nutty flavor.
Substitute: cannellini or pinto beans

Cannellini (white kidney beans) These smaller white beans, also called Tuscan beans, have a mild flavor that becomes permeated with the tastes of the ingredients with which they cook. Their lightness makes them a popular bean to combine with numerous ingredients.
Substitute: navy, haricot, or Great Northern beans

Fave (fava or broad beans) These oval beans have a creamy texture and an earthy flavor. When fresh, *fave* are pale green and have a delicate taste; when dried, their color is tan and their flavor becomes more intense. Unless fresh *fave* are very young and small, their outer skins toughen and need removing. If you are using dried beans, try to purchase them skinned and split.
Substitute: cannellini beans for fresh *fave* and *borlotti* beans for dried

Ceci (chickpeas or garbanzos) These round, ochre-colored legumes have a rich, nutty flavor. They take longer to soak and cook, so it is wise to keep the canned variety on hand. The larger European chickpea is the bean of choice, not the much smaller Chinese bean.

Lenticchie (lentils): There are numerous colors and types, but those used in Italian cooking are the green or small russet brown lentils. They have a delicate, earthy taste and maintain their shape when cooked. Even though lentils do not require soaking, doing so reduces their cooking time by half. Check for any small stones.

Substitute: French *puy* lentils, which have a wonderful earthy taste but stay firmer; if substituting, you may have to puree part to achieve the desired density.

Buying and Storing Legumes

Fresh When they're available there's no real substitute for fresh beans. They should be crisp and free of any brown spots. Keep refrigerated, or shell and freeze them for future use. They can also be cooked and then frozen.

Yield: 1½ pounds unshelled = about 2 cups shelled or 1 cup dried

Frozen Good-quality frozen beans, such as peas, borlotti, or favas, keep their texture and taste to a high degree. Make sure that their packaging is clean and damage-free.

Canned Though somewhat inferior in texture and nutrition, good-quality canned beans are indispensable for convenience. If it's possible, purchase ones that are imported from Italy; they tend to be of very high quality and without the seasonings and preservatives found in many other brands. Do keep in mind that most canned beans have a much higher sodium content and will need to be drained and sometimes rinsed.

Yield: 1 14-ounce can = about 1¾ cups, drained

Dried Contrary to popular belief, dried beans cannot be kept indefinitely. Over time they lose moisture, making their soaking and cooking time correspondingly longer, and if too old, no amount of cooking will soften them. Always buy beans that you can see; the colors should be bright and the skins should not be cracked or shriveled.

Dried beans are best stored in see-through, airtight containers and placed in a cool, darker place in your kitchen. Never store in damp conditions and never freeze or refrigerate dried beans; they will toughen. Beans that are bought several months apart should not be mixed; their cooking times may vary.

When you are increasing the amount of dried legumes in your recipe, the cooking liquid doesn't increase proportionally. As a guideline, when doubling the amount of legumes, add about 25 percent more liquid. It is better to start with less liquid and increase the amount if needed.

Approximate Yields for Chickpeas, Cannellini, and Borlotti Beans

Dried	Soaked and Cooked
½ cup (3 ounces)	1¼ cups
⅔ cup (4 ounces)	1½ cups
1 cup (6 ounces)	2½ cups
1¼ cups (7½ ounces)	3 cups
1½ cups (9 ounces)	3¾ cups
1¾ cups (10½ ounces)	4⅓ cups
2 cups (12 ounces)	5 cups

Verdure Fondamentali/Basic Vegetables Carrots, celery, onions, tomatoes, and potatoes are staples of almost every Italian kitchen. Although you may think there is nothing special to learn about these everyday vegetables, there are types and techniques that yield better-tasting and healthier soups.

Carote (carrots) Whenever possible buy organic carrots; their taste is sweeter and they are indistinguishable from the ones you will find in Italy. To best preserve their nutrients, a light scraping with a sharp knife is all that is needed, and if the carrots are very young and small, no scraping at all is required. Medium-sized carrots tend to have the best flavor.

Cipolle (onions) Yellow onions are as ubiquitous in Italy as they are in America, but other types of onion play an equally important role. Red onions are far more common in Tuscany, while white onions are widely used in the north. Shallots, most associated with French cooking, are becoming more widely used in Italy. Their sharp, somewhat sweeter taste makes them a wonderful alternative. As with garlic, if onions are sautéed at too high a temperature, they can quickly turn dark and bitter.

Buying and Storing Avoid bruised or sprouting onions. The skins should be dry. Keep in a cool, dark spot, unrefrigerated.

Potate (potatoes) For the purpose of cooking soups, you will need to know the difference between the two main types of potatoes: waxy and floury. Their different textures will yield distinctly different results when cooked in your soup.

Baking or floury potatoes have a dryer texture and a higher starch content. These russet potatoes are referred to as baking or Idaho potatoes. When cooked in soup, they break down and thicken its texture.

Boiling or waxy potatoes have a firmer, creamier texture and a lower starch content. When cooked in soups, they hold their shape. Most red potatoes are of the waxy variety.

All-purpose potatoes, somewhere between the waxy and floury varieties, can be used in most soups. These include Superior, Kennebec, King Edward, and Yukon Gold. If they are being used to thicken the soup, chop them finely.

Buying and Storing Potatoes should be firm and feel heavy with no soft spots or discoloration. Keep in a dark, cool place, not refrigerated; brown paper bags work well. Any green parts or potato sprouts contain poisonous alkaloids and should be completely cut out. Washed potatoes store badly.

Sedano (celery) After washing, place the celery round side up. Take the back of a wooden spoon and gently tap the celery to break down the ribs. Unless the celery is extremely woody, this method makes peeling unnecessary.

Pomodori (tomatoes) For cooking, the tomatoes of choice are *pomodoro al sugo,* tomatoes for making sauce. In Italy, this invariably means very ripe plum tomatoes. Not only do they have the fullest flavor, but really ripe tomatoes have few seeds and their skins easily peel off.

Fresh Unless you are using cherry tomatoes, fresh tomatoes will have to be peeled and seeded. Simply plunge in boiling water for about 10 to 15 seconds and peel when cool enough to handle. Any ripe, thin-skinned variety can be used. Fresh tomatoes are best stored at room temperature.

Canned These are the tomatoes most commonly used in the preparation of Italian soups. Whenever possible always choose imported Italian plum tomatoes, preferably the San Marzano variety. Italian tomatoes are picked ripe, at the height of their flavor, and will always be preferable to an insipid, underripe fresh tomato. They can be chopped before adding or broken up in the soup pot using a wooden spoon.

Strained (passato) These pureed tomatoes are a fine alternative. Their flavor is more concentrated and you will need to add about one third to one half less than canned chopped tomatoes.

Tomato Paste (concentrato di pomodoro) When just a light taste of tomato is required or the rosy hue it imparts, tomato paste is used. It is usually diluted with a little hot water before adding. Always try to buy tomato paste imported from Italy.

Tomato Sauce (salsa di pomodoro) The more interesting taste of a homemade tomato sauce can be substituted for pureed or chopped tomatoes (see page 46 for a quick version).

Approximate Yields:
1 14-ounce can = 1¼ cups drained tomatoes
1 pound fresh tomatoes = 1 cup cooked, including their juices
2 pounds fresh plum tomatoes = 1¾ cups, peeled, seeded, and chopped

Preparazioni Fondamentali / Basic Preparations

Brodi/Prepared Broths I like to think of the liquid component of soup, the *brodo,* in several ways. The simplest is the addition of water that becomes infused with the tastes of the other ingredients as the soup cooks, in essence creating a natural broth. Then there are the prepared broths, which can range from the one that has simmered on your stove for hours to water with the simple addition of stock cubes.

The most commonly used prepared *brodi* are meat, vegetable, and chicken. However, when the word *brodo* is used in Italian cookery, it almost always refers to a *brodo di carne* (meat broth). This **classic broth** is a combination of beef, chicken, and aromatic vegetables that have been slowly simmered to yield a flavorful but delicate *brodo*. Unlike French stock, meat, not bones, is the dominant ingredient, resulting in a light-tasting broth. If your preference is for vegetable or chicken broth, these can almost always be used in place of or in conjunction with a meat broth.

Stockpot A tall stockpot is ideal; it encourages the simmering broth to circulate and its smaller surface area minimizes evaporation.

Ingredients All homemade broths include the aromatic vegetables: carrots, celery, and onions and/or leeks, with parsley and bay leaf often added. Carrots and celery need only to be washed, not scraped. Celery tops are as tasty as the stalks and parsley stems as flavorful as the leaves. Just be sure that whatever ingredients you add to your broth are fresh and still have plenty of life.

Cooking Broths are best cooked at a gentle simmer; too high a temperature breaks down the fat, making your broth cloudy and giving it a greasy feel. There are two schools of thought as to when to add the aromatic flavorings. One is to combine everything at once; the other is to add the flavorings after the meat has come to its initial boil. I prefer adding the vegetables and herbs later so they don't float to the top, making it difficult to skim off the surface scum. Although the vegetables are added to hot rather than cold water, the long cooking time still allows for their flavors to fully leach out.

Brodo Classico Rapido

Quick Classic Broth

yield: about 5¹/₂ cups

When time does not permit, this meat broth can be prepared in about 1 hour. The quantity given is for 4 servings.

1 pound lean veal or beef, ground or finely chopped
Few pieces of chicken parts, such as necks or wings (optional)
1 carrot, finely chopped
1 celery rib, finely chopped
1 small onion, unpeeled

1 leek, white and light green parts, finely chopped
1 garlic clove, peeled
1 tomato, chopped (optional)
Pinch of salt
6 whole peppercorns
6 cups cold water

Place all the ingredients in a saucepan and cover with the water. Bring to a boil over medium heat, stirring often. Lower the heat and very gently simmer, covered, for at least 1 hour, or place in a preheated 300°F. oven. Strain through a fine sieve; for a clearer broth, line the sieve with dampened cheesecloth.

Brodo Classico

Classic Meat Broth

Classic meat broth is usually prepared with relatively lean cuts of beef and/or veal, along with smaller proportions of chicken and bones. Pork and lamb are never added; both give too dominant a flavor. A lean stewing beef, such as brisket, rump, or flank, is the meat of choice. If possible, use a well-aged boiling fowl rather than ordinary chicken; it has far more flavor and stands up much better to a long cooking. If adding chicken, buy the most economical cuts, such as backs, necks, and wings.

I find that the proportion of meat to poultry is far less important than the overall advantage of having a homemade broth. If I have a well-aged fowl, it becomes as important an ingredient as the beef. If only ordinary chicken is on hand, I supplement it with beef stock cubes. For a deeper flavor, Fabio Picchi of Cibreo adds a touch of red wine to his *brodo*. If using stock cubes, remember that your broth will reduce considerably as it cooks, so always add them toward the end of cooking.

5 pounds assorted beef, veal, and/or
    chicken , with approximately
    3¹/₂ pounds all meat
About 16 to 18 cups cold water
1 teaspoon coarse salt
2 medium carrots, washed
1 medium onion, peeled and cut
    in half
2 to 3 celery ribs or their leafy tops
1 garlic clove, peeled and flattened

1 bay leaf
1 whole fresh or canned and drained
    plum tomato (optional)
1 leek, white and light green part
    (optional)
¹/₂ cup dry red wine (optional)
1 teaspoon whole peppercorns
    (optional)

1. In a stockpot, combine all the meat and cover with the water. Slowly bring to a boil over moderate heat, uncovered. This will take about 45 to 60 minutes. Avoid stirring and periodically skim off the scum that rises to the surface. When it reaches a boil, add about 1 cup of cold water to cause more scum to rise.

Lower the heat and add the vegetables and herbs. Partially cover and cook at a gentle simmer for a minimum of 3 hours, preferably for 4 to 5 hours.

If you are adding the wine and peppercorns, add them about 20 minutes before the end of cooking.

2. Remove the large pieces of meat and strain the broth into a ceramic or glass bowl. If using right away, skim the surface with a paper towel to absorb the fat. If refrigerating or freezing, allow to cool completely, uncovered.

3. Special care must be taken with broths that contain meat; few cooking basics are as perishable and as potentially dangerous as a flesh-based broth. Unless you intend to use your *brodo* within a few days, it is best to freeze it.

Refrigerating Place in a container with a small surface area so the layer of fat will be thicker and lift off easily. Cover and refrigerate for several hours or overnight, leaving the fat to form on top. Your broth will keep, refrigerated, for 3 days. *Brodo* can be kept indefinitely in the refrigerator by boiling it every few days for about 5 minutes.

Freezing Be sure to remove any fat—frozen fat can turn rancid. Place in containers that allow enough room at the top for expansion. To save space in your freezer, before cooling, boil the broth, uncovered, until reduced. Freeze in ice cube trays and, when solid, place the cubes into airtight plastic bags. When needed, dilute the reduced stock with water. Date your containers, as frozen stock should be used within 3 months.

Brodo di Dadi

Stock Cube Broth

I never allow the lack of a homemade *brodo* to keep me from the abundant pleasures of a good soup. With the exception of clear broth soups, most soups calling for a prepared *brodo* can be successfully made using a commercially made broth or *dadi,* stock cubes.

Most stock cubes have a high salt content and benefit from adding about a third to a half more water than is recommended on the package. Use stock cubes judiciously and always sample the *brodo* as you add them. If you have a little time, they can greatly benefit from cooking with fresh ingredients to make what Italians refer to as *brodo del compromesso* (broth of compromise).

*1 large cube chicken stock
  (see Nota)
1 large cube beef stock or 2 large
  cubes vegetable stock*

*Aromatic vegetables: onion, leeks,
  carrot, celery, and parsley,
  coarsely chopped (optional)
5¹/₂ cups water*

Mince or break up the cubes in hot or boiling water. If adding vegetables, add the cold water and simmer, covered, for about 30 minutes. Add more water to equal the desired amount of broth.

Nota: Canned beef or chicken broth can be invigorated in the same way as stock cubes.

Brodo di Pollo

Chicken Broth

yield: about 10 cups

cooking time: 2½ to 3½ hours

A good chicken broth should be light but not bland. A well-aged fowl makes the tastiest and least fatty broth. If that is unavailable, a roasting chicken and/or necks, backs, and wings can be used. When not using an aged fowl, I add a stock cube or two to deepen the flavor of the less aged chicken. Adding the outer leaf of an onion imparts a subtle golden hue to your stock.

4 to 5 pounds boiling fowl or
*   4 pounds chicken parts such as*
*   necks, wings, and backs*
16 cups cold water
1 large onion, thickly sliced
1 large leek, ends trimmed, white
*   and lighter green parts, cut into*
*   1-inch pieces*

2 carrots, cut into 1-inch pieces
A few celery rib tops with leaves or
*   2 ribs*
2 fresh bay leaves or 1 dried
6 parsley sprigs
1 garlic clove, peeled

1. Wash the chicken, removing the giblets. Place in a stockpot and cover with the water. Bring to a boil over moderate heat, skimming off the scum that rises to the surface (it will take about an hour for it to reach a boil). Pour in a cup of cold water to encourage more scum to come to the surface. Add the remaining ingredients, bring back to a boil, and remove any scum. Lower the heat and cook, partially covered, at a gentle simmer for 2 to 3 hours (if adding stock cubes, add to taste toward the end of cooking).

2. Remove the large pieces of chicken carcass and strain the broth through a cheesecloth or a very fine sieve into a large glass or ceramic bowl. If using the broth immediately, use a folded paper towel to soak up surface fat. If storing, allow to cool completely, uncovered, before refrigerating.

3. Cover and place the cooled broth in the refrigerator. When the fat has congealed on top, spoon off and discard. It can be kept in a covered container in the refrigerator for 3 days or follow the instructions for freezing (page 37).

Brodo Leggero

Light Broth

Many recipes call for a lighter-tasting and less salted broth, which is simply made by diluting classic meat or chicken broth with water. As a general guideline, use 1 part water to 3 parts broth.

Brodo Vegetale

Vegetable Broth

yield: 8 cups

cooking time:
1½ hours

A flavorful vegetable broth can make a fine substitute for a meat-based one. For the depth of flavor necessary, sauté the onions and leeks for as long as possible before adding the other vegetables. I always start the sauté and then prepare all the other vegetables. For a lighter and more delicate broth, simply omit the sauté and add all the vegetables directly to the cold water.

As a general guideline, add 2½ to 3 pounds of vegetables (including the onions and leeks) for every 9 cups of water. The following recipe is the one I use most often. Not only does it always produce a fine-tasting broth but pureed it becomes a wonderful soup, which I serve topped with Parmesan crostini or sautéed mushrooms.

1 large onion, peeled and sliced

2 large leeks, white and light green
  parts, sliced

2 to 3 tablespoons extra-virgin
  olive oil

2 to 3 large carrots, cut into about
  1-inch pieces

2 whole celery ribs with leaves, cut
  into about 1-inch pieces

1 medium turnip, coarsely chopped

1 medium potato, cut into quarters

1 to 2 tomatoes, left whole

2 garlic cloves, crushed

Bunch of parsley, leaves
  and/or stems

2 fresh bay leaves or 1 dried

4 ounces mushroom caps or stems or
  1/4 ounce dried porcini
  mushrooms, rehydrated
  (optional, see Nota)

9 cups cold water

1 tablespoon peppercorns

1/2 cup dry white wine
  (optional, see Nota)

1. Over medium-low heat, sauté the onion and leeks in the oil for at least 10 minutes, or until the *sapori* is ready to add. Add a little hot water if needed (omit this step for a lighter broth, adding the onions and leeks with the other vegetables; see recipe introduction).

2. Add all the ingredients, except for the peppercorns and wine, and cover with the water. Over moderate heat, bring to a boil, skimming off any scum that rises to the surface. Lower the heat and cook at a gentle but steady simmer for about 45 minutes.

3. Add the peppercorns and wine and cook, uncovered, for 10 more minutes. Strain, lightly pressing down on the vegetables to extract their final juices. If storing, allow to cool, uncovered, before refrigerating.

Nota: For a deeper flavored broth, add wine and/or a few dried porcini mushrooms, previously soaked and washed, along with their soaking liquid.

Brodo Vegetale Leggero

Light Vegetable Broth

Follow the vegetable broth recipe on page 40, without sautéing the leeks and onion, or dilute your vegetable broth with water, 3 to 4 parts broth to 1 part water.

Crostini

Croutons

The best bread for crostini is dense, fine-textured, and just slightly stale. Generally only *la mollica,* the center of the bread, is used; however, if the crusts are not too browned, they can be left on. Using a serrated knife, cut the bread into ½-inch-thick slices. Stack the slices one on top the other and cut into ½-inch strips, then cut again into ½-inch strips to make cubes (slice the bread before it becomes too stale and too difficult to cut). The bread squares can now be toasted in the oven or fried in oil and/or butter.

Baking Place in one layer on an ungreased baking sheet. Bake in a preheated 350°F. oven until golden, turning from time to time, for 10 to 12 minutes. If you prefer, toss the cubes in a little oil or melted butter before baking.

Frying Over moderate heat, heat ample oil and/or butter in a large frying pan, preferably nonstick. Add only enough bread cubes to cover the pan in one layer and sauté, turning occasionally, until lightly colored. To prevent burning, don't allow the oil to become too hot. When evenly golden, lift out with a spatula and drain on paper towels.

Storing Place on flat trays and allow to cool, uncovered. To keep overnight, place in foil and reheat before serving. If no oil or butter has been added, they can be stored in an airtight container for up to 2 weeks. Or freeze and use within 3 months.

Crostini al'Aglio/Garlic Croutons Before frying, add 2 cloves of lightly flattened peeled garlic to the butter and oil. After the garlic has turned golden, lightly press with the back of a fork to extract its juices, then remove. Add the cubed bread and sauté, turning frequently, until golden on all sides. Or toss the bread cubes with the heated oil and butter before baking.

Crostini al Formaggio/Parmesan Croutons Preheat the oven to 300°F. To prevent the *crostini* from sticking, use a nonstick baking sheet. Over low heat, melt the butter and oil or just butter. Coat the crostini and then sprinkle with freshly grated Parmesan cheese. Arrange in a single layer and bake until golden.

Crostoni

Grilled Italian Bread

Similar to *bruschetta* without any topping, slices of good country bread are grilled or fried and often rubbed with garlic. Toast the bread on both sides and, if using garlic, rub on one side of the bread while it is still hot.

Crosta di Parmigiano

Parmesan Rind

Adding a Parmesan rind to your soup imparts a subtle and mellow taste, often making the addition of grated cheese unnecessary. Prolonged cooking renders the rind meltingly soft and very flavorful. The rind can be taken out at the end of cooking or, if the pieces of rind are small enough, left in.

Wash the rind well before adding. Soak in cold water for 10 minutes, drain, then scrape the outside with the blade of a knife.

Funghi Porcini Secci

Dried Porcini Mushrooms

Before dried porcini are cooked, they need to be reconstituted in warm water; using water that is too hot can bring out unpleasant tannins. The soaking time will vary according to the quality of the mushroom. Beautiful large, creamy-colored porcini require about 30 minutes; smaller dark bits are best soaked for about 60 minutes. The flavorful liquid the soaked mushrooms yield can be added to enrich your soup or frozen in an ice cube tray for use at a later date.

1. Place the porcini in a small bowl and cover with approximately 1 cup warm water. Allow to soak for 30 to 60 minutes.

2. Lift out the mushrooms, squeezing and adding their juices back to the bowl. Rinse the mushrooms under cold running water, pat dry, and, depending on their size, chop or leave whole.

3. Filter the liquid through a strainer lined with cheesecloth, a coffee filter, or paper towel and collect in a clean bowl.

Pesto

Fresh Basil Sauce

yield: about ¹/₄ cup

Synonymous with the cooking of Liguria, *pesto alla genovese* is made from fresh basil, garlic, olive oil, and grated Romano and Parmesan cheese. Pine nuts are often added—however, for soup it is optional. If you don't have quite enough fresh basil, supplement with some fresh parsley leaves, or blanched spinach leaves.

Using a stone mortar and wooden pestle is the traditional way of making pesto; however, a blender or food processor does the job well in less than a minute. Purists claim that the metal blades alter the taste of the basil; however, sprinkling a little salt on the basil leaves before processing prevents them from oxidizing.

Storing: To keep for a few days, smooth over the top, cover with a layer of olive oil, and refrigerate. If keeping longer, mix the cheese in just before serving.

> 1¹/₂ *cups (about ³/₄ ounce), fresh basil leaves, loosely packed, stripped from their stalks, washed, and patted dry*
> *Coarse salt*
>
> 1 *tablespoon pine nuts (optional)*
> 4 *tablespoons freshly grated pecorino Romano and/or Parmesan cheese*
> 1 *to 2 garlic cloves*
> ¹/₄ *cup extra-virgin olive oil*

Using a food processor Place the basil in a processor or blender and sprinkle with a little coarse salt. Process until finely chopped, then add the rest of the ingredients and process to a creamy paste. If you need to, scrape the ingredients back into the bottom of the bowl and process again. For a less intense pesto and to extend the amount, simply dilute with some broth, particularly when serving on top of a soup.

Using a mortar and pestle Grind the garlic, pine nuts, and a pinch of coarse salt using a forceful circular motion. Add the basil and grind until well amalgamated. Add the cheese gradually and grind in until well combined. Transfer the mixture to a small bowl and mix in the oil, adding a little at a time, until the pesto is creamy.

Salsa di Pomodoro

Tomato Sauce

When a recipe calls for pureed or chopped tomatoes, a more flavorful *salsa di pomodoro* (tomato sauce) can be substituted. Although this may be a staple of an Italian kitchen, it is one we don't readily have available. A noted chef showed me his quick way of making this sauce. Not only is it easy to prepare with vegetables that are almost always on hand, the 15 minutes extra time yields a subtly more flavorful soup.

Sauté a minced *battuto* of 1 small onion, 1 carrot, and 1 stalk celery in extra-virgin olive oil and add to 1 to 2 cups chopped or pureed tomatoes (if you prefer, add garlic and/or dried chili peppers). Cover and cook for 15 minutes or longer.

Preparation of Dried Legumes

A staple ingredient in a wide variety of Italian soups, legumes are most commonly used in their dry form—*legumi secci*. Their preparation may look complicated, but don't be misled; there are just a few basics to know.

Before Soaking Legumes need to be checked for any foreign matter. This holds true particularly for lentils and chickpeas. The easiest method is to spread them on a flat surface, where any pebbles or grit will be easy to pick out. Place the picked over beans in a large strainer and rinse under cold or tepid running water.

Soaking Soaking reduces the cooking time by half, improves the texture, and, most important, breaks down the indigestible sugars thought to cause gas. Simply cover the legumes with 2 to 3 inches of tepid to cool water, about 4 times their volume.

Traditional Soaking Method Allow to soak, uncovered, in a cool, not refrigerated, place for about 6 hours to overnight (chickpeas require at least an overnight soaking and preferably 24 hours). The fresher the legumes, the less time needed.

Quick-Soak Method Add the legumes and cold water to a heavy saucepan. Cover and slowly bring to a boil over medium heat; then simmer for 2 to 3 minutes. Remove from the heat and allow to sit, covered, for about 1 hour.

Soaking Tips

- Never add salt to the soaking water as it toughens the skins.
- Discard any beans or skins that rise to the surface.
- If you have to extend the soaking time for a day or two, be sure to change the water at least once a day and refrigerate in the soaking liquid.
- If the beans are left to soak for too long or in too warm a place, they could ferment. If this happens, throw them out.

Rinsing After soaking, drain the legumes, discarding the soaking liquid. Rinse under tepid to cold water while gently rotating them with your hands.

Cooking I have come across two distinct ways of cooking beans in Italy. The first is what I call the basic method, in which the beans are cooked at a gentle but steady simmer. The second is what I call the Tuscan method, in which an earthenware pot is used and the beans are cooked very gently for hours, either on the stovetop or in the oven.

Whichever method you use, add cold water, cover the pot, and bring to a boil slowly over medium, never high, heat. As a guideline, it will take about 20 minutes to slowly bring 6 cups of cold water to a boil. Salt or any acidic ingredient, such as tomatoes, should not be added until the beans have become tender, otherwise their skins will toughen.

Basic Method In a heavy-bottomed pot, add the beans and the amount of water indicated in the recipe and turn the heat to medium. Cover, and when it reaches a boil, adjust the heat to low and gently simmer, with the lid just slightly ajar to allow the steam to escape. Using a heat diffuser helps to maintain a gentle simmer.

Tuscan Method A glazed earthenware casserole with a lid is essential; if unglazed, it can only be used in the oven. Place the casserole on a heat diffuser and proceed as above. Cook, covered, at a *very* gentle simmer, for 2 to 3 hours. If cooking in the oven, first bring to a boil in a saucepan on the stovetop, then transfer to the earthenware pot and cover. Place on the middle rack of a preheated 350°F. oven. Alternatively, a Crock-Pot set initially at a high temperature and then set at the lowest setting will achieve similar results.

Cooking Tips

- If foam rises to the surface, it's unnecessary to skim it off; during long cooking it disappears. If you prefer, add a small amount of olive oil in the beginning to reduce the foaming, approximately 1 tablespoon per cup of beans.

- It is optimal to add salt or tomatoes after the beans have softened but not cooked completely; in this way they are better able to absorb their flavors.
- Avoid stirring; if needed, use a wooden spoon.
- When cooling cooked beans, keep in their cooking liquid to keep their skins from splitting.

Pureeing Legumes There are several ways of pureeing, all yielding different results. Add some of the cooking liquid with the legumes:

Blender or Food Processor The length of blending will determine the coarseness. For a finer texture, blend long enough so that the skins fully break down. If you are adding to the bowl of a food processor, be careful that the temperature is not too hot, otherwise the plastic will expand, making the top difficult to remove.

Food Mill or Sieve These remove the skins and produce the lightest purees. Generally, using the fine-holed disc of a food mill works best. If you are using a sieve, it is easier first to puree in the food processor and then push through the sieve.

Immersion Blender Easy because the beans stay in the same pot, this method yields the coarsest texture. To avoid a mess, be careful not to lift the blender out of the liquid as you swirl it around.

A Note on Red Kidney Beans Even though dried red kidney beans are not called for in the recipes, should you decide to substitute them, they contain a toxic substance not found in other beans and require extra attention. After bringing to a boil, allow them to cook vigorously for 10 minutes before lowering the heat to a gentle simmer.

Storing Cooked Legumes Cooked legumes will keep, refrigerated, for several days in a covered container. They also freeze well for several months. Before refrigerating or freezing, allow them to cool in their cooking liquid. If they are frozen, thaw them before heating.

Substituting Fresh Legumes Two pounds unshelled weight yields about 1 cup dried. To prepare, shell, rinse under cold water, and cook at a lively simmer for 45 to 60 minutes.

Minestre e Zuppe di Legumi

Legume Soups

*L*egumes are the edible seeds from pod-bearing plants and include beans, peas, chickpeas, and lentils. They can be fresh, dried, canned, or frozen; however, it is their dried form—legumi secci—*that is most used in Italian cooking. Inexpensive, easy to store, and highly nutritious, dried legumes play an important role in a wide variety of Italian soups.*

Along with grains, soups made from legumes represent one of the oldest of food preparations. Since antiquity, Italians have regarded legumes as carne dei poveri, *"meat of the poor." But they are anything but poor when it comes to taste and versatility. Their earthy goodness complements a vast variety of ingredients. Pureed or left whole, legumes create soups that range from refined and delicate to rustic and hearty.*

The earliest known legumes—*lenticchie, ceci,* and *fave*—were first cultivated in southern Italy, where to this day they maintain their prominence. Lentils are widely used in Lazio, chickpeas are a favorite in Abruzzi and Molise, and fava beans are indispensable to the soups of Sicily and Sardinia. Tuscany has a multitude of bean soups that pay homage to their favored *cannellini toscanelli,* and in northern Italy, the magenta-streaked borlotti reigns supreme. And no wonder, the finest borlotti beans—*borlotti di Lamon*—come from the Veneto. The most popular and perhaps the finest rendition of cannellini and borlotti beans are to be found in *pasta e fagioli,* the pasta and bean soups prepared throughout Italy.

A major distinction of legume-based soups is that they are almost always prepared with the simple addition of water and not a prepared broth. When fresh or dried legumes are cooked they lend both flavor and texture to their cooking liquid, and the broth they create is every bit as important as the legumes themselves. This is not to say that canned beans can never be substituted, but they should always be considered a second choice when preparing an authentic *minestra* or *zuppa di legumi.*

It has taken centuries for the humble legumes, once considered unsuitable for refined palates, to be afforded the place of honor they now hold in Italian cooking. Legumes have become a food of choice, and there is no better way to show them off than in soups.

Preparing Legume Soups

Preparing legume soups equates to knowing how to prepare and cook dried legumes; in doing so correctly, their texture and final taste will be optimum in your soup. The only special requirement is that all dried beans, with the exception of lentils, need to be soaked prior to cooking. Pages 29–31 describe the legumes and pages 47–49 describe their preparation.

Battuto Often the *battuto* is added as a flavor base for cooking the beans.

Brodo Most commonly, the broth is created from cooking the dried legumes, usually with herbs, garlic, or some form of prosciutto added for flavoring. If canned beans are used, when only water is called for, a prepared broth or stock cube is added for additional flavor. Be sure not to salt the water or broth until the beans turn tender.

Sapori These ingredients are used to complement the main ingredient, the legumes. If you are pureeing, the shape the *sapori* vegetables is cut in is not important.

Condimenti Most legume soups are served with a fine estate olive oil, which becomes an integral flavoring. Whenever possible, it is preferable to add the oil that corresponds to the particular region of your soup.

The Recipes

With the exception of fresh fava beans, the recipes in this chapter are devoted to the soups that are traditionally prepared with dried legumes. However, should time be a major consideration, a number of these recipes have directions for substituting canned beans. I have chosen recipes that would not be unduly compromised. In the case of chickpeas, this was an easy decision. Chickpeas hold up much better in the canning process than do cannelini or borlotti beans. As for lentils, their obvious superior quality in the dried form and their short cooking time make it unnecessary to use canned ones.

Many of the recipes are written to serve 4 as a main dish or 6 as a first course. This not only indicates they can make wonderful main dishes, but also that legume soups are as delicious when served days later. As with minestrone, reheat over gentle heat, adding more water, and if adding pasta, cook just before serving.

Cooking beans always demands a good heavy-bottomed pot. Earthenware pots are excellent choices, and using a heat diffuser helps to maintain a gentle heat. It is best not to cook beans in excessively large pots. A 2½- to 3½-quart size works well for all of these recipes.

Pasta e Fagioli/Pasta and Bean Soups

Along with minestrone, pasta and bean soups—*pasta e fagioli*—represent one of Italy's most well-known dishes. As its name implies, the legume of choice is *fagioli,* from the kidney or haricot family of beans. In Italy this means *borlotti* or *cannellini.* The other key element is the pasta, which is not just another ingredient, but has equal importance to the beans. Depending on the region, not only does the choice of bean and pasta vary, but so does its preparation. Although all these soups share much in common, this basic combination may be enhanced by a variety of ingredients to yield wonderfully diverse soups.

Because *pasta e fagioli* makes a wonderful main dish, I have made these recipes to serve 4 as a main course or 6 as a first course. The following is a general guideline for using dried beans (it is better to start with the lesser amount of liquid and then add more if needed):

Serves	Dried Beans	Water
4 as first or 2 as a main course	1 cup (6 ounces)	5 to 6 cups
6 as a first or 4 as a main course	1½ cups (9 ounces)	7 to 8 cups
8 as a first or 6 as a main course	2 cups (12 ounces)	9 to 10 cups

Pasta e Fagioli alle Erbe

Pasta and Bean Soup with Fennel and Herbs

serves: 4 to 6

cooking time:
1 to 2 hours

$\mathcal{T}$his aromatic *pasta e fagioli* comes from Sardinia and is prepared with fresh fennel, thyme, and marjoram. A rosy-hued base of pureed cannellini and borlotti beans provides the delicate base for this soup's fresh, assertive flavors. Try to purchase fennel that still has its feathery leaves to use as a garnish.

³/₄ cup (4¹/₂ ounces) dried borlotti
beans, soaked and rinsed
(page 47), or 1 14-ounce can,
lightly drained
³/₄ cup (4¹/₂ ounces) dried
cannellini beans, soaked and
rinsed (page 47), or 1 14-ounce
can, drained

Brodo
7 cups cold water
1 teaspoon coarse salt

Sapori
3 tablespoons extra-virgin olive oil
2 medium fennel bulbs, halved,
cored, and thinly sliced
(about 2¹/₄ cups)

6 thyme sprigs, leaves removed and
chopped, or ¹/₂ teaspoon dried
4 marjoram sprigs, leaves removed
and chopped, or ¹/₂ teaspoon
dried

Condimenti
Salt and freshly ground pepper
5 to 6 ounces (about 2 cups) large
tubular pasta, such as penne or
rigatoni
Finely chopped fennel leaves
(optional)
Extra-virgin olive oil, preferably
estate Ligurian

1. Combine the beans and water in a heavy-bottomed soup pot, cover, and place over medium heat. When it reaches a boil, lower the heat and gently simmer with the lid just slightly ajar, until the beans are tender, about 1¼ hours. Add the salt toward the end of cooking. (If using canned beans, add 4¾ cups light vegetable broth and simmer for 15 minutes.)

Puree half of the beans with a ladle of the broth until smooth. Return to the pot, and using a wooden spoon stir well to combine. Maintain over low heat while preparing the *sapori*.

2. In a separate heavy saucepan, warm the oil over medium-low heat. Add the *sapori* and sauté until softened, stirring often, for 3 to 4 minutes. Cover the pot and sweat the fennel for 10 minutes, stirring occasionally. Add to the cooked beans and simmer together for 10 minutes.

3. Add the salt and pepper to taste and bring the soup to a lively simmer. Add the pasta and cook until *al dente*, stirring occasionally. Add a little boiling water if needed.

Garnish with the fennel leaves and serve with the oil.

Pasta e Fagioli all'Ischitana

Pasta and Bean Soup with Tomatoes

serves: 4 to 6

cooking time:
2¼ hours

*A*specialty of the island of Ischia, tomatoes are given equal importance to the beans. Basil, chili pepper, and fennel seeds create its distinctive flavoring and cooking this soup without sautéing creates its lightness. The pasta is a mixture of the strands that are so popular in this region.

1½ cups (9½ ounces) dried
cannellini beans, soaked and
rinsed (page 47)

Battuto

Finely Chopped Together
1 garlic clove
1 medium celery rib
6 fresh basil leaves

Brodo
6 cups cold water

Sapori
3 to 4 tablespoons extra-virgin olive oil
1 small dried chili pepper or
¼ teaspoon crushed flakes
¾ teaspoon fennel seeds

10 ripe plum tomatoes, peeled and
seeded, or 2 14-ounce cans,
drained and cut into large pieces
3 ounces fatty pancetta, minced and
pounded or processed to a paste
1 teaspoon coarse salt

Condimenti
Salt
6 to 7 ounces (about 1½ cups)
spaghetti, bucatini, or linguine,
broken up
Freshly ground pepper
2 to 3 teaspoons finely chopped fresh
basil (optional)
Freshly grated Parmigiano-
Reggiano cheese

1. Combine the beans, *battuto,* and *brodo* in a heavy-bottomed saucepan. Cover and place over medium heat. When it reaches a boil, lower the heat and gently simmer with the lid just slightly ajar, until the beans are almost tender, about 1 hour.

continued

2. Stir in the *sapori* and cook until the beans are tender, about 30 minutes more.

3. Add the salt to taste and if using a whole chili pepper, remove. Bring the soup to a lively simmer, add the pasta, and cook until *al dente*. Stir occasionally with a wooden spoon and add a little boiling water if needed.

Serve hot or at room temperature with a robust grinding of pepper, a garnish of basil, and Parmesan cheese.

Variante: In Naples, oregano replaces the basil and fennel seeds. Add the celery, thinly sliced, and reduce the tomatoes by half, adding a large pinch of oregano. Use a large tubular pasta, such as ziti, and serve with a light fruity olive oil.

serves: 4 to 6

cooking time: 2¼ hours

Pasta e Fasoi alla Lombarda

Pasta and Bean Soup, Lombardy Style

In Lombardy the borlotti beans are left whole, resulting in a lighter and brothier *pasta e fagioli (fasoi* is the local dialect). The pasta of choice is *maltagliati,* ½-inch-wide strips of egg pasta cut into irregular diamond shapes. Much the same effect can be achieved by cutting fresh fettuccine into about 2-inch irregular diagonal strips. This popular soup's full flavor comes from adding the *battuto* at the end of cooking and serving with a well-aged Parmesan cheese. If you prefer a denser soup, simply puree about half the beans before adding the pasta.

Sapori
1½ cups (9 ounces) dried borlotti
    beans, soaked and rinsed
    (page 47)

Brodo
7 cups cold water
1 teaspoon coarse salt

Battuto
4 to 5 tablespoons extra-virgin
    olive oil

Minced Together
1 small onion
3 ounces fatty pancetta

2 garlic cloves
½ cup packed parsley leaves

1 tablespoon tomato paste, diluted
    with a ladleful of bean broth

Condimenti
Salt and freshly ground pepper
8 ounces fresh maltagliati or
    fettuccine or 5 ounces dried,
    broken into small pieces
Freshly grated Parmigiano-
    Reggiano cheese

1. Combine the beans and water in a heavy-bottomed soup pot, cover, and place over medium heat. When it reaches a boil, lower the heat and gently simmer with the lid just slightly ajar, until the beans are tender, about 1¼ hours. Add the salt toward the end of cooking.

2. In a separate heavy saucepan, combine the oil and minced *battuto* and sauté over low heat, stirring occasionally, for 8 to 10 minutes. Raise the heat to medium, stir in the tomato liquid, and simmer for about 5 minutes. Add to the cooked beans and stir gently with a wooden spoon.

3. Add the salt and pepper to taste and bring the soup to a lively simmer. Add the pasta and cook until *al dente.* Serve with the Parmesan cheese.

Variante: For a vegetarian soup, add 1 small carrot and 1 celery rib to the *battuto,* replace the tomato paste with ⅔ cup pureed tomatoes, and stir in 2 to 3 tablespoons Parmesan cheese at the end of cooking.

Minestra di Pasta e Fagioli alla Siciliana

Pasta and Bean Soup with Cauliflower

Sicily has a long tradition of peasant dishes in which meat is replaced by vegetables combined with beans. This soup's simple earthy combination of tastes requires no fresh herbs and its easy preparation make it a favorite main dish. The key is to sauté the onions long enough to develop their sweetness and not to overcook the cauliflower, keeping its flavor and texture distinct. A fruity olive oil best complements this savory soup.

Battuto

3 tablespoons extra-virgin olive oil
³/₄ cup pancetta, diced
    (3 to 4 ounces)
1 large onion, sliced very thinly
1³/₄ cups (10¹/₂ ounces) dried
    borlotti beans, soaked and rinsed
    (see Nota and page 47)

Brodo

7¹/₂ cups cold water
1 teaspoon coarse salt

Sapori

3 cups (about 12 ounces) small
    cauliflower florets

Condimenti

Salt and freshly ground pepper
6 ounces fresh egg tagliatelle or
    4 ounces dried, cut into short
    pieces
Extra-virgin olive oil, preferably
    estate from Liguria or Puglia

1. In a heavy-bottomed soup pot, sauté the *battuto* over medium-low heat until the onion is a deep golden color, stirring occasionally, for 8 to 10 minutes.

Using a wooden spoon, stir the beans into the *battuto*.

2. Add the water, cover, and raise the heat to medium. When it reaches a boil, lower the heat and gently simmer with the lid just slightly ajar, until the beans are very tender, about 1¹/₂ hours. Add the salt toward the end of cooking.

3. Bring the soup to a lively simmer, add the *sapori,* and cook until the cauliflower is tender, about 10 minutes (if adding dried pasta, slightly undercook the cauliflower).

4. Add the salt and pepper to taste. Add the tagliatelle and stir occasionally with a wooden spoon until *al dente*. Add a little boiling water if needed, and serve with the oil.

Nota: Dried red kidney beans can substitute for the borlotti; just be sure to boil them for 10 minutes to rid them of any toxins (see page 49).

Pasta e Fagioli alla Toscana

Tuscan Pasta and Bean Soup

*A*fter trying this deliciously delicate *pasta e fagioli* at Osteria Numero Uno in Florence, I immediately sought out the owner to find out what made it so extraordinary. Gianni Girardi was kind enough to share his secrets. The best olive oil, flavored with plenty of fresh rosemary and garlic, is stirred into the soup just before adding the pasta. Its delicacy was a result of pureeing the beans through a food mill, eliminating their skins. Signor Girardi unabashedly told me that he always adds *dadi* (stock cubes) for extra flavor.

Sapori
1³/4 cups (10¹/2 ounces) dried
    cannellini beans, soaked and
    rinsed (page 47), or 4¹/4 cups
    canned, with some of its juices

Brodo
7¹/2 cups cold water
2 garlic cloves, peeled
2 fresh bay leaves or 1 dried
1 teaspoon coarse salt

Battuto
3 to 4 tablespoons extra-virgin
    olive oil

Minced Together
1 medium-large red onion
1 medium carrot

1 medium celery rib

¹/3 cup tomato pulp or puree, such
    as Pomi
¹/2 beef stock cube, minced

Condimenti
¹/3 cup extra-virgin olive oil,
    preferably estate Tuscan
2 fresh rosemary sprigs, left whole
    (see Nota)
4 garlic cloves, peeled and left whole
Salt
5 ounces (1¹/4 cups) short pasta,
    such as ditalini or small
    macaroni
Freshly ground pepper

1. Combine the beans and *brodo* except for the salt in a heavy saucepan. Cover and place over medium heat. When it reaches a boil, lower the heat and gently simmer with the lid just slightly ajar, until the beans are very tender, about 1¼ hours. Add the salt toward the end of cooking (if using canned beans, add 6 cups water and simmer for about 30 minutes). Remove the bay leaves.

2. Shortly before the beans have finished cooking, combine the oil and minced *battuto* in a heavy-bottomed soup pot and sauté over medium-low heat, stirring occasionally, for 8 to 10 minutes. Add the tomato and stock cube and cook, stirring, for 2 to 3 minutes more.

3. Drain the beans, adding most of the broth to the sautéed *battuto*. Puree the beans with its remaining broth through the small-holed disc of a food mill and add to the soup pot (if using a food processor, puree with a couple of ladles of broth and push through a sieve to eliminate the skins). Stir well to combine and gently simmer, covered, for 15 to 20 minutes more.

4. Meanwhile, in a small heavy saucepan, combine the oil, rosemary, and garlic. Sauté over low heat until the garlic is golden, about 10 minutes. Gently crush the garlic with the back of a fork to release its juices, then remove along with the rosemary. Stir 2 tablespoons of the flavored oil into the soup and place the remainder in a server, allowing it to cool.

Add the salt to taste and bring the soup to a lively simmer. Add the pasta and cook, stirring occasionally, until *al dente*. The broth should have a silky texture. If necessary, add a little boiling water.

Season with a few twists of freshly ground pepper and serve with the aromatic oil.

Nota: The sprigs of rosemary can be replaced with dried rosemary leaves. Soak 2 tablespoons in warm water to soften, drain, and pat dry. Strain the oil to remove.

Variante: In Milan at Al Capriccio, this soup is topped with shrimp. Omit the stock cube, increase the tomatoes to ½ cup, and add 10 ounces fresh egg fettuccine, cut into short strips.

Pasta e Fagioli alla Trentina

Pasta and Bean Soup, Trento Style

*I*n this delicate *pasta e fagioli* Trento's Austro-Hungarian culinary heritage is evident by the touch of cinnamon and vinegar. Their flavors in this soup are almost indiscernible, but the character they impart is not. Oil infused with the taste of onion and garlic balances out this aromatic soup.

1³/₄ cups (10¹/₂ ounces) dried
    cannellini beans, soaked and
    rinsed (page 47)

Brodo
7¹/₂ cups cold water
1 large celery rib
¹/₈ teaspoon cinnamon

Sapori
3 tablespoons extra-virgin olive oil
¹/₃ cup finely chopped onion
1 to 2 garlic cloves, halved
    lengthwise

2 tablespoons tomato paste
1¹/₂ teaspoons coarse salt

Condimenti
Salt and freshly ground pepper
7 ounces (1¹/₂ cups) short pasta,
    such as ditalini
Freshly grated Parmesan cheese
1 to 2 tablespoons best red wine
    vinegar

1. Combine the beans and *brodo* in a heavy-bottomed soup pot, cover, and place over medium heat. When it reaches a boil, lower the heat and gently simmer with the lid slightly ajar, until the beans are almost tender, about 1 hour.

2. In a separate small heavy saucepan, combine the oil, onion, and garlic and sauté over low heat, being careful not to brown the garlic, for 8 to 10 minutes. Strain the flavored oil into the beans, pressing the garlic and onion to release all their juices, then discard.

Add the tomato paste and salt and continue cooking until the beans are tender, about 30 minutes more. Remove the celery rib.

3. Add the salt and pepper to taste and bring the soup to a lively simmer. Add the pasta and cook until *al dente*. Take the soup off the heat and stir in 2 to 3 tablespoons of Parmesan cheese and the vinegar to taste. Serve with the Parmesan cheese.

Pasta e Fasoi alla Veneta

Pasta and Bean Soup, Veneto Style

*T*he importance of this classic soup is underscored by the fact that it is the only dish from the Veneto that features pasta. In fact, the Veneto even claims to have the most variations. *Pasta e fasoi* (the local dialect) may vary from city to city, but the beans of choice are always the local *borlotti di Lamon*. The first borlotti to be cultivated in Italy, they are prized for their fine texture and plump size. The pasta varies from fresh egg tagliatelle to short tubular cuts, and in Udine *bigoli*, a thick whole wheat spaghetti is added. Characteristic of the soups from this region, they omit tomatoes, giving this *pasta e fagioli* its distinctive ocher hue.

Battuto	*Brodo*
4 to 5 tablespoons extra-virgin olive oil	4 ounces pancetta, left whole (see Nota)
	7¹/₂ cups cold water
Minced Together	
1 small onion	*Condimenti*
1 medium celery rib	Salt and freshly ground pepper
1 medium carrot	10 ounces fresh tagliatelle or
1³/₄ cups (10¹/₂ ounces) dried borlotti beans, soaked and rinsed (page 47)	6 ounces dried, broken into short pieces, or whole wheat spaghetti
	Extra-virgin olive oil, preferably estate

1. In a heavy-bottomed soup pot, sauté the *battuto* over low heat, stirring occasionally until the vegetables soften, 8 to 10 minutes. Add the beans and stir to coat well.

2. Add the *brodo,* cover, and turn the heat to medium. When it reaches a boil, lower the heat and gently simmer with the lid just slightly ajar, until the beans are tender, about 1¼ hours. Remove the pancetta and allow to cool. Cut its meat into thin strips and reserve.

Puree about half the beans with a couple of ladles of broth until smooth. Return to the soup and, using a wooden spoon, stir well to combine.

3. Add the salt and pepper to taste and bring the soup to a lively simmer. Add the pasta and cook until *al dente*, stirring often. Top with the pancetta strips, a robust twist of pepper, and a thread of oil. Serve hot or lukewarm.

Nota: This soup is commonly flavored with fresh pork rind, which is removed at the end of cooking, cut into *listrelle* (thin strips), and used as a garnish. This recipe adds pancetta or a proscuitto end; if you prefer, the pancetta can be minced with the *battuto.*

Variante: For a vegetarian soup, add 1 teaspoon rosemary leaves and 1 garlic clove to the *battuto* and add ⅓ cup chopped tomatoes after the beans become tender.

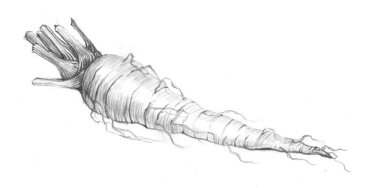

Legumi/Bean, Chickpea, Lentil, and Fava Bean Soups

From the robust dense winter zuppe to the more delicate minestre, legumes take center stage in these soups. For hundreds of years legumes have taken the place of meat in the "poor cooking" of la cucina povera *and, not surprisingly, all of these soups make wonderful main-course dishes or hearty beginnings for the courses to follow.*

serves: 4 to 6

cooking time:
1 hour

Minestra di Ceci e Finocchi

Chickpea and Fennel Soup

The tall dark green stalks of *finocchio selvatico* (wild fennel) is a favorite ingredient of southern Italy. In this flavorful soup from Sardinia, its distinct anise taste combines beautifully with chickpeas, tomatoes, and a savory *battuto*. This recipe uses the sweet fennel bulb, adding the seeds to resemble the taste of wild fennel. Using canned chickpeas makes this soup as short to prepare as it is long on pleasure.

Battuto

3 to 4 tablespoons extra-virgin
  olive oil
1 medium-large onion, halved and
  thinly sliced
2 ounces sausage, casing removed

Minced Together
1 garlic clove
¹/₄ cup parsley leaves

Sapori

³/₄ cup chopped tomatoes, peeled
  and seeded, with their juice
1 scant teaspoon fennel seeds

2 medium fennel bulbs, halved,
  cored, and thinly sliced
  (about 2¹/₂ cups)
2¹/₂ cups canned chickpeas, drained

Brodo
4¹/₂ cups Light Vegetable Broth
  (page 42) or water and
1 stock cube

Condimenti
Salt
3 to 4 ounces (1 cup) small pasta,
  such as ditalini
Freshly ground pepper

1. In a heavy-bottomed soup pot, sauté the *battuto* over low heat, stirring occasionally, for about 10 minutes, breaking the sausage up with a wooden spoon.

2. Stir in the tomatoes and fennel seeds and cook for 3 to 4 minutes. Add the fennel, cover the pot, and sweat until softened, about 8 minutes, stirring occasionally. Stir in the chickpeas.

3. Meanwhile, bring the *brodo* to a boil, then add. Cover and cook at a steady simmer until the fennel is very tender, about 20 minutes more.

4. Add the salt to taste and bring the soup to a lively simmer. Add the pasta and cook until *al dente*, adding a little boiling water if needed. Cover and let the soup rest for about 5 minutes.

Season with a twist of pepper and serve.

Nota: If using dried chickpeas, add 1 cup (7 ounces) and cook as directed for *Pasta e Ceci* (page 70), omitting the rosemary and using its cooking liquid as the *brodo*.

Pasta e Ceci

Pasta and Chickpea Soup

When legumes are combined with pasta in southern and central Italy, chick-peas often replace the beans. The recipes may vary according to region, but they almost always include garlic and rosemary as the natural complement to the nutty taste of chickpeas. This recipe is typical of Rome where this popular soup is made with either *guanciale,* similar to fatty pancetta, or with anchovy on religious days of *magro* when meat is not eaten.

Sapori

1⅓ *cups (9 ounces) dried chickpeas,*
  previously soaked 12 to 24 hours
  and rinsed (page 47), or 3½ cups
  canned, drained

Brodo

7½ *cups cold water*
1 *fresh rosemary branch or*
  2 tablespoons dried (see Nota)
2 *garlic cloves, peeled*
1 *teaspoon coarse salt*

Battuto

2 *to 3 tablespoons extra-virgin*
  olive oil

Finely Chopped Together

2 *garlic cloves*
1 *tablespoon rosemary leaves*
3 *to 4 ounces fatty pancetta or*
  2 anchovy fillets

½ *cup pureed tomatoes or*
  1½ *tablespoons tomato paste,*
  diluted in water

Condimenti

Salt and freshly ground pepper
10 *ounces fresh fettuccine, cut into*
  short pieces, or 7 ounces dried
Estate olive oil

1. Combine the chickpeas and *brodo* except for the salt in a heavy soup pot, cover, and bring to a boil. Lower the heat and gently simmer with the lid slightly ajar, until the chickpeas are very tender, about 2 to 2½ hours. Add the salt toward the end of cooking. (If using canned chickpeas, add 3½ cups water and cook for 45 minutes.) Remove the rosemary and garlic.

2. In a small heavy saucepan, combine the oil and chopped *battuto* and sauté over low heat, stirring occasionally, for about 5 minutes. Stir in the tomato and cook for 15 minutes more. Add to the cooked chickpeas.

3. Puree about half the cooked chickpeas with a couple of ladles of the broth. If using a food processor, puree for 2 to 3 minutes, until the skins have completely broken down; for a thinner soup, pass through the fine-holed disc of a vegetable mill. Add to the *battuto* and, using a wooden spoon, stir well to combine.

4. Add the salt and pepper to taste and bring the soup to a lively simmer. Add the pasta and cook until *al dente*, stirring often to prevent sticking (if using dried pasta, you may prefer to cook it separately in boiling salted water and then add to the chickpeas). If needed, add a little boiling water.

Garnish with a thread of oil, and serve the remaining oil at the table.

Nota: To prevent the rosemary leaves from dispersing into the *brodo,* either tie the branch with colorless thread or place the loose leaves in a muslin bag.

Zuppa alla Norma

Chickpea and Vegetable Soup

*I*magine my delight when the celebrated chef Giampiero Gemignani showed me his new spring menu for Solferino and there was a soup named after me! A delicate puree of chickpeas and cannellini beans provides the backdrop for ten colorful vegetables. After tasting this soup, both beautiful to the eye and palate, I could not have been more honored. If you lack one vegetable, simply increase the amounts of the others. Serve with your finest olive oil.

*1¼ cups (8 ounces) dried chickpeas,
     soaked, or 2 14-ounce cans,
     drained*
*½ cup (4 ounces) dried cannellini
     beans, soaked, or 1 14-ounce can,
     drained*

Brodo

7 cups cold water
1 garlic clove
1 rosemary branch
1 teaspoon coarse salt

Sapori

*2 to 3 ounces (about ⅔ cup, diced)
     of the following: zucchini; carrots;
     celery; asparagus tips, left whole;
     fennel; brown mushrooms,
     preferably chestnut or shiitake;
     boiling potato; leeks, thinly sliced*
*1 to 2 ounces (about ⅓ cup) of the
     following: zucchini flowers, cut
     into thin strips (optional); fresh
     ripe tomatoes, peeled,
     seeded, and chopped; spring
     onions, white and light green
     parts, thinly sliced*

Condimenti

Salt and freshly ground pepper
2 tablespoons minced fresh basil
*Estate olive oil, preferably from
     Lucca*

1. Rinse the chickpeas and cannellini beans with cold water and combine in a heavy-bottomed soup pot. Add the water, garlic, and rosemary, cover, and place over medium heat. When it reaches a boil, lower the heat and gently simmer, the lid slightly ajar, until the chickpeas are tender, about 2 hours. Add the salt toward the end of cooking (if using canned legumes, reduce the water to 5½ cups and cook for 30 minutes).

Remove the rosemary branch. Puree the legumes through the small-holed disc of a vegetable mill, readding to the soup pot.

2. Over moderate heat, bring the soup to a simmer. Add the *sapori,* one vegetable at a time, maintaining the soup at a constant simmer. Cook, uncovered, until the vegetables are just tender, 10 to 15 minutes. Stir occasionally and, if needed, add a little boiling water; the broth should be fairly thin but still have body.

3. Add the salt and pepper to taste. Garnish with the basil and a thread of oil and serve with the rest of the oil.

Zuppa del Frantoio

Bean and Vegetable Soup with First-Pressed Oil

A specialty of Tuscany, most notably the area surrounding Arezzo, this traditional soup pays homage to the first pressing of the olives through the *frantoio* (olive mill). It is thought that nothing better shows off these deep golden threads of virgin oil than a base of pureed beans flavored with the seasonal vegetables. The beans may vary from the nutty taste of borlotti to the earthier flavor of black-eyed beans.

*1¹/₂ cups (8¹/₂ ounces) dried borlotti
    beans, soaked and rinsed
    (page 47), or see Nota*

Brodo
5 cups cold water
1 teaspoon coarse salt

Battuto
6 tablespoons extra-virgin olive oil

Finely Chopped Together
1 medium onion
5 to 6 ounces pancetta

Sapori
*1 medium leek, white and light
    green parts, finely sliced*
*2 medium celery ribs, scraped and
    coarsely chopped*
2 medium carrots, coarsely chopped

*2 medium zucchini, coarsely
    chopped*
*8 ounces coarsely chopped pumpkin
    flesh*
*6 to 8 ounces shredded kale or Savoy
    cabbage*

Condimenti
1/4 cup chopped parsley
*1 teaspoon chopped fresh thyme
    leaves or 1/2 teaspoon dried*
2 garlic cloves, minced
Zest from 1/2 lemon
1 tablespoon tomato paste
Salt and freshly ground pepper
*4 to 6 slices of country bread,
    preferably stale*
Estate olive oil, preferably Tuscan

1. Combine the beans and water in a heavy saucepan, cover, and place over medium heat. When it reaches a boil, lower the heat and gently simmer with the lid just slightly ajar, until the beans are tender, about 1¼ hours. Add the salt toward the end of cooking.

2. In a separate heavy soup pot, sauté the *battuto* over low heat for about 10 minutes.

3. Stir in the *sapori* and stir well to combine with the *battuto*. Cover and sweat the vegetables for 10 minutes.

Puree the cooked beans and their liquid through the small-holed disc of a vegetable mill, adding to the sautéed vegetables (if using a food processor, puree until very smooth, adding a little hot water). Cook at a gentle but steady simmer, covered, for about 30 minutes.

4. Stir in the herbs, garlic, lemon zest, and tomato paste and cook for 30 minutes more. Add the salt and pepper to taste and a little hot water if needed.

5. Toast the bread on both sides and place a layer in a soup tureen or in each bowl, drizzle with abundant oil, and ladle over with the soup. Repeat the layers. Or if you prefer a lighter soup, add only one layer of bread. Garnish with a thread of oil and serve.

Nota: If using black-eyed beans, cook for about 45 minutes.

Zuppa di Fagioli con Insalata di Radicchio

Borlotti and Radicchio Soup

*I*n taste and color, *fagioli borlotti* and *radicchio rosso* have a great affinity. The borlotti beans are cooked in an aromatic broth and pureed, providing a mellow but flavorful base for the tart taste of the radicchio. Fresh parsley and basil delicately garnish this elegant soup.

Instead of pancetta, prosciutto is used for its taste and leanness. It can be part of the *battuto,* or a prosciutto end can be cooked with the beans and then discarded. To shred the radicchio, roll its leaves over one another and slice finely. To keep its taste from turning bitter, the radicchio is added after the soup is taken off the fire.

1 cup (6 ounces) dried borlotti
*   beans, soaked and rinsed*
*   (page 47), or 2¹/₂ cups canned,*
*   drained (see Nota)*

Battuto
2 to 3 tablespoons extra-virgin
*   olive oil*

Minced Together
1 small carrot
1 small celery rib
1 garlic clove
2 shallots or 1 small red onion
2 ounces prosciutto

Brodo
4 cups cold water
1 fresh bay leaf or ¹/₂ dried
4 cups Light Vegetable Broth
*   (page 42) or water and 1 stock*
*   cube*

Condimenti
3 tablespoons extra-virgin olive oil
1 teaspoon good-quality wine
*   vinegar, preferably white*
2 tablespoons minced parsley
2 tablespoons minced fresh basil
2 to 3 ounces (about 2 cups) finely
*   shredded radicchio*
Salt and freshly ground pepper

1. In a heavy-bottomed soup pot, sauté the *battuto* over medium-low heat until softened, stirring occasionally, 4 to 5 minutes.

2. Add the beans and, using a wooden spoon, stir to coat well. Add the water and bay leaf, cover, and turn the heat to medium. When it reaches a boil, lower the heat and gently simmer with the lid slightly ajar, until the beans are tender, about 1¼ hours. Remove the bay leaf and drain the beans, reserving the liquid.

Put aside a ladleful of the beans. Puree the remainder of the beans in a food processor, adding enough hot bean broth to achieve a smooth puree.

3. In a soup pot, combine the puree and vegetable broth and bring to a simmer. The broth should be creamy, not dense. Add some of the reserved bean broth if needed.

4. In a small bowl, whisk together the vinegar, oil, and herbs of the *condimenti*. Take the soup off the heat and stir in the herb mixture and radicchio. Add the salt and pepper to taste.

Serve with a garnish of the whole borlotti beans placed in the center of each serving.

Nota: If using canned beans, add 4½ cups vegetable broth and the bay leaf and gently simmer, covered, for 30 minutes.

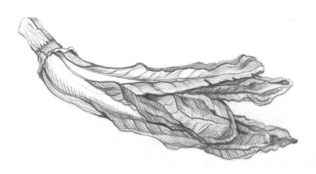

Zuppa di Fave Fresche con Cipolle

Fresh Fava Bean Soup with Spring Onions

*O*ne of the irresistible signs of an approaching Roman summer is the arrival of the first small, tender fava beans. Their deliciously sweet earthy taste is commonly offset with the piquant flavor of sheep's milk cheese. This recipe calls for the milder taste of *caciotta,* a soft fresh sheep's milk cheese. If unavailable, sprinkle the bread with pecorino Romano cheese.

Sapori

2 to 3 tablespoons extra-virgin
    olive oil
2 to 3 ounces fatty pancetta, finely
    chopped
12 ounces spring onions and/or leeks,
    white parts only, finely sliced
    (about 2 cups)
2¹/₂ cups shelled fava beans (3 to 4
    pounds fresh unshelled), see Nota
Coarse salt

Brodo

2¹/₂ cups water and 2¹/₂ cups
    Vegetable Broth (page 40) or
    substitute

Condimenti

4 slices of country bread, preferably
    stale
2 to 3 ounces caciotta or pecorino
    Romano
Extra-virgin olive oil
¹/₃ cup chopped mixed fresh parsley
    and basil

1. Sauté the oil and pancetta in a heavy-bottomed soup pot over medium-low heat until the pancetta fat melts, 5 to 7 minutes.

Add the onions and sauté until soft, stirring often, for about 5 minutes. Then add the fava beans, season with a few pinches of salt, and gently sauté, stirring occasionally, for 15 minutes. If needed, add a little hot water to prevent the beans from sticking.

2. Bring the *brodo* to a boil and add. Continue cooking until the beans are very tender, 10 to 15 minutes.

3. Meanwhile, toast the bread on both sides. Spread one side with a thin layer of cheese and place in each soup bowl. Drizzle the bread with oil, ladle over with the hot soup, and sprinkle with the herbs.

Nota: Using fresh *fave* calls for patience, as one pound of unshelled beans yields far less than half their shelled weight. If using the larger *fave,* their outer tough skins need removing. You can supplement the fresh beans with frozen. Canned ones are best not used.

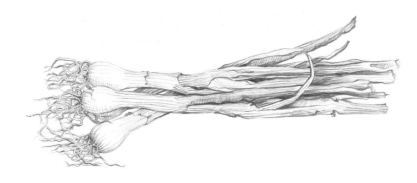

Minestra di Fave Passate con Lattuga

Pureed Fava Bean Soup with Lettuce and Prosciutto

*T*his recipe from Calabria combines pureed fresh fava beans with lettuce for a deliciously fresh-tasting soup, perfect for warm weather.

Sapori

1½ cups fava beans (about
    2 pounds fresh unshelled or
    8 ounces frozen, defrosted)
1 baking potato, peeled and coarsely
    chopped (about 2 cups)

Brodo

3½ cups water and 1 cube vegetable
    or chicken stock

Battuto

3 tablespoons extra-virgin olive oil

Minced Together

3 ounces prosciutto
1 medium onion

Condimenti

1 small head of Boston lettuce, cored
    and cut into thin strips
Salt and freshly ground pepper
Crostini fried in oil or butter
    (optional)

1. Place the *sapori* in a soup pot and add just enough cold water to cover. Bring to a boil over moderate heat, then lower the heat and simmer until the potato turns tender, about 20 minutes. If needed, add a little boiling water. Puree until smooth.

2. Bring the *brodo* to a simmer in the soup pot, then add the fava puree and stir well to combine. Maintain over low heat while preparing the *condimenti*.

3. In a separate heavy saucepan, sauté the *battuto* over moderate heat until the onion lightly colors, 3 to 4 minutes. Add the lettuce and stir with a wooden spoon until it wilts and is well coated with the *battuto*. Add to the soup and stir well.

Add the salt and pepper to taste and serve garnished with the crostini.

Minestra di Lenticchie e Zucca al Guanciale

Lentil and Pumpkin Soup with Pancetta

serves: 4 to 6

cooking time:
1½ hours

*P*articularly favored in central Italy, *guanciale* is made from pig's jowl. Though similar to pancetta, its higher fat content and more flavorful taste make it much appreciated in pasta sauces and soups. This splendid Roman soup also combines two other ingredients favored in this region—lentils and mint.

Battuto
2 tablespoons extra-virgin olive oil
2 ounces fatty pancetta, diced

Minced Together
1 medium onion
1 garlic clove
1 small celery rib
1 small carrot

Sapori
1 cup (7 ounces) brown lentils,
    picked over, rinsed, and
    drained well

2 cups pumpkin or butternut squash,
    cut into small cubes
    (about 8 ounces)

Brodo
5½ cups light Classic Meat Broth
    (page 36) or water and 2 stock
    cubes (1 chicken, 1 beef)
1 bay leaf

Condimenti
Salt and freshly ground pepper
1 tablespoon chopped parsley
1 tablespoon chopped fresh mint or
    1 teaspoon dried (see Nota)

1. In a heavy-bottomed soup pot, combine the oil and pancetta over medium-low heat. After the pancetta has started to release its fat, 3 to 4 minutes, add the minced *battuto* and sauté, stirring occasionally, for about 5 minutes.

2. Add the lentils and, using a wooden spoon, stir for 2 to 3 minutes to coat well.

continued

3. Meanwhile, bring the *brodo* to a boil, then add. Cover and simmer until the lentils are tender, about 45 minutes. Add the pumpkin, lower the heat, and gently simmer, covered, until tender without disintegrating, about 15 minutes. Remove the bay leaf.

4. Add the salt and pepper to taste. Gently stir in the herbs and serve.

Nota: If using dried mint, add about 5 minutes before the end of cooking.

serves: 4

cooking time:
1½ hours

Zuppa di Lenticchie e Castagne

Lentil and Chestnut Soup

Fresh chestnuts are available in Italian markets from the late autumn through winter, which is the best time for enjoying this delicious soup from Abruzzi. Good-quality vacuum-packed or canned chestnuts can be substituted, making its preparation easy.

Brodo
6 cups cold water
1 teaspoon coarse salt
2 fresh bay leaves or 1 dried

Sapori
1 cup (7 ounces) brown or green
   lentils, picked over and rinsed
3 tablespoons extra-virgin olive oil
3 to 4 (about 2/3 cup) ounces diced
   pancetta
4 fresh basil leaves, finely shredded

8 ounces chestnuts, fresh roasted
   (see page 226), or vacuum-
   packed or canned, peeled and
   drained
Pinch of thyme and marjoram
2 teaspoons tomato paste
2/3 cup dry white wine
Salt and freshly ground pepper

Condimenti
4 slices country bread

1. Combine the *brodo* and lentils in a heavy-bottomed soup pot. Bring to a boil, then lower the heat and simmer, covered, until tender, about 1 hour.

2. About 10 minutes before the lentils have finished cooking, in a separate heavy saucepan, combine the oil, pancetta, and basil and sauté over medium-low heat. Add the chestnuts and herbs and sauté, stirring often, for 5 minutes.

Add the tomato paste and wine and cook until evaporated, about 10 minutes. Using a wooden spoon, stir the entire mixture into the cooked lentils and cook for 10 minutes more. If needed, add a little water and salt and pepper to taste.

3. Meanwhile, toast the bread on both sides, place the warm slices in each bowl, and ladle over with the hot soup.

Zuppa Senese di Lenticchie

Lentil Soup with Red Onion

*F*ollowing the same Sienese tradition found in the preparation of *ribollita,* this deliciously savory soup is topped with thinly sliced red onions and drizzled with the finest olive oil. This recipe adds fried fresh sage leaves to the *condimenti* for an even more intensely flavored soup.

Battuto
2 to 3 tablespoons extra-virgin
    olive oil
5 to 6 sage leaves, shredded, or
    1 teaspoon dried

Minced Together
1 medium red onion
2 ounces pancetta or prosciutto

Sapori
1³/₄ cups (12 ounces) brown or
    green lentils, picked over and
    rinsed well

Brodo
7 cups cold water
1 teaspoon salt
2 garlic cloves, coarsely chopped
1 celery rib with leaves, left whole

Condimenti
Extra-virgin olive oil
6 to 8 fresh sage leaves, shredded
    (optional)
4 to 6 slices of coarse country bread,
    cut into ¹/₂-inch-thick slices
2 garlic cloves, peeled
Coarsely ground black pepper
1 large red onion, cut into paper-
    thin slices

1. In a heavy-bottomed soup pot, sauté the *battuto* over low heat, stirring occasionally, for 8 to 10 minutes, adding a little hot water if necessary.

2. Add the *sapori* and *brodo* and bring a boil. Lower the heat and simmer, partially covered, until the lentils are tender, about 40 minutes. Remove the celery stalk and add salt to taste. Maintain over low heat while preparing the *condimenti*.

3. If adding fresh sage leaves, heat the oil over moderately high heat in a frying pan, preferably nonstick, and fry the leaves until crisp. Remove and set aside. In the same pan, adding more oil if needed, sauté the bread slices on both sides until lightly browned. Rub one side of the bread with garlic.

4. Place a bread slice in each soup plate, season with a robust twist of freshly ground pepper, and ladle over with the soup. Top with the fried sage leaves and sliced onions. Drizzle with oil, serving the remaining oil and onions at the table.

Minestroni

"Big" Vegetable Soups

Minestra *in Italian means "soup." When "one"—or its plural form—"oni"— is added to the end of an Italian word, it means "big." And true to its name, everything about a minestrone is big. Distinguished from other soups by its notable variety of ingredients, minestrone is prepared with an abundance of fresh vegetables, aromatic herbs, legumes or grains, and potatoes or squash to add body. Pancetta is often a small but essential flavoring and pasta or rice are commonly added. Freshly grated Parmesan or pecorino cheese or a good flavorful olive oil complete this chorus of tastes and textures.*

From the substantial minestroni *of the north to the herb-filled lighter* minestroni *of the south, every region and indeed every cook have created their own inter-*

pretation. The locally produced products, the climate, and most of all, the gastronomic traditions of each area go into creating *minestroni* of distinct differences. It is no wonder that the densest *minestroni* come from the colder mountainous areas, while the *minestroni* of the south are bursting with the tastes and colors of the Mediterranean.

What every minestrone has in common is the predominance of fresh vegetables cut into small pieces and gently simmered to create a soup of unusual richness. No one single flavor ever dominates. A minestrone becomes infused with the tastes and aromas of all its ingredients. Delicious when served immediately and even days later, minestrone becomes more flavorful when allowed "to sit" for a few hours or overnight.

A meal in itself, there is nothing dainty about a minestrone. Served in earthenware bowls deep enough to stir in freshly grated cheese or a flavorful olive oil, minestrone is enjoyed year-round: hot in the cooler months and *tiepido* (at room temperature) in the spring and summer. The pleasures that come from using all available ingredients to create these soups of seemingly endless variety make minestrone one of the most popular soups throughout Italy.

Preparing Minestrone

Nowhere in Italian soup cookery is the idea of orchestration more apparent than with minestrone's varied and abundant vegetables. For example, potatoes and squash used to thicken the soup are always added first, while peas and spinach would lose their character if added too early. Fresh herbs may be added at the start of cooking for a gentle flavoring or at the end for greater emphasis.

The most efficient way to cook minestrone is to prepare the ingredients in the order they are to be added. While the *battuto* is cooking, you can wash and chop the vegetables; while one vegetable is cooking you can prepare the next. Not only does this save time, but it maintains a consistent cooking temperature.

Battuto The *battuto* is almost always sautéed. To prolong the sauté until the *sapori* is ready, sweat the sautéed *battuto* by adding a little hot water and covering the pot.

Sapori Almost all *minestroni* use potatoes or pumpkin to thicken and bind the soup. To ensure that they fully break down, chop them very finely—using a food processor makes this easy. The other *sapori* vegetables are chopped into about ⅓-inch pieces. The uniformity of size matters more than their shape. The vegetables are either sautéed, *col soffritto,* or added raw, *a crudo.*

Brodo With minestrone's robust *battuto* and varied *sapori,* usually just the addition of lightly salted water as the *brodo* suffices. However, if you prefer, add a stock cube or a prepared broth for more flavor. Depending on the recipe, the temperature at which the *brodo* is added can vary.

The temperature you cook minestrone plays a major role in the final result. The more robust—*robusto*—*minestroni* require a very gentle heat. This allows the legumes, potatoes, or squash that bind the soup to release their starches while at the same time maintaining the texture of the other vegetables. Using a heat diffuser is a great help. The lighter—*leggeri*—*minestroni* are cooked over a higher heat.

Condimenti Pasta and rice can be substituted for one another or, if you prefer, omitted altogether. Before adding uncooked pasta or rice, bring the soup to a lively simmer. Stir with a wooden spoon to prevent sticking; the denser the soup, the more you will need to stir. Cook until *al dente;* they will continue to cook after the soup has been taken off the heat. Alternatively, cook separately and add just before serving.

Vegetables that require a short cooking time are often added with the pasta or rice. If green vegetables are added at the end of cooking, leave the lid off to maintain their greenness.

Minestrone is almost always served with freshly grated Parmesan or pecorino cheese, stirred in at the end of cooking and/or passed around at the table. If you are serving with olive oil instead, a good estate oil is always preferable.

The Recipes

More than any other type of soup, minestrone lends itself to numerous variations. And while any number of combinations can yield wonderful results, there are certain ones that give each minestrone its distinctive character. The introduction to each recipe describes these essential ingredients.

Minestrone is a soup you will want to make in larger quantities to be enjoyed the day you cook it as well as many days later. The recipes in this chapter are for 6 to 8, serving 6 as a main course or 8 as a first course.

The recipe you choose to prepare will not only be determined by the availability of ingredients but also by the season and cooking time. To make your selection easier, the recipes are divided into two categories: *robusti,* the heartier *minestroni,* which take 1½ hours or longer to cook, and *leggeri,* the lighter *minestroni,* which take 1 to 1½ hours to cook.

Making Vegetarian Minestrone If you omit meat, part of minestrone's true character will be lost. To compensate, substitute a flavorful vegetable *brodo* for water, add a few ripe tomatoes, increase the amount of herbs, and/or add a Parmesan rind (page 44).

Preparing Ahead of Time If you are not planning to serve the minestrone when it has finished cooking but later that day, allow it to sit in a cool place in your kitchen, unrefrigerated, before reheating or serving at room temperature. For best results, cook the pasta or rice separately and add just before serving. Minestrone will keep, refrigerated, for about 4 days in a tightly sealed container.

When reheating, add more water and place over low heat. Stir frequently with a wooden spoon to prevent sticking and add more water as needed. Reheating in the oven or in the microwave works well.

A Note on Dried Beans Although using dried beans is preferable, in all but a few recipes canned beans can be satisfactorily substituted. The cooking time can be substantially shortened by substituting canned or precooked beans for dried ones.

Robusti/Robust Minestrone Soups

These hearty minestroni are popular throughout central and northern Italy. Most are served from the autumn through spring, some being wintertime staples of Italy's remote mountainous towns. They all require a somewhat longer cooking time and make wonderful main-course soups.

Jota Triestina

Bean and Sauerkraut Minestrone

serves: 6 to 8

cooking time: 2 hours

This classic winter minestrone is closely linked to Friuli-Venezia Giulia's strong Austro-Hungarian heritage. A staple of the poor mountain villages surrounding Gorzia and Trieste, *jota* was prepared from easily obtained ingredients, both fresh and preserved. There are numerous variations of *jota,* but its most defining feature is *crauti acidi* (sauerkraut). In this richly satisfying soup, its mildly acidic taste is balanced by the savory taste of *pancetta affumicata* (smoked bacon).

Although this recipe can be made with store-bought sauerkraut, I much prefer the far more interesting and fresher taste of homemade *crauti acidi*. Not only is it simple to make but the sauerkraut can be cooked in a separate pot as the beans are cooking. In Friuli *brovada,* "shredded turnips," replace the cabbage; for this interesting variation, either substitute or supplement the cabbage with turnips. I always make extra so I can prepare *zuppa di crauti* (see *Variante*).

continued

1²/₃ cups (10 ounces) dried borlotti
    beans, soaked and rinsed
    (page 47)

Brodo

8 cups cold water
2 fresh bay leaves or 1 dried

Battuto

3 tablespoons extra-virgin olive oil
8 ounces minced veal or pork

Minced Together

1 large onion
2 garlic cloves
¹/₂ cup parsley leaves

¹/₄ cup polenta cornmeal

Sapori

2 tablespoons olive oil
¹/₂ cup minced onion

5¹/₂ cups shredded Savoy cabbage,
    light inner leaves only
    (about 12 ounces)
1 teaspoon salt
4 whole peppercorns
2 fresh bay leaves or 1 dried
3 juniper berries
3 tablespoons white wine vinegar or
    1¹/₂ cups (12 ounces) prepared
    sauerkraut, well drained
    (see Nota)

Condimenti

4 to 5 ounces smoked pancetta or
    smoked bacon
3 tablespoons extra-virgin olive oil
6 to 8 slices of country bread

1. Combine the beans and *brodo* in a large heavy-bottomed soup pot and place over medium heat. When it reaches a boil, lower the heat and gently simmer, with the lid just slightly ajar, until the beans are partially cooked and start to turn tender, 45 to 60 minutes.

2. In a separate, small, heavy saucepan, combine the oil and veal and gently sauté until the veal renders its fat, 5 to 7 minutes. Add the minced *battuto* and sauté for 5 minutes more. Add the polenta and stir with a wooden spoon until thickened. Stir into the partially cooked beans and continue to cook until the beans are tender, about 30 minutes more.

3. Meanwhile, prepare the sauerkraut. Combine the oil and onion in a heavy saucepan and sauté over medium-low heat until the onion turns pale golden, stirring occasionally, for about 5 minutes.

Turn the heat to medium. Add the cabbage, salt and pepper, and spices and stir until softened. Add ⅔ cup of water, cover, and simmer, stirring occasionally, for about 40 minutes. Check periodically to see if more water needs to be added, keeping in mind there should hardly be any liquid left at the end of cooking; add the water in small amounts. If there is too much liquid, remove the cover and increase the heat.

Add the vinegar and cook, uncovered, until it evaporates, about 10 minutes. Remove the bay leaf, juniper berries, and peppercorns.

4. Meanwhile, prepare the *condimenti*. If using pancetta, chop finely; if using bacon, cut into ¾ to 1-inch pieces. In a frying pan, preferably nonstick, sauté the pancetta with the oil over moderate heat until it has rendered its fat. Add the cooked sauerkraut and sauté, stirring often, for about 5 minutes. Using a wooden spoon, stir the sauerkraut-bacon mixture into the soup and cook for 15 minutes more.

Toast the bread in the oven and serve the soup piping hot with the still warm bread.

Nota: If using prepared sauerkraut, combine with ¾ cup water, the juniper berries, and bay leaf and gently simmer, uncovered, until its liquid has almost evaporated.

Variante: This simple sauerkraut soup is prepared in neighboring Trentino-Alto Adige. Melt 4 tablespoons butter, add ½ cup flour, and stir until a dark golden color. Adding a little at a time, stir in 6½ cups light meat or vegetable broth. Bring to a boil, then add the sauerkraut with a pinch of cumin seeds and simmer for 30 minutes.

Minestrone col Farro

Minestrone of Beans and Farro

Vegetables take a back seat to the grains and beans in this hearty-textured minestrone. This recipe is typical of Umbria and the richly cultivated area of Garfagnana where *farro* is grown and some of Italy's finest olive oil is produced. This substantial but surprisingly mellow soup is served hot or at room temperature with *una fila,* a thread of first-pressed *lucchese* oil.

$1^{3}/_{4}$ *cups (10 ounces) dried borlotti*
  or cannellini beans, soaked and
  rinsed (page 47)
$1^{1}/_{2}$ *cups (8 ounces) farro or spelt,*
  soaked for 4 hours or overnight
  and rinsed

  Brodo
8 cups cold water
$1^{1}/_{2}$ *teaspoons coarse salt*

  Battuto
3 to 4 tablespoons extra-virgin
  olive oil
1 medium-large onion, chopped
  (about $^{3}/_{4}$ cup)
1 fresh sausage, casing removed,
  or 3 to 4 ounces minced pancetta

2 garlic cloves, peeled
3 to 4 fresh sage leaves or 2 dried,
  chopped

  Sapori
3 medium carrots, thinly sliced
  (about $1^{1}/_{2}$ cups)
3 medium celery ribs, thinly sliced
  (about $1^{1}/_{4}$ cups)
2 tablespoons tomato paste, diluted
  in $^{2}/_{3}$ cup hot water
3 cups (6 ounces) finely shredded
  kale or Savoy cabbage

  Condimenti
Salt and freshly ground pepper
Extra-virgin olive oil, preferably
  estate Lucchese or Tuscan

1. Over moderate heat, combine the beans and *brodo* except for the salt in a heavy saucepan. Cover, and when it reaches a boil, lower the heat and gently simmer with the lid slightly ajar, until the beans are tender, about 1¼ hours. Add the salt toward the end of cooking.

Remove about half the beans and set aside. Puree the rest with its cooking liquid until smooth and add to a heavy soup pot. Bring to a simmer, add the *farro,* and cook until the grains are tender but still slightly firm, about 20 minutes. Stir occasionally with a wooden spoon.

2. Meanwhile, in a heavy saucepan, sauté the *battuto* over medium-low heat for 8 to 10 minutes, breaking up the sausage meat with a wooden spoon. Remove the garlic.

3. Add the carrots and celery to the *battuto* and stir well to combine. Add the diluted tomato paste and simmer for about 5 minutes. Add the vegetables, kale, and whole beans to the pureed beans and *farro* and cook for 15 minutes more, stirring occasionally. If needed, add some boiling water. Add the salt and pepper to taste, drizzle with the oil, and serve.

Variante: For a vegetarian soup, omit the sausage and serve with Parmesan cheese instead of oil.

Minestrone alla Ligure con Soffritto
Porcini and Eggplant Minestrone

serves: 6 to 8

cooking time:
2½ hours

*I*t is said that basil is the king of herbs in Liguria and rosemary its queen. A *soffritto,* a sautéed *battuto* of both these herbs, crowns this splendid minestrone. Pairing the earthy flavors of porcini mushrooms and eggplant with the sweetness of pumpkin and carrots creates a subtle but assertive combination of tastes. Their beautiful autumnal colors prepare you for the richness of tastes to follow.

continued

¹/₂ ounce dried porcini mushrooms,
    soaked in 1¹/₂ cups warm water
    for 30 minutes
³/₄ cup (4¹/₂ ounces) dried borlotti
    beans, soaked and cooked
    (see Nota), or 1 14-ounce can,
    drained and rinsed

Sapori

4 tablespoons extra-virgin olive oil
1 medium eggplant, trimmed and
    chopped (about 3 cups), see Nota
2 medium carrots, diced
    (about 1¹/₄ cups)
1 pound pumpkin or butternut
    squash, peeled, seeded, and finely
    diced (about 3 cups)
8 ounces green beans, trimmed and
    cut into ¹/₂-inch pieces
    (about 1¹/₂ cups)
¹/₄ head of Savoy cabbage, tender
    inner leaves shredded
    (about 4 cups)

Brodo

7 cups cold water
Porcini soaking liquid
1¹/₂ teaspoons coarse salt

Battuto

2 tablespoons extra-virgin olive oil

Minced Together

1 small onion
1 small garlic clove
¹/₂ cup fresh basil leaves
1 tablespoon fresh rosemary leaves
2 ounces prosciutto (optional)

1¹/₄ cups chopped tomatoes, peeled
    and seeded (1 14-ounce can,
    lightly drained)

Condimenti

Salt and freshly ground pepper
²/₃ cup (4 ounces) long-grain rice
Freshly grated Parmesan or pecorino
    cheese

1. Rinse and chop the porcini mushrooms as described on page 44, reserving their soaking liquid. Strain the soaking liquid through a filter and set aside.

2. In a large heavy-bottomed soup pot, lightly heat the oil over moderate heat. Add the eggplant, carrots, pumpkin, and porcini and sauté, rotating the vegetables, for about 5 minutes.

3. Add the *brodo* and bring to a boil. Lower the heat and gently simmer, partially covered, until the eggplant and pumpkin break down, about 2 hours. Stir in the cooked borlotti beans, green beans, and cabbage. Cook, uncovered, for about 15 minutes more.

4. Meanwhile, in a small heavy saucepan, sauté the *battuto* over low heat for 5 to 7 minutes. Stir in the tomatoes, cover and cook for 30 minutes, stirring occasionally, adding a little water if needed.

5. Add the salt and pepper to taste and bring to a lively simmer. Add the rice and cook until *al dente*. Stir occasionally with a wooden spoon to make sure the rice isn't sticking and add a little boiling water if needed.

Add the tomato sauce and stir well to combine. Serve with the grated cheese.

Nota: The borlotti beans can be cooked separately while the soup is cooking. The eggplant is cooked until it melts into the soup. Only if the eggplant is very fresh and firm should you include the skin. After chopping, rinse well under cold running water.

Variante: In the summer, this soup is cooked *a crudo*. Replace the pumpkin with potatoes and the dried porcini with 6 to 8 ounces fresh wild mushrooms. Bring the water and salt to a boil, add the *sapori,* and gently simmer, covered, for 2 hours. Add 1¼ cups, short pasta, such as ditalini, and stir in ¼ cup pesto.

Virtù (Minestrone Abruzzese)

Springtime Minestrone of Legumes

A dish of profound tradition, *Virtù* is a springtime specialty of Abruzzi, a cuisine renowned for not wasting anything. Legend has it that the first time this soup was prepared, seven beautiful and virtuous maidens each in turn added a different ingredient. Perhaps less poetic, but more realistic, this was a dish created by the virtuosity of the housewife who combined her dwindling winter pantry with the abundance of the fresh May harvest. When she added fresh marjoram and mint, this minestrone filled the kitchen with the aromas of spring.

And true to its name, *Virtù* seems to use practically everything—beans, chickpeas, lentils, fava beans, greens, tomatoes, meat, and vegetables—even the pasta is made up of whatever diverse types are on hand. The broth is created by cooking pork belly (or unsmoked bacon) and prosciutto rind in water, yielding a light and naturally salted broth.

Making this soup is not difficult, but it requires some orchestration and several pots. The dried legumes cook in one pot as the broth cooks in another; the *battuto* cooks separately as the greens are blanched before being added. Prepare this soup in the spirit of the *Abruzzesi,* who claim that the care this soup takes recalls the patience of the seven maidens, the thought of which makes this wonderful soup even better.

1/2 cup dried borlotti beans, soaked
and drained, or 1 1/4 cups canned

2/3 cup brown or green lentils,
rinsed well and drained
(see Nota)

1 1/4 cups canned chickpeas, well
drained, or 1/3 cup dried
(see Nota)

Brodo

6 1/2 cups water

8 ounces pork belly or unsmoked
bacon

Prosciutto rind or end
(about 8 ounces) or 3 to 4 ounces
pork belly

Sapori

3 medium carrots, cut into large dice
(about 2½ cups)
1 large celery rib, chopped
(about 1 cup)
¾ cup shelled fresh or frozen fava
beans

Battuto

4 tablespoons extra-virgin olive oil
1 tablespoon chopped fresh marjoram
leaves
1½ tablespoons chopped fresh mint
leaves

Finely Chopped Together
1 large onion
2 ounces pancetta

½ cup fresh parsley leaves
2 garlic cloves

¾ cup chopped tomatoes, peeled
and seeded

Condimenti

8 ounces spinach or Swiss chard,
tough stems removed
¼ small curly-leaf endive
¾ cup shelled and defrosted frozen
or fresh peas (about 1 pound
unshelled)
5 ounces (about 1¼ cups) diverse
small pasta
Freshly grated pecorino Romano
cheese

1. In a heavy casserole, combine the borlotti beans and lentils, cover with 4 cups of cold water, and place over medium heat. When it reaches a boil, lower the heat and gently simmer with the lid just slightly ajar, until all the legumes turn tender, about 1¼ hours (if using precooked chickpeas, add at this point; see *Nota*).

2. Meanwhile, add the *brodo* to a soup pot and simmer for about 1 hour, skimming off the scum that rises to the surface. Drain, returning the liquid to the pot. After the pork and prosciutto cool, trim away the fat, cut its meat into thin strips, and readd to the broth.

Drain the cooked legumes, reserving the cooking liquid. Add the legumes and about 1 cup of the bean broth to the soup (if using any canned legumes, add at this point).

continued

3. Bring the broth to a lively simmer, add the *sapori,* and cook for about 15 minutes.

4. Meanwhile, in a separate heavy saucepan, sauté the *battuto* except for the tomatoes over low heat, stirring occasionally, for about 5 minutes. Stir in the tomatoes and cook for 5 minutes more, then add to the soup (if adding fresh peas, add with the tomatoes).

5. Plunge the spinach and endive in a large pot of lightly salted boiling water for about 1 minute. Drain, coarsely chop, and add to the soup.

Bring the soup to a lively simmer and add the defrosted peas. Add the pasta and cook until *al dente,* stirring occasionally with a wooden spoon.

Serve hot or at room temperature and accompany with the pecorino cheese.

Nota: Chickpeas require a longer cooking time than other legumes. They can be precooked for about 1 to 1½ hours and then added to the other legumes after they have been brought to a simmer. If using canned borlotti and chickpeas, cook the lentils for about 45 minutes, then add to the broth with the canned legumes.

serves: 6 to 8

cooking time:
3 hours

Minestrone alla Milanese

Minestrone with Rice

"*Tanti Milanesi, tante ricette*"—"so many Milanese, so many recipes." Nowhere does this expression hold more true than for this classic northern Italian soup. This rich minestrone adds a risotto rice for its mellow texture, known as *legante,* or "bound." A staple of the trattoria, this colorful soup is served hot in the winter and at room temperature in warmer weather.

2/3 cup (4 ounces) dried borlotti or
    cannellini beans, soaked and rinsed
    (see Nota), or 1 14-ounce can,
    drained

Battuto
3 to 4 tablespoons extra-virgin olive oil
5 to 6 ounces pancetta, diced in small
    cubes (about 1 cup)

Minced Together
1 medium-large onion
1/3 cup parsley leaves
1 large garlic clove
3 to 4 fresh sage leaves (optional)

Sapori
3 medium carrots, diced
    (about 1 1/2 cups)
2 medium celery ribs, diced
    (about 3/4 cup)
2 medium leeks, white and light green
    parts, finely sliced (about
    1 cup)
2 baking potatoes, peeled and finely
    chopped (about 2 1/2 cups)

1 cup chopped tomatoes, peeled and
    seeded (1 14-ounce can, drained)

1/4 head of Savoy or green cabbage,
    outer leaves and tough core
    removed, coarsely shredded (about
    3 1/2 cups)
3 medium zucchini, diced
    (about 2 1/2 cups)

Brodo
9 1/2 cups cold water
2 teaspoons coarse salt
Parmesan rind, washed and scraped
    clean (optional, page 44)

Condimenti
Salt and freshly ground pepper
1 cup fresh or defrosted frozen peas
    (about 1 pound unshelled)
1 cup (6 1/2 ounces) risotto rice, such
    as Arborio or Vialone Nano
Freshly grated Parmigiano-Reggiano
    cheese
1/4 cup chopped fresh basil
    (optional)

1. In a large heavy-bottomed soup pot, sauté the *battuto* over low heat, stirring occasionally, for about 10 minutes.

continued

2. Over medium heat, add the *sapori,* except for the cabbage and zucchini. Sauté with the *battuto,* stirring, for 4 to 5 minutes.

3. Add the *brodo* and bring the soup to a boil. Lower the heat and cook at a very gentle simmer with the lid just slightly ajar, for about 2½ hours.

Add the cabbage, zucchini, and cooked borlotti beans and cook for about 15 minutes more. Remove the Parmesan rind.

4. Add the salt and pepper to taste, bring the soup to a steady simmer and add the peas and rice. Stir occasionally until the rice just turns *al dente* (the rice will continue to cook after the soup has been taken off the heat). If needed, add boiling water to thin the soup.

If a Parmesan rind has not been added, stir in 3 to 4 tablespoons of grated Parmesan cheese to taste. Sprinkle with the basil and serve with the Parmesan cheese.

Nota: If using soaked dried beans: Cook in a separate pot while the rest of the soup is cooking, adding a garlic clove and bay leaf to its cooking water (4 cups). Let stand in its liquid until needed, then drain.

Variante: For a springtime soup, omit the cabbage and add asparagus tips (6 to 8 ounces) with the peas. Use long-grained rice or a short tubular pasta and replace the Parmesan with fresh pesto or a *battuto* of minced fresh basil, parsley, and garlic.

Ribollita

Twice-Cooked Tuscan Minestrone and Bread Soup

serves: 8 to 10

cooking time:
2½ to 3 hours

A specialty of Siena and the surrounding area, *ribollita* pays homage to the local riches—cannellini beans, black cabbage, and the finest olive oil. Unlike in other *minestroni,* bread takes the place of pasta or rice. Its best flavor and density is thought to be achieved after sitting overnight and then—*ribollita*—reboiled, with the bread dissolving into the soup. There are many ways of preparing this classic dish. My favorite is to add thinly sliced raw onions.

Tuscan tradition calls for preparing this soup after the first frost when black cabbage (*cavolo nero*) is at its most flavorful. Unlike its name suggests, *cavolo nero* is not a cabbage nor is it black; its dark bluish-green leaves are part of the kale family. If kale is unavailable, substitute Savoy cabbage, adding the dark outer leaves as well as the inner tender ones. Turnip greens can be used for a lovely springtime *ribollita*.

2 cups (12 ounces) dried cannellini
    beans, soaked and drained
    (page 47)

Brodo

8 cups cold water
1 garlic clove, peeled and left whole
Prosciutto bone (optional)
1½ teaspoons coarse salt

Battuto

5 to 6 tablespoons extra-virgin
    olive oil
1 large red or white onion, finely
    chopped (about 1 cup)

Sapori

2 medium celery ribs, sliced
    (about ¾ cup)
3 medium carrots, sliced
    (about 1½ cups)

2 medium potatoes, peeled and
    coarsely chopped (about 2 cups)
1½ tablespoons tomato paste,
    diluted in ½ cup hot water
1 pound black cabbage or kale, stalks
    removed and leaves coarsely
    shredded (about 8 ounces trimmed
    weight)
Salt and freshly ground pepper

Condimenti

8 to 10 slices slightly stale country
    bread, cut ⅓ inch thick
2 to 3 garlic cloves, peeled
2 to 3 medium red or white onions,
    sliced paper-thin (optional,
    see Nota)
Freshly ground black pepper
Estate olive oil, preferably Tuscan

1. Combine the beans and *brodo* except for the salt in a heavy saucepan. Cover and bring to a boil over medium heat. Lower the heat and gently simmer with the lid just slightly ajar, until the beans are tender, about 1¼ hours. Add the salt toward the end of cooking.

2. In a heavy-bottomed soup pot, sauté the *battuto* over medium-low heat until the onion becomes lightly colored, stirring occasionally, 5 to 7 minutes.

3. Add the celery, carrots, and potatoes and stir well to combine. Add the tomato liquid, cover, and sweat the vegetables for about 10 minutes. Add 5 cups cold water and bring to a simmer, then add the kale.

4. Set aside about half the cooked cannellini beans. Puree the remaining beans with the cooking liquid through the fine-holed disc of a food mill and add to the vegetables (if using a food processor, puree only about a third of the beans and process until smooth).

Add the bean puree to the vegatables and gently simmer, covered, for about 1 hour. Add the salt and pepper to taste and the whole beans and cook for 10 minutes more. If needed, add more water.

5. Toast the bread in the oven until it starts to color, then rub one side with garlic.

There are several ways to serve *ribollita*. Place a slice of bread in each soup bowl, ladle over with the soup, top with a thin layer of onions (optional), season with a few twists of pepper and a generous drizzle of oil, and serve.

Or make 2 to 3 layers with the bread and allow to sit overnight. The next day, bring to a simmer over moderate heat. Alternatively, using ovenproof bowls or a large casserole, cover and bake in a preheated 325°F. oven until heated through, about 30 minutes. Using a wooden spoon, break up the bread in the soup, adding more water if needed. Season with the pepper and serve with the oil.

Nota: To soften the taste of the *condimenti* onions when preparing *ribollita,* cover the sliced onions with boiling water, then drain before adding.

Leggeri/Light Minestrone Soups

These lighter minestroni *are most commonly served from spring to autumn. Not surprisingly, many of these recipes come from the Italian Riviera and southern Italy. Their shorter cooking time and fresher tastes make them ideal warm weather main-course soups.*

Minestrone Primavera col Pesto

Springtime Minestrone with Pesto

serves: 6 to 8

cooking time:
40 minutes

Although pesto is closely associated with the cooking of Liguria, its ability to transform an ordinary minestrone into an extraordinary one is appreciated throughout Italy. In this light minestrone, a generous amount of garden vegetables and pasta fortify this popular soup. The pasta will not reheat well, so add it to the soup just before serving or substitute rice.

continued

²/₃ cup (4 ounces) dried cannellini and/or borlotti beans, soaked and cooked (page 47), or 1 14-ounce can, drained

Brodo

8 cups cold water

2 chicken or vegetable stock cubes or about 1¹/₂ teaspoons coarse salt or bean cooking liquid

2 tablespoons extra-virgin olive oil

Sapori

2 medium leeks, white and green parts, thinly sliced (about 1 cup)

3 to 4 ripe plum tomatoes, peeled, seeded, and coarsely chopped

2 medium zucchini, diced (about 2¹/₄ cups)

2 medium celery ribs, diced (about ³/₄ cups)

3 medium carrots, diced (about 1¹/₂ cups)

2 small eggplants, trimmed and diced (about 3 cups)

2 medium boiling potatoes, peeled and diced (about 1¹/₂ cups)

8 ounces wild mushrooms or ¹/₂ ounce dried porcini (page 44, optional)

Condimenti

7 to 8 ounces pasta, such as small penne or bucatini, broken up, or rice (³/₄ cup)

¹/₄ cup Pesto (page 45)

Freshly grated Parmesan cheese

1. Combine the *brodo* and *sapori* in a large soup pot and bring to a boil. Lower the heat and cook, covered, at a steady simmer until the vegetables are tender, about 20 minutes. Add the cooked beans.

2. Bring the soup to a lively simmer, add the pasta and cook until *al dente*. Remove from the heat and stir in the pesto or mix a little broth into the pesto and place a dollop on each serving. Serve with the Parmesan cheese.

Variante: For a *minestra di verdura,* omit the beans and pasta and reduce the water to 6¹/₂ cups.

Minestrone Napoletano

Minestrone with Roasted Peppers

*A*s delicious as it is beautiful, this minestrone uses the riches of the Naples countryside—eggplant, tomatoes, zucchini, and sweet peppers. A final addition of a basil-parsley pesto heightens all their flavors. This soup is cooked *a crudo,* and both the *battuto* and *sapori* are added raw. Half of the *battuto* is added at the beginning; the other half is combined with the grated cheese and oil to make a pesto.

*²/₃ cup dried borlotti beans, soaked
and cooked (see Nota), or
1 14-ounce can, drained*

Sapori

*2 large celery ribs, peeled and cut into
¹/₂-inch slices (about 1¹/₄ cups)*

*2 medium carrots, diced
(about 2 cups)*

*1 medium potato, peeled and
coarsely chopped (about ³/₄ cup)*

*1 small red onion, finely chopped
(about ¹/₂ cup)*

*3 to 4 ripe fresh or canned plum
tomatoes, peeled, seeded, and
chopped (about ³/₄ cup)*

*1 small eggplant, cut into small
cubes (about 2¹/₄ cups)*

*2 medium zucchini, diced
(about 2 cups)*

Brodo

6¹/₂ cups cold water

1 teaspoon coarse salt

Battuto

Minced Together

2 garlic cloves

¹/₂ cup fresh basil leaves

¹/₂ cup fresh parsley leaves

3 tablespoons extra-virgin olive oil

*¹/₄ cup freshly grated pecorino Romano
or Parmigiano-Reggiano cheese*

Condimenti

2 large red and/or yellow peppers

Salt and freshly ground pepper

¹/₂ cup fresh or defrosted frozen peas

*³/₄ cup (3 ounces) short pasta, such
as conchigaliette (little shells)*

continued

1. Combine the *sapori* and *brodo* in a large soup pot and bring to a boil.

2. Stir half of the minced *battuto* into the soup. Lower the heat and simmer, covered, for 1 hour. Place the other half of the *battuto* in a small bowl, beat in the oil and cheese to make a pesto, and reserve.

3. Meanwhile, roast the peppers (see page 180).

4. Ten to 15 minutes before the soup has finished cooking, add the cooked borlotti beans.

Add the salt and pepper to taste, roasted peppers, and peas.

Bring to a lively simmer, add the pasta, and cook until *al dente*. Stir occasionally with a wooden spoon, adding boiling water if needed.

Take the soup off the heat and stir in the pesto or mix a little broth into the pesto and place a dollop on each serving.

Nota: The soaked dried borlotti beans can be cooked separately while the rest of the soup is cooking.

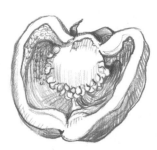

Minestrone Sardo

Sardinian Minestrone with Fennel

serves: 6 to 8

cooking time:
1½ hours

*F*inocchio selvatico* (wild fennel) is used extensively in the cooking of Sardinia. Its distinctive anise flavor combines with tomatoes and sausage to create a full-flavored, but wonderfully light minestrone. This minestrone gets its body from borlotti beans and chickpeas, not the customary potatoes or squash. Sardinia's well-known cheese, *pecorino sardo*, also known as *fiore sardo*, is an essential addition.

1 pound fresh unshelled cranberry beans
    or 1 14-ounce can, drained, or ²/₃ cup
    dried borlotti beans, cooked (page 47)

Battuto

3 to 4 tablespoons extra-virgin
    olive oil
1 medium onion, chopped
1 scant teaspoon fennel seeds
4 ounces mild fresh sausage, casing
    removed

Minced Together

½ cup parsley leaves
1 medium carrot
1 medium celery rib
2 garlic cloves

Sapori

1 pound fennel bulbs (trimmed weight),
    quartered and cut into ½-inch slices,
    feathery leaves reserved (see page 166)

4 ripe plum tomatoes, peeled, seeded,
    and coarsely chopped, or
    1 14-ounce can Italian tomatoes,
    drained and chopped
Coarse salt
1 14-ounce can chickpeas, rinsed
    and drained

Brodo

6½ cups boiling water

Condimenti

3 ounces (about ¾ cup) short pasta,
    such as ditalini
½ cup chopped fresh Italian parsley
Freshly grated pecorino Sardo or
    Romano cheese
Salt and freshly ground pepper
Reserved fennel leaves, finely
    chopped (optional)

continued

1. Combine the oil, onion, fennel seeds, and sausage in a heavy-bottomed soup pot. Sauté over low heat, breaking up the sausage meat and stirring occasionally until the onion lightly colors, 5 to 7 minutes. Add the minced *battuto* and continue to sauté, stirring occasionally, for 4 to 5 minutes.

2. Lower the heat to medium and stir in the fennel and tomatoes. Season with a few generous pinches of salt and sauté until the fennel softens, stirring often, for about 8 minutes.

Add the fresh borlotti beans (if adding canned borlotti beans, add with the chickpeas).

3. Add the *brodo* and cook at a slow but steady simmer, partially covered, for about 45 minutes. About 15 minutes before the end of cooking, add the chickpeas (if using canned or cooked borlotti beans, add at this point).

4. Bring the soup to a lively simmer. Add the pasta and cook until *al dente*, stirring occasionally with a wooden spoon. If needed, add a little boiling water.

Take the soup off the heat and stir in the parsley and 3 to 4 tablespoons pecorino and salt and pepper to taste. Garnish with the fennel leaves and serve with the pecorino cheese.

Variante: For a vegetarian soup, slightly increase the tomatoes and use half vegetable broth. The beans or chickpeas can be replaced with 8 ounces coarsely chopped potato and the fennel seeds with rosemary.

Minestrone alla Sicilia

Squash and Herb Minestrone

serves: 6 to 8

cooking time:
1½ hours

Characteristic of Mediterranean cooking, this minestrone uses abundant fresh herbs: basil, rosemary, parsley, and marjoram. Their tastes and aromas perfume this colorful fall soup made with Silician *zucca gialla* (yellow squash). Striped green on the outside, its sweetish orange flesh is similar to pumpkin or butternut squash, which is what this recipe calls for. Served hot or at room temperature, this minestrone demands the clean sharp taste of a well-aged pecorino cheese to complement its earthy sweetness. Don't let the absence of an herb keep you from making this refreshing soup; just increase the amount of the others.

continued

1½ cups fava beans, fresh or frozen, skins removed or 1¾ cups cooked cannellini beans, 4 ounces dried (see Nota), or 1 14-ounce can, rinsed and drained

Battuto
3 to 4 tablespoons extra-virgin olive oil

Finely Chopped Together
1 tablespoon fresh rosemary leaves
⅓ cup fresh basil leaves
2 ounces smoked pancetta or bacon
1 small celery rib
1 small onion
¼ cup fresh parsley leaves

Sapori
1 pound pumpkin or butternut squash (trimmed weight) peeled, seeded, and diced (about 3 cups)

1 medium potato, diced (about 1½ cups)
2 medium zucchini, diced (about 2 cups)
2 medium carrots, diced (about 1¾ cups)

Brodo
7 cups boiling water
1½ teaspoons coarse salt or 2 cubes vegetable or chicken stock

Condimenti
Salt and freshly ground pepper
1 cup peas, fresh or frozen, defrosted
4 to 5 ounces pasta, such as small shells or macaroni (1¼ cups)
2 tablespoons finely chopped mixed fresh basil and marjoram
Freshly grated pecorino Romano cheese

1. In a large heavy-bottomed soup pot, sauté the *battuto* over medium-low heat, stirring occasionally, for about 5 minutes.

2. Add the *sapori* and sauté, stirring often, for 3 to 4 minutes.

3. Add the *brodo* and cook, partially covered, at a slow but steady simmer for about 1 hour. Stir in the fava or cooked cannellini beans and cook for about 15 minutes more.

4. Add the salt and pepper to taste, then add the fresh peas and cook, uncovered, for about 10 minutes (if using defrosted peas, add with the pasta). Bring the soup to a lively simmer, add the pasta and cook until *al dente*, stirring occasionally with a wooden spoon. If needed, add a little boiling water to thin the soup. Take the soup off the heat and stir in the herbs.

Season each serving with a robust twist of pepper and a sprinkling of cheese, serving the remaining cheese at the table.

Nota: The dried cannellini beans (soaked) can be cooked separately as the rest of soup is cooking: start cooking as described on page 48 before you begin preparing the soup.

Minestrone Verde col Pesto

Green Minestrone with Pesto Sauce

*O*ne of Italy's best-loved soups, *Minestrone Verde col Pesto,* has numerous variations. What they all have in common are the freshest vegetables and a generous addition of freshly made pesto sauce. Many Genovese claim this classic soup should be made with only green vegetables.

The broth, simply water thickened by potatoes, is cooked first. The vegetables are then added raw, *a crudo,* as they are prepared. This not only saves time, but it maintains the soup at a constant simmer. To obtain the freshest quality of the vegetables, they are cooked uncovered at a steady simmer.

*²/₃ cup dried cannellini beans,
soaked and cooked (page 47), or
1 14-ounce can, drained*

Brodo
*7 cups cold water
1 teaspoon coarse salt or 1 cube
vegetable or chicken stock
1 large baking potato, peeled and
finely chopped (about 1³/₄ cups)*

Sapori
*2 to 2¹/₂ pounds assorted vegetables,
such as:
²/₃ cup finely chopped white and/or
spring onion or shallots
²/₃ cup sliced leeks, white and light
green parts*

*1 pound (about 4 cups) cubed
zucchini
6 to 8 ounces chopped green beans
(about 1¹/₂ cups)
6 to 8 ounces broccoli florets
(about 2¹/₂ cups)
6 ounces (1 cup) shelled fresh or
defrosted frozen peas*

Battuto
*1 cup packed fresh basil leaves,
washed and dried (reserve
6 to 8 whole leaves)
1 tablespoon lightly toasted pine nuts
2 small garlic cloves*

Pinch of salt and freshly ground
 pepper
$^1/_3$ cup freshly grated pecorino
 Romano cheese
3 tablespoons extra-virgin olive oil

Condimenti
Salt and freshly ground pepper
8 ounces shredded spinach
 (2 to 3 cups)
5 to 6 ounces flat pasta, such as
 linguine, broken up

1. In a large soup pot, bring the *brodo* to a boil. Lower the heat and simmer, covered, for about 20 minutes. In the meantime, prepare the vegetables.

2. Add the *sapori* according to their cooking time: first the onions, leeks, and zucchini, followed by the green beans and broccoli. Simmer, uncovered, until the vegetables just turn tender, about 20 minutes. Add the cannellini beans and fresh peas 10 minutes before the end of cooking. Add the defrosted peas with the pasta.

3. Meanwhile, prepare the *pesto battuto.* Combine the basil, pine nuts, and garlic in the bowl of a food processor and sprinkle with a pinch of salt and a twist of pepper. Pulse until finely minced. Add the cheese and oil and process to a pastelike consistency. Transfer to a small bowl and mix in a few tablespoons of hot broth.

4. Lightly add the salt and pepper to taste and bring the soup to a lively simmer. Add the spinach and pasta and cook until *al dente*, stirring occasionally with a wooden spoon. If needed, add some boiling water.

Take the soup off the fire. Either stir in all of the pesto or stir in half the pesto and place a dollop on each serving. Garnish the center of each serving with a fresh basil leaf.

Variante: For a warmer weather soup, substitute shredded lettuce for the spinach and long-grain rice for the pasta. If you prefer, omit the cannellini beans.

Minestre in Brodo

Broth Soups

*A*ny number of diminutive word endings are used in the description of these broth-based soups. Contrasting to the rustic zuppe *and the more* substantial minestre, *these light and refined soups are commonly served as part of the evening meal. All are defined by a good homemade broth with the addition of just a few delicate elements.*

The simplest of these soups is called minestrina, *"little soup." These are simply broth with the addition of* pastina—*small shapes of pasta, described by endings that mean "tiny," such as* quadretti *(squares),* anellini *(rings),* tempestina *(ovals), and* stelline *(stars). Strands of thin pasta, such as* capelli d'angelo *(angel's hair) and* taglierini, *are often used as well. The choice may be a matter of regional preference,* but more often it is a result of whatever small pasta is on hand. And if none is available, *spaghettini* or another thin pasta is simply broken up into little pieces. Peas, asparagus tips, or other delicate vegetables may enrich these soups.

Perhaps somewhat more elaborate are the broth soups made with a specially prepared filled pasta. Northern Italy is renowned for its *primi piatti* made with filled pasta, which are either served as *pastascuitta*—"dry pasta" with a sauce—or as *pasta in brodo*—"pasta in broth." With fillings ranging from savory meat to bread crumbs and cheese, the types of small filled pasta most commonly added are *tortellini, cappelletti,* and *anolini.*

When pasta is not added, there is no shortage of the inventive elements that Italians come up with to enrich their broth soups. Dumplings come in a variety shapes, flavorings, and names. In the Alto Adige and Trentino, *canederli* are preferred, in Tuscany *gnocchetti* are added, and in Emilia-Romagna, the Marche, and Veneto, the spaetzlelike *passatelli* are added. Not only do they vary with the region but subtle differences abound from city to city. In Venice, *passatelli* may be prepared with grated lemon, while in Bologna nutmeg is preferred, and in Mantua pancetta and garlic are added.

For centuries, broth soups have enjoyed the reputation as being a perfect, easy-to-digest dish to serve the very young, the very old, and the unwell. Their curative and nutritious qualities are thought to depend on the quality of the broth; and so too it is with their culinary effect, these popular soups depend on the *brodo*.

Preparing Broth Soups

Once you have a good homemade broth on hand, other than adding or making the elements to be added, these soups require no real preparation. They are all more or less made the same way: the broth is brought to a boil, then the ingredients are added and cooked until done.

Brodo For the best presentation and taste, homemade broth should be as fat-free as possible. Take extra care in skimming away any fat.

Many of the elements are cooked in the simmering broth, and depending on the amount of time required, part of the broth may evaporate. Have extra broth or boiling water on hand to replenish the broth. Keep in mind that if a substantial portion evaporates, the broth may become overly strong if only more broth, and not water, is added.

Sapori When adding pasta, first bring the broth to a boil, then after the pasta has been added, lower the heat to a steady simmer. If using freshly made filled pasta, be careful about letting the boil become too strong as the pasta could easily burst open. As a guideline the amount of pasta per person is 1 to 1½ ounces dried and 2 to 2½ ounces fresh. For the most refined presentation, cook the pasta separately to keep it from clouding the broth.

If adding dumplings, many of these contain flour and need to be cooked long enough to get rid of their raw taste. Their floating to the top does not necessarily indicate doneness.

Condimenti Most of these soups are served with Parmesan cheese. Use a good-quality Parmigiano-Reggiano, preferably grated at the table.

The Recipes

These recipes have purposely omitted *pasta ripiena* (filled pasta) for two reasons. First, so many good-quality prepared pastas, both fresh and frozen, are available commercially. Second, there are so many fine cookbooks that go into explicit detail about preparing filled pasta that I decided to leave this to those much abler than myself.

For the most part, these recipes are wonderfully easy alternatives to preparing a filled pasta, and I think you will find them a nice change as well. Once you do several types, it becomes easy to make your own variations. In some recipes the cooking time includes the baking or sitting times. When two serving numbers are indicated, they both refer to first-course servings.

Bomboline di Riso in Brodo

Little Rice Balls in Broth

*T*his recipe is adapted from a nineteenth-century recipe in Italy's best-known cookbook, *La Scienza in cucina e l'arte di mangiar bene,* by Pellegrino Artusi. Its simple preparation can easily be adapted to using leftover risotto.

Sapori
1 cup (7 ounces) risotto rice
2¼ cups milk
3 tablespoons unsalted butter
Salt
3 tablespoons freshly grated
    Parmesan cheese

Pinch of grated nutmeg
2 large egg yolks
All-purpose flour
1 large egg and 1 egg white
Olive oil

Brodo
5 to 7 cups Classic Meat Broth (page 36)

1. Combine the rice and milk in a heavy-bottomed saucepan. Cook over moderate heat, stirring often, until all the liquid has been absorbed and the rice is *al dente*, 16 to 18 minutes. At the end of cooking, stir in the butter and a pinch of salt. Transfer the mixture to a bowl and mix in the Parmesan, nutmeg, and egg yolks, adding one at a time. Allow the mixture to cool.

2. In 2 separate bowls, put the flour in one and beat together the egg and egg white in the other. Take a heaping tablespoon of the rice mixture and roll into small balls. Lightly cover with the flour and then the egg.

Fry the balls until golden, either by deep frying in hot oil or by frying in a skillet, preferably nonstick. Place on kitchen towels to absorb the excess oil.

3. Bring the *brodo* to a boil. Place the rice balls in each soup plate and ladle over with the hot broth.

Variante: In Naples *pallottoline* (little balls) are prepared. Replace the milk with water and fry the balls in lard or pancetta-flavored oil.

Canederli in Brodo

Dumplings in Broth

serves: 6

cooking time:
1 hour

A specialty of the Alto Adige, *canederli* is the translation of *knodel,* the German word for dumpling, reminiscent of when this region was under Hapsburg rule. These large balls of stale bread soaked in milk and eggs may be embellished with any number of ingredients (see *Variante*). Typically they are prepared with *speck* (smoked prosciutto); my favorite is adding the guinea fowl left over from making the broth. *Canederli* are not just served in soup, they are an accompaniment to stewed meat or become a first course, topped with a tomato or ragout sauce.

Sapori

10 ounces slightly stale country
    bread, crusts removed and
    crumbled into small pieces
    (2 1/2 cups) (see Nota)
4 ounces (about 1 cup) finely
    chopped cooked fowl, chicken,
    or turkey
2/3 cup milk, at room temperature
2 eggs

2 tablespoons unsalted butter, melted
2 tablespoons minced parsley
Generous pinch of grated nutmeg
    and salt
2/3 cup unbleached flour

Brodo

5 to 7 cups Classic Meat Broth
    (page 36)

1. Combine the *sapori* in a bowl and mix well to combine. Leave to rest in a cool spot in your kitchen for 30 minutes. The mixture will feel sticky but should be able to be formed into balls; if needed, add a little flour or milk (see *Nota*).

continued

Roll the mixture into balls 1½ to 2 inches. This will yield about 8 dumplings; if you want more or less, adjust their size. These dumplings become much larger when cooked; if you are adding less broth, make the balls small enough so they stay covered by the broth and use a pot that is deeper than wider.

2. Meanwhile, over moderate heat, bring the *brodo* to a lively simmer. *Canederli* are best cooked using a slow, steady simmer, not a rolling boil. Add the *canederli* a few at a time to maintain the broth at a constant simmer. Cover and cook at a slow but steady simmer for 20 minutes.

Nota: If your bread is not stale, dry it in the oven until it can be crumbled by hand. The dryness of your bread will determine the amount of milk and flour to be added.

Variante: For vegetarian dumplings, replace the meat with 1 medium onion, minced and sautéed in butter. For *canederli neri,* use seedless rye bread and buckwheat flour, add the onion, and replace the fowl with 6 ounces smoked pancetta.

Canederli di Spinaci in Brodo
Spinach Dumplings in Broth

serves: 4

cooking time:
1 hour

*T*his variation of these classic dumplings (page 121) derives from *la cucina integrale* (healthy cooking) and reinterprets *canederli* in a new and nutritious way. Made with whole wheat bread, spinach, and *farina di grano saraceno,* the buckwheat flour typical of this area, they are not only healthier, but wonderfully light and delicious.

Sapori

1½ cups (about 5 ounces) soft
 whole wheat bread crumbs or
 4 to 5 slices dry whole wheat
 bread, crusts removed and broken
 into small pieces
¼ cup skim milk
8 ounces spinach, washed, well
 drained, and finely chopped
1 egg

1 small garlic clove, minced
Pinch of grated nutmeg
¼ cup ricotta cheese
2 tablespoons grated Parmesan
 cheese
Salt
1 tablespoon olive oil
¾ cup buckwheat flour

Brodo

5½ cups Vegetable Broth (page 40)

1. In a bowl, mix together the *sapori* to combine well; using your hands works best. Allow to rest in a cool spot in your kitchen for about 30 minutes.

The ingredients should form a dough that is not too wet, but dense enough to form a ball; add more flour or milk if needed. Form into balls about 1½ inches in diameter and place on a plate.

2. Meanwhile bring the *brodo* to a lively simmer. Add the *canederli* a few at a time and cook, covered, at a steady simmer for 20 minutes, without letting the soup come to a rolling boil.

Gnocchetti in Brodo ai Funghi

Porcini Dumplings in Broth

*T*hese Tuscan dumplings are a wonderful alternative to mushroom or meat-filled pasta. The mushrooms are first simmered in the broth, which not only cooks them, but lends a subtle mushroom flavor to the broth. Should you want to increase the amount of broth, add the porcini soaking liquid.

*1 ounce dried porcini mushrooms, soaked
in 1 cup warm water (page 44)*

Brodo
6½ cups Classic Meat Broth (page 36)

Sapori
*4 tablespoons unsalted butter, at
room temperature*

Salt and freshly ground pepper
1⅓ cups flour
2 small eggs
1 heaping tablespoon minced parsley
*⅓ cup grated Parmesan cheese,
preferably grana padano*

1. Bring the *brodo* to a boil. Rinse the mushrooms under cold water and cook in the broth for 5 minutes. Drain the mushrooms, chop finely, and return the broth to the pot.

2. In a small heavy saucepan, melt 2 tablespoons of the butter over medium-low heat. Add the mushrooms and sauté for 10 minutes, stirring occasionally. Add the salt and pepper to taste. Drain the mushrooms and place on paper towels to absorb excess moisture.

Sift the flour with a pinch of salt into a mixing bowl. Add the eggs, parsley, mushrooms, and the remaining 2 tablespoons butter (the butter should be soft enough to easily mix in—if not, warm slightly). Mix with a wooden spoon until well amalgamated. Using your hands, form into small balls around ¾ inch in diameter.

3. Bring the *brodo* to a lively simmer and drop in the *gnocchetti*. After they float to the top, cook for 10 minutes, then serve with grated cheese.

Gnocchetti di Ricotta in Brodo

Ricotta Dumplings in Broth

serves: 4

cooking time:
5 minutes

*T*hese delicate dumplings of ricotta, pecorino, and parsley are a specialty of Calabria. Substituting fresh coriander for all or part of the parsley makes for a lovely aromatic variation.

Sapori

12 ounces ricotta cheese, well
   drained
1 large egg and 1 egg yolk
2 tablespoons minced fresh Italian
   parsley
1$\frac{1}{2}$ tablespoons grated pecorino
   Romano cheese

$\frac{1}{2}$ to $\frac{3}{4}$ cup soft bread crumbs
Freshly ground pepper to taste

Brodo

5 to 6 cups Classic Meat Broth
   (page 36) or Vegetable
   Broth (page 40)

1. Drain the ricotta of as much liquid as possible and combine in a bowl with the rest of the *sapori*. Mix together, adding just enough bread crumbs to hold the mixture together.

2. Bring the *brodo* to a boil. Pinch off cherry-sized pieces of the ricotta mixture and drop into the broth. The mixture will be feel wet, but once dropped into the broth it should hold together. Drop one in. If it separates, add some more bread crumbs. Cook for a few minutes from the time the last *gnocchetto* is added.

Minestra di Frittata

Broth Soup with Omelet

A tasty and colorful alternative to fresh pasta, these thin strips of herb-flavored "omelet" are a specialty of the Alto Adige. The *frittata* is the Italian equivalent of the omelet, the difference being that it is cooked on both sides and is not stuffed or rolled. In this recipe, milk and flour are added, resulting in a delicate *frittata* more akin to a crepe.

Sapori
3/4 cup flour
1 cup milk
4 medium eggs
1/4 cup chopped parsley
1 teaspoon chopped chives (optional)
Pinch of salt and freshly ground
    pepper
1 to 2 tablespoons unsalted butter

Brodo
5 1/2 to 7 cups Classic Meat Broth
    (page 36)

Condimenti
Freshly grated Parmesan cheese

1. Sift the flour into a bowl. Using a wooden spoon, mix in the milk, adding a little at a time. Add the eggs, herbs, salt, and pepper and beat together until well combined.

In a frying pan, about 6 inches in diameter and preferably nonstick, melt the butter over moderate heat. Add just enough of the egg mixture to cover the pan. Cook until it becomes set enough to be flipped, then sauté on the other side (see *Nota*). Carefully lift or slide out, placing on a plate. Repeat until all of the egg mixture is used up.

2. When the *frittata* cools, roll up and cut into about ½-inch slices. Meanwhile, bring the *brodo* to a boil.

3. Distribute the *frittata* strips in each serving bowl, ladle over with the boiling broth, and serve with the Parmesan cheese.

Nota: If you are uncertain of your flipping skills, after the eggs have cooked on one side, put a plate upside down over the pan. Reverse the pan, then slide the *frittata* back into the pan and sauté on the other side.

Variante: In Friuli-Venezia Giulia this soup is known as *minestra celestina* and varies slightly. Replace the herbs with 2 tablespoons grated Parmesan cheese and a pinch of grated nutmeg.

Stracciatella alla Romana

Egg and Broth Soup

The word *stracciatella* is synonymous with Rome. Simple to prepare, the eggs are beaten into the soup, becoming *stracci,* "rags." Similar versions of this classic soup are prepared throughout Italy. In the Marche, lemon zest replaces the nutmeg and in Emilia-Romagna and Lombardy, flour replaces the bread crumbs. (If doing so, you will need to increase the cooking time by 3 to 4 minutes to cook the flour.)

Sapori

4 eggs

4 tablespoons freshly grated
    Parmesan cheese

2 tablespoons fine bread crumbs

1/8 teaspoon grated nutmeg

Brodo

5 cups Classic Meat Broth (page 36)
    or Chicken Broth (page 39)

1. In a bowl, beat the eggs. Whisk in the rest of the *sapori* and mix until well blended.

2. Over medium-heat, bring the *brodo* to a boil. While continuously stirring with a whisk or fork, slowly pour the egg mixture into the boiling *brodo*. When the soup returns to a boil and small ribbons have formed, serve.

Variante: In springtime *stracciatella primavera* is prepared with peas or lettuce. Sweat about 2 to 3 cups shredded lettuce in butter for 10 minutes, then cook in the soup for 5 minutes before adding the egg mixture. Or add 1 cup peas and 2 tablespoons minced parsley and serve with toasted crostini. If you prefer, simply add some mixed fresh herbs, such as basil, mint, parsley, and coriander.

Minestra di Passatelli

Egg and Parmesan Strands in Broth

serves: 6

cooking time:
5 minutes

A specialty of Romangna, these delicate golden strands of eggs, Parmesan cheese, and bread crumbs create one of northern Italy's most popular broth soups. This soup achieved great popularity after appearing in Pellegrino Artusi's classic book of 1897, in which he recommends adding either lemon zest and/or nutmeg.

Sapori
1 cup fine dry bread crumbs
1/2 cup freshly grated Parmigiano-
  Reggiano cheese
1/4 teaspoon grated nutmeg or
  1/2 teaspoon grated lemon rind
  or both
2 large eggs

Brodo
6 1/2 cups Classic Meat Broth
  (page 36)

Condimenti
Freshly grated Parmigiano-Reggiano
  cheese

1. In a bowl, mix the *sapori* together to form a dough with the consistency of pasty cornmeal.

2. Bring the *brodo* to a boil. While holding the sieve of choice (see *Nota*) over the broth, push the *passatelli* mixture through the holes and cook for 3 minutes.

Serve with Parmesan cheese.

Nota: From the verb *passare,* "to pass through," the mixture is pushed through a special perforated disc with holes about 1/4 inch in diameter. Any tool, such as a potato ricer, the coarse disc of a food mill, or the holes of a colander, can be used.

Zuppa alla Bolognese

Mortadella Dumplings in Broth

*T*racing its origins back to the fourteenth century, Bologna's famous mortadella takes its name from the time it was made by its ingredients being pounded in a *mortaio* (mortar). In this soup it lends a lightly smoked flavor to these dumplings cut into the shape of *dadini,* little cubes. These will keep up to 3 days in the refrigerator.

This recipe calls for the addition of *semolino,* the ground durum hard wheat flour from which pasta is made; its English translation is semolina. The Parmesan cheese should be very finely grated.

Sapori
3 large eggs
³/4 cup (2¹/2 ounces) freshly grated
    Parmigiano-Reggiano cheese
4 tablespoons unsalted butter,
    softened to room temperature
¹/2 cup semolina (durum wheat
    flour)

2 ounces minced mortadella
¹/8 teaspoon grated nutmeg
Pinch of salt

Brodo
5¹/2 to 7 cups Classic Meat Broth
    (page 36)

1. Preheat the oven to 350°F.

2. Place the *sapori* in a bowl and mix together until thoroughly combined. Smear a small 5 × 9-inch baking pan with butter and spread the egg mixture to a thickness of about ¹/2 inch. Place in the uppermost part of the oven and bake for 10 minutes. Allow to cool, then cut into small ¹/3 to ¹/2-inch cubes.

3. Bring the *brodo* to a boil. Add the dumplings and when the soup returns to a boil, cook for 5 minutes.

Zuppa di Lattuga Ripiena alla Genovese

Stuffed Lettuce Soup in Broth

serves: 4 to 6

cooking time:
1¼ hours

A tradition of the Ligurian Easter, lettuce leaves are filled with a delicate veal stuffing and served in broth. I particularly like this variation, which adds dried porcini mushrooms and the inner leaves of the lettuce too small to be stuffed. Its name *zuppa* comes from serving this soup with toasted bread. Accompanied with the bread, it is a supremely delicate soup; placing the stuffed leaves on top of the bread can turn it into an elegant, light main course.

*¹/₃ ounce dried porcini mushrooms,
    soaked, drained, and chopped
    (page 44)*

Battuto
*2 tablespoons extra-virgin olive oil
2 tablespoons unsalted butter*

Minced Together
*1 medium onion
1 small carrot
¹/₂ small celery rib
1 garlic clove*

Sapori
*12 ounces veal, cut into 1-inch pieces
All-purpose flour
1 large head of romaine lettuce, base
    trimmed and leaves washed, or
    2 heads of Boston lettuce*

*1 egg and 1 egg yolk
¹/₃ cup milk
¹/₄ teaspoon grated nutmeg
¹/₃ to ¹/₂ cup soft bread crumbs
¹/₃ cup freshly grated Parmesan
    cheese
3 tablespoons minced parsley
1 teaspoon minced fresh marjoram
    or ³/₄ teaspoon dried*

Brodo
*6 to 7 cups Classic Meat Broth
    (page 36)*

Condimenti
6 thin slices of toasted country bread

continued

1. Over medium-low heat, combine the oil and butter in a wide heavy-bottomed saucepan or a nonstick frying pan. When the butter melts, add the minced *battuto* and sauté, stirring occasionally, for about 5 minutes.

2. Pat the veal to remove excess moisture and add to the *battuto*. Sprinkle with a little flour, stir to coat well, and sauté over medium heat until the veal lightly browns on all sides, about 10 minutes. Transfer everything to a small heavy-bottomed saucepan, add enough broth (about ¾ cup) to almost cover the veal, and bring to a simmer.

Add the chopped porcini and the small inner lettuce leaves. Cook until the liquid almost completely evaporates, about 30 minutes. Stir occasionally to rotate the veal and prevent it from sticking. Using a knife, very finely chop the mixture or pulse in a food processor for a few seconds and reserve.

3. Meanwhile, bring a large pot of lightly salted water to a boil. Add the large lettuce leaves a few at a time, and blanch just long enough to soften, about 5 to 10 seconds. Remove, drain, and carefully open on a flat surface. Allow to cool, then cut away the tough bottom part of the ribs and any blemished parts.

4. In a medium bowl, beat together the egg, egg yolk, milk, and nutmeg. Add the bread crumbs, Parmesan cheese, and herbs and mix thoroughly. Add the reserved veal-porcini mixture and mix until well amalgamated. If the mixture seems too liquid, add some more bread crumbs.

With the leaf rib side down, place 1 heaping tablespoon of the filling at the narrower end and form into a narrow sausage shape. Roll up each leaf, tucking in the sides before the roll is finished (these can be kept refrigerated for several hours).

5. Arrange the stuffed leaves side by side in the bottom of a shallow heavy-bottomed saucepan about 10 inches in diameter. Pack the leaves tightly, seam side down. Cover with about a third of the *brodo* and gently simmer, covered, for 15 minutes (20 minutes if refrigerated). In a separate pot, bring the remainder of the *brodo* to a simmer.

6. There are two ways to serve this soup—the stuffed lettuce can be place on top of the toasted bread; or for a more delicate rendition, serve accompanied with the bread.

Distribute the stuffed lettuce leaves in each soup plate, cover with the boiling *brodo,* and serve immediately.

Variante: For a vegetarian soup, increase the porcini to $\frac{1}{2}$ ounce, omitting the milk and the small lettuce leaves, and add $1\frac{1}{2}$ cups ricotta cheese directly to the egg mixture.

Minestre e Zuppe di Verdure

Vegetable Soups

Vegetables permeate every aspect of Italian life. From the soft leafy greens to the prickly violet artichokes, the landscape of every region is defined visually and gastronomically by the vegetables that sprout from its soil. Streets and markets come to life with the vivid colors of the beautiful displays and sweet aromas of freshly picked vegetables. With few exceptions, all of these magnificent specimens find their way into a limitless range of soups.

The Italian passion for the best and freshest vegetables is abundantly evident in their soups. In Italy, fresh vegetable soups are synonymous with a stagione, "seasonal." Not only will you not find the same soup made year-round but when a particular vegetable has reached its optimum flavor is when a particular soup will most likely be prepared. Autumn heralds in soups prepared with freshly picked porcini, winter is the time for the tastiest cabbage soups, spring is the time for preparing fresh fennel and pea soups, and summer is the season for aromatic soups perfumed with fresh herbs.

As important as the season, so too is the region where the soup originates. Not surprisingly, the soups of the sun-drenched Italian Riviera and the south are more likely to contain tomatoes, sweet peppers, eggplant, and zucchini; those of central and northern Italy are more likely to contain mushrooms, potatoes, and pumpkin. While you cannot always identify a soup by its ingredients, particularly with the availability of most foodstuffs throughout Italy, there are numerous soups that still retain their distinct regional character.

From the refreshing warm weather vegetable *minestre* to the filling winter *zuppe,* vegetable soups can be as simple as a single ingredient with just a few flavorings or as complex as the soups more akin to a light minestrone. Vegetables that are pureed into a creamy richness or vegetables that remain distinct from the broth, whatever their preparation, when it comes to *minestre and zuppe di verdura* soups, Italians have a knack for combining just the right tastes and textures.

Preparing Vegetable Soups

Preparing vegetable soups is foremost about its ingredients, and this means freshness for quality and seasonality for optimum taste. Perhaps when it comes to preparing these soups, what you don't do is as important as what you do. Most important, do not overcook vegetable soups or they may lose their essential freshness, flavor, and texture.

Sapori The preparation begins by making certain that all fresh vegetables are thoroughly washed under cold running water. Leafy greens need to be soaked and zucchini scrubbed to remove any grit.

How thinly you cut vegetables will help to determine their character and cooking time. Page 14 describes the various ways to cut vegetables. It is never possible to give precise cooking times for vegetables since so much depends on their quality. Vegetables that have not been initially sautéed will take longer to cook.

Brodo Though some vegetable soups require a prepared broth, most are made just with the addition of water. Unlike most *minestroni,* these soups are cooked over a higher heat at a steady simmer. Vegetables have natural salts that release as they cook; it is always best to salt very lightly in the beginning and reserve the main seasoning for the end of the cooking.

Reheating As with all soups, reheat over moderate heat and add more liquid. Take special care with soups that contain cream. If allowed to boil rapidly, they will separate.

The Recipes

Miste —mixed vegetable soups
Verdure —one main vegetable soups
Zucche —zucchini and pumpkin soups
Funghi —mushroom soups
Ortaggi a Foglia —soups of leafy greens

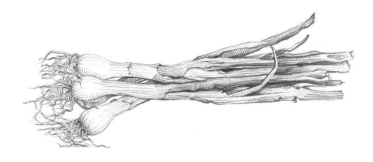

Miste/Mixed Vegetable Soups

These soups get their character from a combination of vegetables, with no single one dominating. Although many share much in common with minestrone, their lighter character and shorter cooking time distinguish these mixed vegetable soups.

Minestra alla Calabrese

Sweet Pepper Soup

serves: 4 to 6

cooking time:
50 minutes

Zucchini, sweet peppers, and young, skinny green beans herald an Italian spring. This recipe comes from Calabria, where the simple addition of water is more customary than a prepared broth. An abundance of fresh basil and adding the vegetables raw create a delicate and fragrant soup.

Battuto
3 to 4 tablespoons extra-virgin
    olive oil
1 to 1^1/$_2$ cups spring onions or leeks,
    white parts only

Sapori
12 ounces small zucchini, cut into
    ^{1}/$_2$-inch-thick slices
    (about 3 cups)
12 ounces green beans, preferably
    thin ones, trimmed and cut into
    short pieces (about 3 cups)

2 small sweet red and/or yellow
    peppers, ribs and seeds removed
    and cut into thin, short strips
8 ounces new potatoes, cut into bite-
    sized pieces (1^1/$_2$ cups)
^{1}/$_4$ cup shredded basil
10 zucchini flowers, cut into thin
    strips, pistils removed (optional)

Brodo
5^1/$_2$ cups cold water
2 ounces prosciutto, slivered
Salt and freshly ground pepper

1. In a heavy-bottomed soup pot, sauté the *battuto* over medium-low heat, stirring often, until the onions become soft without coloring, 4 to 5 minutes.

2. Stir in the *sapori,* cover, and sweat for about 10 minutes. There should be enough water left on the vegetables from washing; if not, add a little hot water and stir occasionally to prevent sticking.

3. Add the water and prosciutto and bring to a boil. Lower the heat and simmer, covered, for about 30 minutes. Add the salt and pepper to taste towards the end of cooking.

Variante: Replace the potatoes with 4 ounces fresh *tagliolini;* cut into short pieces and add at the end of cooking.

Minestra al Cerfoglio

Vegetable Soup with Cilantro

*U*sed as a subtle flavoring or in combination with other herbs, cilantro is an herb not often associated with Italian cookery. Its generous addition in this recipe transforms basic everyday vegetables into an aromatic and refreshing soup.

Brodo
4¹/₂ cups Chicken Broth (page 39)
or Vegetable Broth (page 40) or
1¹/₂ chicken or vegetable stock
cubes dissolved in 4¹/₂ cups water

Sapori
2 to 3 medium leeks, white and light
green parts, cut in half
lengthwise and chopped
(about 1³/₄ cups)
12 ounces (about 2 cups) peeled and
diced boiling potatoes

3 medium carrots, chopped
(about 1¹/₂ cups)
2 medium celery ribs, chopped
(about ³/₄ cup)

Condimenti
1 bunch of fresh cilantro
1 tablespoon and 1 teaspoon unsalted
butter
1 tablespoon and 1 teaspoon flour
Salt and freshly ground pepper

1. Combine the *brodo* and *sapori* in a soup pot and bring to a boil. Adjust the heat and simmer, covered, until the vegetables are tender, 15 to 20 minutes.

2. Meanwhile, in a separate pot, plunge the cilantro into lightly salted boiling water for just a few seconds. Drain and rinse with cold water. Remove the stems, finely chop the leaves, and reserve.

3. In a small heavy saucepan, melt the butter over medium heat. Add the flour and stir vigorously to combine the butter and flour. Whisk in 1 to 2 ladles of the soup broth, adding a little at a time. Add to the soup and stir well to combine. Add the salt and pepper to taste.

Stir in the chopped cilantro to taste, 3 to 4 tablespoons, and serve.

Variante: For a *crema,* instead of dicing, cut the vegetables into larger pieces. When cooked, puree with the cilantro and add with the sautéed flour mixture.

Minestra di Magro con Fagioli

Eggplant Soup with Cannellini Beans

serves: 4

cooking time:
½ to 2 hours

Originally, the word *magro,* "meager," referred to meatless meals prepared on religious days of abstinence. In present-day Italian gastronomy, *magro* refers to vegetarian dishes or lean cuts of meat. This deliciously healthful soup from Liguria demonstrates how a meager dish is turned into one of substance.

The eggplant should be small and very fresh so it exudes no bitterness. Brown mushrooms are called for; however, if only cultivated white ones are available, supplement them with just a touch of dried porcini, about ¼ ounce (page 44).

continued

1⅛ cups (7 ounces) dried cannellini
    beans, soaked and rinsed
    (page 47), or 2¾ cups canned,
    drained (see Nota)

Brodo
5 cups cold water

Sapori
2 small eggplants, peeled and diced
    (about 2⅓ cups)
4 ounces (about 1¾ cups) thinly
    sliced brown mushrooms, such as
    cremini or chestnut

2 tablespoons extra-virgin olive oil
1 cup coarsely chopped peeled
    tomatoes (1 14-ounce can,
    drained)
1 teaspoon minced garlic
1 teaspoon coarse salt

Condimenti
Salt and freshly ground pepper
⅓ cup (3 ounces) long-grain rice
2 tablespoons chopped fresh basil
    and/or parsley

1. Over moderate heat, combine the beans and *brodo* in a heavy-bottomed soup pot and bring to a boil. Adjust the heat and gently simmer with the lid slightly ajar, until the beans are tender, about 1¼ hours.

2. Add the *sapori* and continue to simmer, covered, for about 15 minutes.

3. Add the salt and pepper to taste and bring the soup to a lively simmer. Add the rice and cook, stirring occasionally with a wooden spoon, until done, about 15 minutes. If needed, add a little boiling water. Sprinkle with the herbs and serve.

Nota: If substituting canned cannellini beans, reduce the *brodo* water to 4 cups, add 1 cube vegetable stock, and add the beans with the rice.

Fruffella

Piquant Cabbage and Bean Soup

serves: 4 to 6

cooking time:
1¼ hours

*T*he highly mountainous regions of Abruzzi and Molise share a common tradition of rural, simple cooking. *Diavolilli,* "little devils," is the name *Molisani* and *Abruzzesi* fondly call their red chili peppers, which they add with great abandon to liven up their winter-warming dishes. In this soup, a *condimento* of chili pepper, pancetta, garlic, and parsley transforms good basic ingredients into a memorable soup, substantial enough to be served as a meal in itself.

Brodo

6 cups water

1 tablespoon tomato paste

1 teaspoon coarse salt

Sapori

1 medium-large onion, chopped
  (about 1¼ cups)

1 medium celery rib, sliced into
  ½-inch pieces

1 medium carrot, diced
  (about ¾ cup)

1 large baking potato, peeled and
  diced (about 2 cups)

1¾ cups cooked borlotti beans or
  1 14-ounce can, drained

4 cups (about 12 ounces) thinly
  shredded Savoy cabbage

Condimenti

2 tablespoons extra-virgin olive oil

3 ounces (about ⅔ cup) diced
  pancetta

2 whole garlic cloves, smashed, or
  1 teaspoon minced (see Nota)

1 small dried chili pepper or
  ¼ teaspoon crushed (see Nota)

¼ cup chopped fresh Italian parsley

1. In a soup pot, bring the *brodo* to a lively simmer.

2. Add the onion, celery, carrot, and potato and simmer, covered, for about 30 minutes. Add the borlotti beans and cabbage and stir for a few minutes until the cabbage has reduced, completely covered by the broth. Simmer, uncovered, until the cabbage is very tender, 25 to 35 minutes.

3. Meanwhile, in a heavy saucepan, gently sauté the *condimenti* over very low heat, stirring occasionally, for about 15 minutes (see *Nota*). If using whole garlic and pepper, remove. Stir into the soup and serve.

Nota: The *condimenti* must be slowly cooked over very low heat to allow the pancetta to release its fat and the garlic and chili pepper their essence. For the mildest flavor, leave the chili pepper and garlic whole, then remove.

Garmugia

Springtime Soup of Lucca

serves: 4

cooking time:
45 minutes

This ancient soup, dating back to the sixth century, pays homage to the first vegetables of spring: artichokes, fresh fava beans, peas, asparagus, and *cipolle novelle* (new onions). Its name derives from the medieval Florentine word *miscuglio,* which means "mixture." For noted *lucchese* chef Giampiero Gemignani, *Garmugia* has particular meaning; it was the favorite dish of Mario Tobino, an author and friend who did much of his writing while at Ristorante Solferino.

For a lighter and fresher result whenever possible, Giampiero replaces meat with vegetables. In this recipe, the meat broth and lard used in the original recipe are replaced by a vegetable broth made from a sampling of the *sapori* vegetables. He adds wine to the *sapori* and at the very end purees the broth with a touch of *grano duro* (pasta flour) to add just the right amount of body.

Brodo

8 ounces (about 2 cups) combined
    and prepped sapori vegetables:
    onions, peas, green beans, and
    asparagus stems
10 cups cold water
1 cube vegetable stock

Sapori

1 tablespoon butter
3 to 4 tablespoons extra-virgin
    olive oil
8 ounces new spring onions and/or
    leeks (white and very light green
    parts), thinly sliced (about
    2$^1/_2$ cups) (see Nota)
8 ounces minced lean veal or beef
$^3/_4$ cup white wine
1$^1/_2$ cups shelled fava beans
    (2 pounds unshelled or 7 ounces
    frozen)

1$^1/_2$ cups peas (1 pound fresh
    unshelled or 8 ounces frozen,
    defrosted)
3 artichokes, prepared as described on
    page 154 and cut into
    quarters
1 lemon
6 to 8 ounces green beans, cut into
    $^1/_3$-inch pieces (about 2 cups)
1 pound asparagus, woody ends
    discarded, tips cut off and
    reserved, and stems cut into thin
    rounds
Salt and freshly ground pepper

Condimenti

1 teaspoon pasta flour (see Nota)
4 slices of country bread, toasted in
    the oven with butter

1. Put the *brodo* in a soup pot and bring to a lively simmer. Cook, uncovered, while the *sapori* cooks. Keep at a lively simmer; the broth will reduce substantially.

2. Over moderate heat, combine the butter and oil in a heavy-bottomed wide casserole, preferably with low sides. When the butter melts, add the onions and sauté until very soft, about 5 minutes.

3. Add the minced veal and while stirring, sauté for a few minutes until it loses its pink color. Add the wine and cook for 2 to 3 minutes more.

continued

Stir in the fava beans and cook for 5 minutes. Add the artichokes and lemon and cook for 5 minutes more, adding some broth if necessary. Add the green beans, asparagus stems, peas, and 1 to 2 ladlefuls of the simmering broth. Season with salt and pepper and cook until all the vegetables are very tender, about 15 minutes. Add the asparagus tips and cook at a lively simmer for 5 minutes more. The vegetables should be covered by the simmering *brodo*. Add more broth as needed and stir occasionally with a wooden spoon.

4. In a blender or food processor, add the reduced *brodo* and the pasta flour and puree until well blended. Stir into the vegetables. The broth should be just barely visible; add more boiling water if needed. Add the salt and pepper to taste.

Serve with the bread placed on the side of the soup plates.

Nota: Cipolle novelle are very large versions of our spring onions. All spring onions can be used, or they can be used in combination with leeks, but substitute no other type.

If pasta flour is unavailable, substitute polenta flour.

serves: 4

cooking time:
45 minutes

Giardiniera

Gardener's Soup

A Piedmontese meal almost never commences without a soup. This garden-fresh combination of vegetables and leafy greens is a springtime favorite. Sweating the vegetables in butter with a pinch of sugar brings out their sweetest taste.

Sapori

4 to 5 tablespoons unsalted butter

*2 medium-large carrots, thinly sliced
(about 1½ cups)*

*1 large celery rib, thinly sliced
(about ⅔ cup)*

*1 leek, white and light green parts,
thinly sliced (about ½ cup)*

*2 small turnips, peeled and thinly
sliced (about 1 cup)*

Sugar

*3 cups thinly shredded green
cabbage (about 8 ounces)*

*4 cups thinly shredded Boston
lettuce (about 4 ounces)*

Brodo

*4½ cups light classic broth
(page 40) or substitute*

Condimenti

*1 cup shelled fresh or defrosted
frozen peas*

Freshly grated Parmesan cheese

1. Over medium heat, melt the butter in a heavy soup pot. Add the vegetables and sprinkle with a little sugar. Cover and sweat for about 10 minutes.

Meanwhile, add the cabbage and lettuce to a pot of lightly salted boiling water and cook for 5 minutes. Drain and rinse with cold water.

2. Add about 3 cups of the *brodo* to the vegetables and bring to a steady simmer. Stir in the blanched greens and cook, uncovered, for about 30 minutes (if adding fresh peas, reduce time to 20 minutes).

3. Add the remaining *brodo* and return to a simmer. Add the peas and cook until tender, 2 to 3 minutes for frozen and 10 to 15 minutes for fresh.

Serve with the Parmesan cheese.

Minestra alla Marsigliese

Genovese Vegetable Soup

*T*his soup comes from a small town outside Genoa and is prepared with a variation on the classic pesto sauce. It omits the customary addition of cheese, resulting in a light and fragrant flavoring that makes this springtime soup even more refreshing.

Brodo
6 1/2 cups Light Vegetable Broth
  (page 42) or Chicken Broth
  (page 39) or substitute
2 1/2 cups diced baking potatoes
  (about 12 ounces)

Sapori
1/2 cup cooked or canned cannellini
  beans, drained
2/3 cup chopped ripe tomatoes,
  peeled and seeded
2 1/2 cups diced zucchini (about 8 ounces)

Condimenti
Salt and freshly ground pepper
3 ounces small macaroni or ditalini
  (about 3/4 cup)
3 tablespoons minced fresh basil
  leaves
1/2 teaspoon minced garlic
2 tablespoons extra-virgin olive oil

1. In a soup pot, bring the *brodo* to a steady simmer and cook, covered, for 15 minutes.

2. Add the *sapori* and cook for 15 minutes more.

3. Add the salt and pepper to taste and bring the soup to a lively simmer. Add the pasta and cook until *al dente*.

Meanwhile, combine the basil, garlic, and oil in a small bowl and whisk until well blended. Stir into the soup and serve.

Variante: A similar soup from Sicily replaces the cannellini beans with 2 chopped celery ribs. Sauté 1 small chopped onion in oil, stir in the *sapori,* then add the *brodo.*

Minestra alla Piemontese con Zucca
Vegetable Soup with Pumpkin

serves: 4 to 6

cooking time:
45 minutes

The Piedmontese have a gift for combining many elements to create rich and substantial dishes, often enriched with flavorful sauces. In this soup perfect for fall, a basil and garlic sauce enhances its mellow variety of vegetables. To maintain their character, all the vegetables are cut into large bite-sized pieces and cooked at a fairly brisk simmer. Much of the cooking liquid will evaporate; be careful not to over-salt.

continued

Sapori

8 ounces green beans, cut in about
    ³/₄-inch pieces
8 ounces new potatoes, cut into bite-
    sized pieces (about 1³/₄ cups)
12 ounces pumpkin or butternut
    squash (trimmed weight), cut
    into bite-sized pieces
    (about 2¹/₂ cups)
8 ounces zucchini, cut into bite-
    sized pieces (about 2 cups)
1 small garlic clove, chopped

Brodo

7¹/₂ cups cold water
1 teaspoon coarse salt or 1 cube
    vegetable stock

Condimenti

4 ounces (²/₃ cup) peas
4 to 5 ounces short pasta, such as
    farfalle (about 1¹/₄ cups)
¹/₂ cup packed fresh basil leaves
¹/₂ garlic clove
2 tablespoons extra-virgin olive oil
Salt and freshly ground pepper

1. Over moderate heat, combine the *sapori* and *brodo* in a soup pot and cook at a steady simmer, uncovered, for about 30 minutes.

2. Bring to a lively simmer, then add the peas and pasta. Cook until the pasta is *al dente* and add a little boiling water if needed.

3. In the meantime, prepare the basil sauce. Mince or process the basil and garlic together (if using a food processor, add a pinch of salt). Transfer to a small bowl and beat in the oil.

After the soup has finished cooking, stir the basil sauce into the soup. Add the salt and pepper to taste and serve.

Variante: In Liguria, artichokes replace the zucchini and pasta. Sauté 3 to 4 slivered artichokes (page 154) in butter and add about 10 minutes before the end of cooking. Omit the pasta, serving over toasted bread. Or turn this into an autumn minestrone and add 1 cup cooked cannellini beans and serve with grated pecorino or Parmesan cheese.

Minestra di Primavera

Springtime Soup

serves: 4

cooking time:
1 hour

This light soup from Umbria is a delicious way to make use of springtime vegetables. The flavors of the vegetables are brought out by sautéing them in a pancetta-flavored oil. Umbrian olive oil is among the finest, so choose your best *olio d'oliva extra vergine*.

I particularly like the combination of celery, cauliflower, zucchini, and green beans for their different tastes and textures. If lacking one, increase the amount of the others or add peas, but avoid vegetables such as leafy greens or mushrooms, whose flavors blend into each other.

Battuto

3 tablespoons extra-virgin olive oil

2 ounces (about $^1/_2$ cup) diced
    pancetta or fatty prosciutto

Sapori

2 celery stalks, cut into $^1/_4$-inch
    slices (about $^3/_4$ cup)

1 small cauliflower, cut into small
    florets (3 to 4 cups)

2 medium zucchini, diced (about
    2 cups)

6 to 8 ounces (about $1^3/_4$ cups) diced
    green beans

Brodo

$4^1/_4$ cups cold water

1 teaspoon coarse salt

$^1/_2$ cup pureed tomatoes
    (9-ounce can)

Condimenti

Salt and freshly ground pepper

Chopped fresh parsley or Crostini
    (optional, page 42)

Freshly grated Parmesan cheese
    (optional)

1. Combine the oil and pancetta in a heavy-bottomed soup pot. Gently sauté over medium-low heat until the pancetta has rendered its fat, 8 to 10 minutes.

continued

2. Stir in the *sapori* and sauté, stirring occasionally, until softened, 8 to 10 minutes. There should be enough water left on the vegetables from their washing to prevent sticking. If not, add a little hot water while cooking.

3. Add the *brodo* and bring to a boil. Lower the heat and gently simmer, uncovered, until the vegetables are very tender, 30 to 40 minutes. Salt and pepper to taste and sprinkle with the parsley or accompany with crostini, and serve with the Parmesan.

Zuppa di Verdure alla Veneta

Vegetable Soup, Venetian Style

serves: 4

cooking time:
30 minutes

When I tasted this simple Venetian soup, it was so flavorful that I assumed it was made with a homemade *brodo*. In fact, its broth is a result of cooking very finely cut vegetables quickly. Carrots and potatoes act as a base for the seasonal vegetables. This recipe adds the winter combination of cabbage and cauliflower, but any very fresh vegetables, cut finely, can be added. Use a food processor fitted with the thinnest slicing blade to cut the carrots and potatoes and this soup is wonderfully easy to prepare.

Battuto

3 tablespoons extra-virgin olive oil

1/4 cup minced shallots or onion

Sapori

1 pound carrots, preferably organic,
  peeled and very thinly sliced

12 ounces boiling potatoes, peeled
  and very thinly sliced

1 small cauliflower, cut into small
  florets (about 2 cups)

1/2 head of small Savoy cabbage,
  inner leaves finely shredded
  (about 3 cups)

Brodo

5 cups boiling water

3/4 teaspoon coarse salt

Condimenti

Freshly grated Parmigiano-
  Reggiano cheese

1. In a heavy-bottomed soup pot, sauté the *battuto* over moderate heat, stirring occasionally, until the shallots turn golden, about 5 minutes.

2. Add the carrots and potatoes and stir to coat well. Add the cauliflower and cabbage and stir until the cabbage wilts, about 5 minutes.

3. Add the *brodo* and cook, uncovered, at a lively simmer for 20 minutes. The broth should substantially reduce, concentrating the flavors of the vegetables.

Top with a generous sprinkling of Parmesan cheese and serve with the remaining cheese at the table.

Verdure/One Main Vegetable Soups

These soups—thick, thin, and pureed—pay homage to the many wonderful vegetables of Italy.

Carciofi/Artichokes From bright green and bulbous to violet and tapering, artichokes come in a variety of shapes and sizes. As in all Italian dishes, every part of the artichoke that is served is meant to be eaten, which means that any thorny leaves and hairy choke need to be removed. Unless tender baby artichokes are used, extensive trimming will be required, but this will more than be made up for by the distinctive taste your soup will have.

   Choosing Artichokes should feel solid; those that feel light have lost moisture and have started to dry up. The leaves should be blemish-free and tightly formed. Artichokes will stay fresh longer by trimming the stem and immersing in about ½ inch of water; covering with a damp cloth also helps to maintain moisture.

   Preparation You need to use lemons to prevent artichokes from darkening and from staining your skin (wearing rubber gloves will prevent any discoloration). Have a bowl of cold water ready, with the juice of ½ lemon and another half to rub on the just cut parts. Aluminum pots should be avoided; they will turn artichokes black.

1. Bend back and snap off the tough layers of leaves until you arrive at the tender inner yellow leaves. Always rub the exposed, tender parts with the cut lemon or drop in the acidulated water.
2. If there is a stalk, break it off rather than cutting it. This will pull away the tough fibers from the artichoke hearts. Cut away any tough fibers around the base.
3. With a serrated knife, cut off the tops of the leaves just above the choke. Cut the choke into halves and, using a melon-baller or paring knife, scrape out the inside hair of the choke. Tear out any leaves that have red on them, as they are prickly.
4. Cut the hearts and tender leaves into slices and place in the acidulated water.

Crema di Carciofi

Cream of Artichoke Soup

serves: 4

cooking time:
45 minutes

*A*rtichokes pureed with potatoes is one of my favorite bases, which can easily be turned into several wonderful soups. For a heartier soup, I add cooked barley and cream; for a delicate soup, I simply garnish with slivers of cooked artichoke and top with garlic crostini.

This soup is the perfect way to use artichoke stalks. As a guideline, the proportion of trimmed artichoke to potato should be about three to one. For a silky texture, use a food mill.

Battuto

3 to 4 tablespoons extra-virgin olive oil

Minced Together

1 medium onion

1 small celery rib

1 small carrot

Sapori

4 artichokes, prepared as described on page 154 and thinly sliced, or 1 10-ounce package frozen artichoke hearts

8 to 12 ounces peeled and cubed floury potatoes (about 1³/₄ cups)

Brodo

4¹/₄ cups hot water

³/₄ teaspoon coarse salt

Condimenti

1 cup cooked pearl barley (see Nota)

¹/₃ to ¹/₂ cup heavy cream

2 to 3 tablespoons chopped parsley or garlic crostini (page 42)

Salt

1. In a heavy-bottomed soup pot, sauté the *battuto* over medium-low heat until soft, about 5 minutes.

continued

2. Add the *sapori* and stir well to combine.

3. Add the *brodo* and bring to a boil. Lower the heat and cook at a steady simmer, covered, until the artichokes are tender, about 30 minutes.

Remove a few artichoke slices and reserve (optional). Puree the soup through the fine-holed disc of a food mill or in a food processor and strain to remove the artichoke fiber. Return the puree to the soup pot and reheat over low heat.

4. Stir in the cooked barley, cream, parsley, and salt to taste. Or serve garnished with the artichoke slices and crostini.

Nota: If adding barley, cook ⅓ cup, rinsed well, in about 2 cups of water until tender, about 45 minutes. Drain well before adding.

Minestra di Carciofi e Pasta

Artichoke and Pasta Soup

serves: 4

cooking time:
1 hour

Fields of the silvery green leaves of the artichoke plant are an integral part of the Italian Riviera and the southern Italian coastline. The smallest artichokes, with their less developed fibers, are preferred for their tenderness and flavor. This recipe from Liguria combines their slightly musky taste with tomatoes, pancetta, and pecorino cheese for an assertive but delicate soup. Fresh tagliatelle is the pasta of choice.

Battuto

2 teaspoons olive oil

2 tablespoons unsalted butter

Minced Together

2 ounces pancetta

1 small onion

Sapori

4 globe artichokes, prepared as
described on page 154 and thinly
sliced, or 1 10-ounce package
frozen artichoke hearts

3 ripe tomatoes, peeled, seeded, and
chopped (about ³/₄ cup)

Brodo

4¹/₄ cups water or light vegetable
broth (see Nota)

1 teaspoon coarse salt

Condimenti

Salt and freshly ground pepper

5 to 6 ounces fresh tagliatelle, cut
into short pieces, or 3 ounces
dried

1 to 2 tablespoons chopped fresh
parsley

Freshly grated pecorino Romano
cheese

1. Over medium-low heat, combine the oil and butter in a heavy-bottomed soup pot. When the butter melts, add the minced *battuto* and sauté, stirring occasionally, for about 5 minutes.

2. Add the *sapori* and sauté until the artichokes start to soften, stirring often, for 5 minutes.

3. Add the *brodo* and bring to a slow, steady simmer. Cover and cook until the artichokes are very tender, 30 to 40 minutes.

4. Add the salt and pepper to taste and bring the soup to a lively simmer. Add the pasta and cook until *al dente.* Stir in the parsley and serve with the pecorino cheese.

Nota: If using frozen artichokes, replace the *brodo* water with a light vegetable or chicken broth.

Crema di Asparagi e Patate

Asparagus and Potato Soup

*I*n this Piedmontese soup, the subtle flavor of tomato brings the asparagus and potatoes into perfect harmony. As is customary in this region, a *crema* often has the addition of flour and butter; if you prefer, replace with a touch of mascarpone or cream added at the end of cooking.

Brodo
4 cups water
3/4 teaspoon coarse salt
2 1/2 tablespoons unsalted butter
2 1/2 tablespoons all-purpose flour

Sapori
1 pound asparagus, tough ends
    removed, stalks cut into large
    pieces, tips cut off and reserved

2 tablespoons unsalted butter
1 tablespoon olive oil
12 ounces potatoes, peeled and cut
    into small cubes (about 2 cups)
1 tablespoon tomato paste, diluted in
    1/3 cup hot water
Salt and freshly ground pepper

Condimenti
Crostini, fried in butter (page 42)

1. Bring the water and salt to a boil. In a separate heavy saucepan large enough to hold the water and asparagus stalks, melt the butter over moderate heat. When it starts to foam, add the flour and stir until lightly colored. While continuing to stir, slowly pour in the boiling salted water and stir until completely amalgamated. Add the asparagus stalks, cover, and simmer until tender, about 15 minutes.

2. Meanwhile, in a separate heavy-bottomed soup pot, combine the butter and oil over medium heat. When the butter melts, add the potatoes and sauté until golden, stirring often, for about 5 minutes. Add the tomato liquid, cover, and sweat for about 10 minutes, stirring occasionally to keep the potatoes from sticking. Add the asparagus tips and cook, uncovered, until crisp-tender, about 3 minutes.

3. Puree the asparagus stalks with its cooking liquid until smooth. Add to the potatoes and asperagus tips, and using a wooden spoon, stir well to combine. Add the salt and pepper to taste and bring to a simmer. If the soup appears too dense, add a little boiling water.

4. Serve with the crostini.

Minestra di Broccoli alla Romana
Broccoli Soup with Pasta

serves: 4

cooking time:
35 minutes

*I*n late summer, the vivid lime-green buds of *cavolbroccolo* appear throughout the Roman countryside. This member of the broccoli family has a delectable flavor that I describe as the best of broccoli and cauliflower combined. In this typical country soup, its taste is complemented by garlic and pancetta. Green broccoli also yields wonderful results, but if you have some cauliflower on hand, add a little and you may come a little closer to the heavenly taste of *cavolbroccolo*.

Battuto

2 tablespoons extra-virgin olive oil

Minced Together

1 medium onion

2 to 3 ounces pancetta

2 garlic cloves

Sapori

1 pound broccoli

2 teaspoons tomato paste, diluted in
  1/2 cup hot water

Brodo

1 cube chicken or vegetable stock
  dissolved in 5 cups water or
  3/4 teaspoon coarse salt

Condimenti

Salt and freshly ground pepper

7 ounces spaghetti, broken into short
  pieces, or tubetti

Freshly grated Romano or Parmesan
  cheese

continued

1. Over low heat, sauté the *battuto* in a heavy-bottomed soup pot, stirring often, until the pancetta has rendered its fat, 8 to 10 minutes.

2. Meanwhile, prepare the broccoli. Separate the florets from the stems and cut into small buds. Peel the remaining stems and cut into ½-inch pieces. Plunge into cold water and drain. Add to the *battuto* and stir well to combine. Add the diluted tomato paste, cover the pot, and sweat for about 5 minutes.

3. Add the *brodo* and bring to a boil. Lower the heat and simmer, covered, until the broccoli is tender, about 10 minutes.

4. Add the salt and pepper to taste and bring the soup to a lively simmer. Add the pasta and cook until *al dente*. Serve with the grated cheese.

Variante: For a similar soup from the Veneto, replace the pasta with ¾ cup rice and add 1 small carrot and celery rib to the *battuto* and omit the tomato paste.

Crema di Carote e Rape

Cream of Carrot and Turnip Soup

A simple but perfect coupling of tastes, this soup pairs the sweetness of carrots with the slight tartness of turnips. When I was served this soup, it was presented with a beautiful swirl of parsley cream sauce. All the vegetables are pureed, so the shape you cut them is not important; just be sure to chop them small enough so they cook quickly.

Sapori

3 cups (12 ounces) chopped carrots

2 cups (6 to 8 ounces) chopped turnips

2 leeks, white and light green parts, sliced (about 1 cup)

1 cup (5 to 6 ounces) diced potato

Brodo

4 cups Vegetable Broth (page 40)

1 cup milk

Condimenti

6 tablespoons chilled heavy cream

1 tablespoon minced parsley and whole parsley leaves

1. Combine the *sapori* and broth in a soup pot and bring to a boil. Lower the heat and gently simmer, partially covered, for about 30 minutes.

2. Puree and readd to the soup pot. Over low heat, add the milk and reheat.

3. In a small bowl, whisk the cream and parsley together. Garnish each serving with the parsley cream, making a circle, S shape, or other design, and top with a few whole parsley leaves.

Crema Fredda di Carote al Prosecco

Cold Cream of Carrot Soup with *Prosecco*

*T*his elegant summer soup was created by Chef Graziano Bettiol for the Gran Ristorante Quadri in Venice. A touch of *prosecco,* the Italian equivalent of champagne, is added *al servizio,* just before serving. Graziano stresses this makes the soup even more refreshing. He also suggests serving the *prosecco* at the table to be added to taste. Needless to say, this soup is preceded by an aperitif of champagne.

Battuto
1 tablespoon extra-virgin olive oil
3 tablespoons unsalted butter
1/4 cup minced shallots

Sapori
1 1/2 pounds carrots, preferably
    organic, scraped and coarsely
    chopped

Brodo
4 cups Chicken Broth (page 39) or
    Vegetable Broth (page 40) or
1 1/2 cube chicken or vegetable
    stock dissolved in 4 cups water

Condimenti
1/4 cup heavy cream
Prosecco or champagne

1. Over medium-low heat, combine the oil and butter in a heavy-bottomed soup pot. When the butter melts, add the shallots and sauté until soft, 2 to 3 minutes.

2. Over moderate heat, add the *sapori* and *brodo.* Bring to a steady simmer and cook, covered, until the carrots are tender, about 30 minutes. Add a little water if the soup becomes too dense. Take off the heat and let cool.

3. Stir the cream into the soup, then puree in a blender or food processor until smooth.

Serve the soup lightly chilled or at room temperature. Add the *prosecco* to taste, stirring into the soup, and bring the bottle to the table.

Crema di Cavolfiore con Peperoni

Pureed Cauliflower Soup with Red Peppers

serves: 4

cooking time:
1 hour

A garnish of red pepper is a great visual and taste complement to pureed cauliflower. This recipe calls for simply sautéing the peppers, but for a more intense flavor they can first be roasted (page 180). This elegant soup goes equally well if served before a fish or meat course.

Brodo
4¹/₂ *cups Vegetable Broth (page 40)*
  or Chicken Broth (page 39) or
  substitute

1 medium baking potato, peeled and
  diced (about 1 cup)
Salt and freshly ground pepper,
  preferably white

Sapori
2 medium leeks, white and light
  green parts, thinly sliced
  (about 1 cup)
1 pound cauliflower (see Nota)

Condimenti
2 tablespoons extra-virgin olive oil
1 large sweet red pepper, stemmed,
  seeded, and diced

1. In a soup pot, bring the *brodo* to a boil. Add the *sapori,* adjust the heat, and cook at a lively simmer for about 30 minutes.

Finely puree and then return to the soup pot. Reheat over very low heat and add the salt and pepper to taste.

2. Meanwhile, in a nonstick frying pan, heat the oil over moderate heat. Add the peppers, sprinkle with a pinch of salt, and sauté until the peppers are lightly browned, stirring occasionally, for about 10 minutes.

Place a generous garnish of the peppers in the center of each serving.

continued

Nota: As much of the cauliflower should be used as possible. Trim the base of the stalk and remove the dark outer leaves; the light green leaves can be chopped and used. Cut the curds into small florets and coarsely chop the stems. Soak in cold salted water until ready for cooking.

Variante: For a delicate *vellutata,* add ½ cup cream, stirred into the pureed cauliflower, and replace the red pepper with Parmesan crostini (page 43).

serves: 4

cooking time:
45 minutes

Zuppa con Cavolfiore e Patate

Cauliflower and Potato Soup

This simple Tuscan soup combines cauliflower and potatoes with onions and pancetta. Ladled over slices of country bread, this soup is deliciously rustic; topped with crostini, it becomes more refined, but no less satisfying.

Battuto
3 tablespoons extra-virgin olive oil

Finely Chopped Together
2 ounces pancetta
1 medium red onion

Brodo
4³/₄ cups Classic Meat Broth
    (page 35) or Chicken Broth
    (page 39) or substitute

Sapori
8 ounces boiling potatoes, peeled and
    diced (about 1¹/₂ cups)
8 ounces cauliflower florets
    (about 2 cups)
Salt and freshly ground pepper

Condimenti
4 slices ¹/₂-inch-thick country bread
    or garlic crostini (page 43)
1 to 2 garlic cloves, peeled

1. In a heavy-bottomed soup pot, sauté the *battuto* over moderate heat, stirring occasionally, for about 5 minutes. Meanwhile, in a separate pot, bring the *brodo* to a boil.

2. Stir the potatoes and cauliflower into the *battuto,* then add the boiling *brodo.* Adjust the heat and simmer, covered, for 30 to 40 minutes. If needed, add a little boiling water. Add the salt and pepper to taste.

3. Meanwhile, lightly toast both sides of the bread under the grill and rub one side with garlic or prepare the garlic crostini.

Ladle the soup over the toasted bread or top with the crostini and serve.

Variante: In Sardinia, this combination becomes the base for a summer minestrone. Add 2 thinly sliced artichokes, prepared as described on page 154, and sauté with the *battuto* for 5 minutes. Omitting the bread, add ½ cup long-grain rice and ½ cup peas toward the end of cooking and serve with grated pecorino cheese.

Finocchio/Fennel   There are two types of fennel used in Italian cooking. One is the herb, the tall green stalks of *finocchio selvatico,* wild fennel. Grown in Italy since the sixteenth century, wild fennel is prized not only for its distinctive anise flavor but for its abundance of healthy qualities. The other is the vegetable, grown for its bulb. When cooked in soups, the mild licoricelike flavor of this fennel, also known as Florentine fennel, becomes delicately sweet.

Choosing   Italian cooks distinguish between the rounder male fennel bulb and the flatter elongated female bulb. The less stringy and more fragrant male fennel is more desirable, particularly when eaten raw; however, both work well for soup cookery. Select pearly white, tightly packed bulbs; if the tops are still attached, they should be bright green. Try to avoid deeply cracked outer layers; too much of the bulb will have to be discarded.

Fresh fennel should be used within a few days, but if the bulbs are in very good condition they will keep longer. If the stalks are attached, trim them, wrap the bulbs and stalks separately in plastic, and refrigerate.

Yield   1 pound = 12 ounces trimmed = 2½ to 3 cups chopped

Preparation   The fennel bulb is a bunch of tightly gathered stems attached to a central core much like celery. When you slice and remove its base, the layers fall apart. Save the stalks and trimmings for flavoring your *brodo* and reserve the edible feathery leaves for flavoring or garnishing.

1. Trim the fennel by cutting off the stalks where they meet the bulb. Detach and discard any blemished outer layers. If the outer layer is very stringy, scrape it with a peeler.
2. Cut the bulb in half lengthwise and cut off the woody root end.
3. Cut into ¼-inch slices and wash under cold running water.

Minestra di Finocchi e Porri con Pesto Rosso

Fennel and Leek Soup with Sun-Dried Tomato Pesto

serves: 4

cooking time:
45 minutes

*T*he delicate pairing of leeks and fennel comes to life with the final flourish of a pesto made with sun-dried tomatoes. Its simplicity and short cooking time belie its complex, heady flavor—making this one of my favorite soups.

Battuto

3 tablespoons extra-virgin olive oil

1 teaspoon dried fennel seeds

2 medium leeks, white and light green parts, thinly sliced (about 1 cup)

Sapori

2 garlic cloves, coarsely chopped

1 pound fresh fennel bulbs (trimmed weight), coarsely chopped (see page 166)

Brodo

5 cups light Chicken Broth (page 39) or Vegetable Broth (page 40) or substitute

Condimenti

1 cup fresh basil and/or flat parsley leaves

6 to 7 sun-dried tomatoes, preserved in oil

1/4 cup freshly grated Parmesan cheese

1 to 2 tablespoons extra-virgin olive oil

1. In a heavy-bottomed soup pot, sauté the *battuto* over medium-low heat until the leeks are pale golden, stirring occasionally, for 8 to 10 minutes.

2. Add the *sapori,* stirring well to combine, for 1 to 2 minutes.

3. Add the *brodo* and cook at a steady simmer, covered, until the fennel is very tender, about 30 minutes.

continued

4. Combine the *condimenti* in the bowl of a food processor and pulse to form a paste. Depending on how much oil is in the tomatoes, add 1 to 2 tablespoons olive oil.

Take the soup off the heat and stir in the pesto or ladle into individual soup bowls and garnish each serving with a dollop of pesto.

Variante: Omit the pesto and you have a soup of supreme delicacy. Garnish with abundant fresh parsley and/or basil.

serves: 4

cooking time:
40 minutes

Zuppa di Finnochi e Scalogni con Rucola

Fennel and Shallot Soup with Arugula

The sweetness of fennel and shallots contrasts with peppery arugula in this delicate but wholly satisfying soup. Potato gives it body and the arugula is used much like an herb, judiciously. This recipe calls for partial pureeing, but for an even more elegant soup make it into a *passato* and puree all of it before adding the arugula. Watercress or sorrel can be substituted.

Battuto

2 tablespoons unsalted butter
1 tablespoon olive oil
$^{1}/_{2}$ cup finely chopped shallots

Sapori

1 pound fennel bulbs (trimmed
   weight), chopped into small slices
1 large baking potato, peeled and
   very finely chopped (see Nota)
2 tablespoons chopped fennel greens,
   if available

Brodo

5 cups cold Chicken Broth (page 39)
   or Vegetable Broth (page 40) or
   1$^{1}/_{2}$ cubes chicken or
   vegetable stock minced in 5 cups
   cold water
Salt and freshly ground pepper

Condimenti

1 ounce arugula, stems removed,
   finely chopped (about $^{3}/_{4}$ cup)
Garlic crostini (page 43, optional)

1. Over medium-low heat, combine the butter and oil in a heavy-bottomed soup pot. When the butter melts, add the shallots and sauté until softened, stirring occasionally, for 3 to 4 minutes.

2. Add the *sapori* and *brodo* and bring to a boil. Lower the heat and cook at a steady simmer, covered, until the vegetables are tender, about 30 minutes.

Puree half the soup, readd, and stir well to combine. Add the salt and pepper to taste and return the soup to a simmer.

3. Take the soup off the heat and stir in the arugula. Serve with the crostini sprinkled on top.

Nota: The potato should be very finely chopped to ensure it fully breaks down; a food processor makes this easy.

Variante: This recipe easily adapts to a cold soup. To the *passato,* add ½ to ¾ cup cream along with the arugula. To ensure the soup is not too hot when you add the cream, first combine it with a ladleful of soup. Serve cold or at room temperature.

Minestra di Lasagnette e Porri

Pasta and Leek Soup

Piemonte means "at the foot of the mountains." Its cooking derives as much from the simple rustic cooking of the mountains as it does the elegant cooking of the French court. This wonderful soup has a decidedly Italian touch with the addition of garlic, sage, and *lasagnette,* a wide flat egg pasta similar to fettuccine.

Sapori

1 tablespoon unsalted butter

1 tablespoon oil

10 ounces peeled and diced potatoes
   (about 1³/₄ cups)

1¹/₄ to 1¹/₂ pounds leeks, white and
   light green parts, thinly sliced
   (about 4 cups)

Coarse salt

Battuto

1 tablespoon unsalted butter

2 tablespoons olive oil

Reserved leeks (see *Nota*)

Finely Chopped Together

1 medium onion

1 medium celery rib

1 garlic clove

3 to 4 sage leaves

Brodo

4¹/₂ cups Classic Meat Broth
   (page 36) or substitute

Condimenti

5 ounces dried fettuccine or 10
   ounces fresh, cut into about
   2-inch pieces

¹/₄ cup freshly grated Parmigiano-
   Reggiano

1. Over medium-low heat, combine the butter and oil in a heavy saucepan. When the butter melts, stir in the potatoes and half the leeks and sprinkle with a few pinches of salt. Add enough water to barely cover the leeks. Gently simmer, covered, for about 30 minutes, adding a little water if needed. Allow the leeks to cool slightly, then puree until smooth.

2. Meanwhile, in a heavy-bottomed soup pot, sauté the *battuto* until softened, stirring occasionally, for about 5 minutes.

Add the *brodo* and the leek puree and stir to combine. Cook at a gentle but steady simmer, partially covered, for about 30 minutes.

3. When the soup has almost finished cooking, cook the pasta in lightly salted boiling water until *al dente.* Drain well, add to the soup, and serve with the Parmesan cheese.

Nota: Half the leeks are cooked and pureed with the potatoes, the other half sautéed with the *battuto*.

Carabaccia

Florentine Red Onion Soup

*D*eriving from the Greek word *karabos,* a boat in the shape of a nutshell, the name *carabaccia* refers to the tureen once used to serve this sixteenth-century soup. The original recipe has the typical Renaissance flavorings of almonds, sugar, cinnamon, and lemon juice. This simplifies the sweet-and-sour flavors with a touch of balsamic vinegar, which not only has a great affinity to onions but makes this soup very easy to prepare.

Sapori

5 tablespoons extra-virgin olive oil

2 pounds red onions, very thinly
 sliced (see Nota)

Coarse salt

3 tablespoons balsamic vinegar

Brodo

5 cups Classic Meat Broth (page 36)
 or Chicken Broth (page 39) or
 substitute

Salt and freshly ground pepper

Condimenti

4 to 6 slices of white or whole wheat
 country bread

Freshly grated Parmesan cheese

1. In a heavy saucepan, warm the oil over low heat. Add the onions, sprinkle with a few pinches of salt, and gently sauté until very soft, 10 to 15 minutes. Stir occasionally and add a little hot water if needed. Add the vinegar and cook until almost evaporated, 3 to 4 minutes more. Meanwhile, bring the broth to a boil.

2. Add the boiling broth to the onions and simmer, covered, for about 1 hour. Lightly add the salt and pepper to taste.

3. Toast the bread, place a slice in each soup bowl, and ladle over with the soup. Serve with the Parmesan cheese.

Nota: The onions can be easily sliced in a food processor using the thinnest slicing blade. For a milder onion flavor, blanch the sliced onions in lightly salted boiling water for a few minutes and drain well before adding.

Variante: Using Spanish onions, sauté 1 thinly sliced carrot and 1 thinly sliced celery rib with the onions. Replace the vinegar with ½ cup white wine and just before the end of cooking, add 1 cup peas.

Cipollata

Tuscan Onion Soup

serves: 4

cooking time:
1½ to 2 hours

Translating as "onion stew," *cipollata* is a specialty of central Italy. The onions are slowly simmered with a pancetta *battuto,* yielding a deliciously sweet and savory soup. In Tuscany, sausage is added and the *brodo* is a rich pork broth, while in Umbria tomatoes and a Parmesan-egg sauce enrich the soup (see *Variante*). This recipe adapts the Tuscan way, using a leaner meat broth.

continued

Battuto

$^1/_4$ cup extra-virgin olive oil

2 ounces mild sausage, casings
    removed and cut into small
    pieces, or minced pork

Finely Chopped Together

2 ounces fatty pancetta

1 small carrot

1 small celery rib

Sapori

4 large Spanish onions (about
    2 pounds), very thinly sliced
    and soaked (see Nota)

Brodo

5 cups Classic Meat Broth (page 36)
    or substitute

Salt

Condimenti

4 slices country bread

2 garlic cloves, peeled

1. In a heavy-bottomed soup pot, sauté the *battuto* over medium-low heat for about 10 minutes. Stir with a wooden spoon, breaking up the sausage meat.

2. Drain the onions, add to the *battuto,* and stir until most of its soaking liquid has evaporated, 3 to 4 minutes. Add just enough broth to barely cover the onions, about 2 cups, and simmer, covered, for 1 hour. Add the remaining broth and salt to taste; continue to simmer, uncovered, for about 20 minutes.

3. Toast the bread on both sides under the broiler and rub one side with garlic. Place the bread in each bowl and ladle over with the soup.

Nota: To slice the onions easily, use the fine slicing blade of a food processor. The sliced onions are then soaked to soften their flavor. Cover with cold water and leave overnight or cover with boiling water and allow to soak for at least 30 minutes, then drain.

Crema di Piselli Novelli alla Menta

Cream of Pea and Lettuce Soup with Mint

serves: 4

cooking time:
20 minutes

A touch of fresh mint makes this the perfect hot-weather soup. Prepared with *piselli novelli,* the first young peas of spring, this refreshing Roman soup has lightly pureed vegetables and a touch of cream. For a vegetarian soup, sprinkle with freshly grated Parmesan cheese.

Battuto

2 tablespoons unsalted butter

Minced Together
2 ounces pancetta
2 large shallots
1/2 small celery rib

Sapori

1 3/4 cups shelled fresh or defrosted
frozen peas
2 teaspoons chopped fresh mint
1 small head of Boston lettuce, end
removed and leaves shredded

Brodo

4 cups Vegetable Broth (page 40) or
Chicken Broth (page 39) or
2 cubes vegetable or chicken
stock dissolved in 4 cups water

Condimenti

1/4 cup heavy cream
1 to 2 teaspoons chopped fresh mint
Salt and freshly ground pepper
Crostini, sautéed in butter (page 42)

1. Over low heat, melt the butter in a heavy-bottomed soup pot. Add the minced *battuto* and sauté until the pancetta has rendered its fat, stirring occasionally, 8 to 10 minutes.

2. Add the peas and mint and stir to coat well for 1 to 2 minutes. Add the lettuce and stir until it wilts. Meanwhile, in a separate pan, bring the *brodo* to a boil.

continued

3. Add the boiling *brodo* and cook over medium-high heat, uncovered, until the peas are crisp-tender, 3 to 10 minutes, depending on whether the peas are frozen or fresh.

Using an immersion blender, coarsely puree the peas and lettuce. Or drain the vegetables, readding the liquid to the soup pot, and coarsely puree in a food processor, using short pulses, then readd to the broth.

4. Lower the heat to a simmer. Stir in the cream and mint to taste and cook for about 2 minutes. Add the salt and pepper to taste. Serve garnished with the crostini.

Variante: In Lombardy, ½ cup rice replaces the cream. After draining the peas and lettuce, cook the rice in their broth before readding. Replace the mint with fresh parsley and if you prefer, replace the lettuce with additional peas.

Minestra di Piselli con Quadrucci

Pea and Prosciutto Soup with Pasta

*T*his popular soup from Lazio contrasts the sweetness of peas and basil with the savory taste of prosciutto. To ensure the peas do not overcook, the pasta of choice is *quadrucci,* small squares of fresh egg pasta. Fresh fettuccine, cut into small squares, makes a fine substitute or dried pasta, broken into small pieces, can be used.

Battuto

3 tablespoons extra-virgin olive oil

Minced Together

1 medium onion

1/4 cup fresh basil leaves

1 garlic clove

Sapori

1 1/2 cups fresh or defrosted frozen
shelled peas (about 8 ounces)

3 ounces lean prosciutto, cut into
small cubes (see Nota)

1 teaspoon tomato paste, diluted in
3/4 cup hot water

Brodo

5 cups light Classic Meat Broth
(page 36) or 1 1/2 cubes meat
stock dissolved in 5 cups water
(see Nota)

Condimenti

Salt and freshly ground pepper

7 ounces fresh egg pasta, such as
fettuccine or 4 ounces dried, cut
into short pieces

2 to 3 fresh basil leaves, shredded

Freshly grated Parmesan cheese

1. In a heavy-bottomed soup pot, sauté the *battuto* over low heat, stirring occasionally, for 3 to 4 minutes.

2. Add the peas and prosciutto and stir to coat well for 1 to 2 minutes. Turn the heat to medium, add the tomato liquid, and simmer until the peas are almost tender, 8 to 10 minutes for fresh, and 2 to 3 for frozen (if using dried pasta, reduce by a few minutes).

3. Bring the *brodo* to a boil and then add to the peas and prosciutto. Lightly add the salt and pepper to taste. Bring to a lively simmer, add the pasta, and cook until *al dente*. Garnish with the basil and serve with Parmesan cheese.

Nota: The diced prosciutto can be replaced with a prosciutto end, cooked in the broth, its meat shredded and readded to the soup. If you are using fresh peas, their pods can be used to flavor the *brodo*. Simmer with carrot, celery, and onion for about an hour, adding enough water to equal 5 cups.

Passato di Peperone Giallo

Pureed Yellow Pepper Soup

*T*his recipe comes from the Florentine restaurant Cibreo, where I watched chef and owner Fabio Picchi perform his alchemy turning yellow peppers to gold. He pointed out that its superb flavor derives from the simple addition of bay leaves and a well sautéed *battuto*. An artistically arranged garnish of small mounds of Parmesan cheese, parsley, and crostini completes this elegant soup.

Battuto

3 tablespoons extra-virgin olive oil

Minced Together
1 medium red or yellow onion
1 medium carrot
1 medium celery rib

Sapori

4 large yellow bell peppers, cored, seeded, and cut into large chunks
2 baking potatoes (about 1 pound), peeled and cut into large chunks

Brodo

3½ cups hot water
2 fresh bay leaves or 1 dried
1 teaspoon coarse salt
Freshly ground pepper

Condimenti

2 teaspoons extra-virgin olive oil
1 cup Italian bread, cut into ¼-inch cubes
3 to 4 ounces coarsely grated Parmesan cheese
¼ cup chopped fresh Italian parsley

1. In a heavy-bottomed soup pot, sauté the *battuto* over medium-low heat, stirring occasionally, until the onion is golden, about 10 minutes.

2. Add the *sapori,* water, bay leaves, and salt, and bring to a boil. Reduce the heat and simmer, uncovered, until the peppers and potatoes are soft, about 30 minutes.

Remove the bay leaves and puree the soup through the fine-holed disc of a food mill (see *Nota*). Reheat over low heat and season with the pepper.

3. In a frying pan, preferably nonstick, heat the oil over medium-high heat. Toss the bread cubes until crisp, 2 to 3 minutes. Top each serving with individual mounds of the crostini, Parmesan cheese, and parsley and serve immediately.

Nota: Using a food mill is necessary to remove the pepper skins. Alternatively, puree in a food processor or blender and push through a sieve.

Zuppa di Peperoni con Pollo
Roasted Pepper Soup with Chicken

serves: 4

cooking time:
30 minutes

One of my favorite warm weather soups, this recipe was created by master chef Giampiero Gemignani. The sweet but intense taste of roasted peppers combined with fresh basil, mint, and marjoram yields a perfectly flavored soup. A garnish of slivered chicken and basil completes this masterpiece. Try to use red, yellow, and green peppers. If you need to increase the amount of one type, keep the green peppers to one third the total.

The tastes of this soup are so appealing, I prepare it in a number of ways. Giampiero purees the peppers with a touch of *grano duro* (pasta flour) to a fine consistency. This is certainly the most elegant presentation. Alternatively, for a light main-course soup I increase the amount of chicken and only partially puree the peppers or them leave whole (omitting the flour). A pinch of dried oregano can replace the fresh marjoram.

continued

Sapori

3 tablespoons extra-virgin olive oil

2 tablespoons butter

2 pounds sweet peppers (2 red,
 2 yellow, and 2 green), roasted
 and cut into thin, short strips
 (see *Nota*)

2 to 3 tablespoons finely chopped
 basil, mint, and marjoram

Brodo

4³/₄ cups Chicken Broth (page 39)

Salt

2 tablespoons grano duro (pasta
 flour) or semolina (polenta flour)

Condimenti

8 ounces cooked chicken breast, cut
 into thin strips

3 to 4 large basil leaves, shredded

1. Over medium-low heat, combine the oil and butter in a heavy-bottomed soup pot. When the butter starts to bubble, add the roasted peppers and sauté, stirring occasionally, for about 10 minutes. Stir in the herbs and sauté for 2 to 3 minutes.

2. In a separate pot, bring the chicken broth to a simmer and add to the peppers. Add the salt to taste and cook for about 10 minutes. Reserve the broth and strain the peppers.

Add the peppers to a food processor and puree until smooth, adding the broth and flour a little at a time. Readd to the soup pot and return to a simmer.

3. Add the chicken and simmer until cooked, 5 to 7 minutes. Sprinkle each serving with the fresh basil.

Nota: To roast peppers, cut them in half lengthwise, remove the seeds, then place, cut-side down, in a pan about 5 inches from the broiler, and broil until lightly and evenly charred, about 7 minutes. Place in a plastic bag or under an inverted bowl to allow them to steam for a few minutes. When they are cool enough to handle, scrape (rub) off the skins. Cut the peppers into thin strips (avoid rinsing them) and reserve.

Minestra di Pomodori e Porri

Tomato and Leek Soup

serves: 4 to 6

cooking time:
1 hour

*I*n this favorite summertime soup, fresh rosemary gently perfumes a simple combination of leeks, carrots, and tomatoes. Using a food processor to finely chop the carrots and potato makes this soup easy to prepare. In the winter, a small addition of cream makes it even more comforting. If possible, use organic carrots, or season with a generous pinch of sugar.

Sapori
3 to 4 tablespoons extra-virgin olive oil
8 medium leeks, white and light green parts, thinly sliced (about 3 cups) (see Nota)
Coarse salt
1 14-ounce can imported Italian tomatoes, with their juice
3 medium carrots, peeled and finely chopped (about 2 cups)
1 medium baking potato, peeled and finely chopped (about 1 cup)

2 teaspoons chopped fresh rosemary leaves or 1 teaspoon dried

Brodo
3 cups Chicken Broth (page 39) or Vegetable Broth (page 40) or 1 cube chicken or vegetable stock dissolved in 3 cups water
Salt and freshly ground pepper

Condimenti
2 to 3 tablespoons chopped fresh parsley

1. In a heavy-bottomed soup pot, combine the oil and leeks and sprinkle with a pinch of salt. Cover the pot and sweat over medium-low heat for about 10 minutes, turning the leeks occasionally, until they become very soft. If needed, add a little hot water.

continued

Stir in the tomatoes, breaking them up with a wooden spoon. Add the rest of the *sapori* and cook about 5 minutes, stirring often.

2. Add the *brodo* and bring to a boil. Lower the heat and simmer, covered, for about 45 minutes. Add the salt and pepper to taste, sprinkle with the parsley and serve.

Nota: Trim the root end of the leeks, cut lengthwise, and while separating the layers, wash under cold running water. While the leeks are cooking, prepare the *sapori.*

Zucche/Zucchini and Pumpkin Soups

Part of the gourd family of plants known as *zucca,* pumpkin and zucchini are the squashes of choice when it comes to Italian soup cookery. The orange-colored flesh of pumpkin melts easily when cooked, lending its vibrant taste and brilliant color. Zucchini, with its thin dark skin and mild flavor, acts as a foil for stronger-tasting vegetables and herbs. Either as the main or complementary ingredient, both are popular additions to a large variety of soups.

Pumpkin (*zucca, zucca gialla*) The winter squashes you are most likely to find in Italy come from Chioggia or Mantua. At the market, since many are sold as slices, it is often hard to know what variety you may be purchasing. However, whichever type you do purchase, make sure it is firm, without bruising or soft spots. The larger pumpkins tend to be less flavorful, so choose the smaller pumpkins with the brightest orange flesh. As a general rule, the more intense the color of the flesh, the more taste it has. Butternut squash is sweeter, but can still be used interchangeably in almost every recipe, though you may want to reduce the amount, not only taking into account the sweeter taste, but the lessened wastage when trimming.

Preparation Depending on the size and thickness of its skin, the pumpkin, once peeled and seeded, may yield only about one half of its original weight. The easiest and least wasteful way to remove the flesh is to cook it in the oven or microwave until it begins to soften, and then scoop out its flesh.

Zucchini (*zucchine*) The diminutive of *zucca, zucchina* means 'little gourd' in Italian. These summer squashes are thin-skinned and are always best when very young and small, when the skin is as delicate as the flesh. Choose zucchini that are firm and preferably no more than 6 inches long.

Preparation Zucchini require careful washing. If there is time, it helps to first soak it in warm water to loosen any grit. A good scrubbing with a vegetable brush and running water completes the job.

Zuppa di Zucca e Cannellini

Pumpkin and Cannellini Bean Soup

This Tuscan soup perfectly balances the sweetness of pumpkin and basil with pancetta and chili pepper for a distinctive *zuppa*. For an equally delicious *minestra*, replace the bread with fresh tagliatelle. The pancetta is cooked as part of the *battuto*, then removed and used as part of the *condimenti*; be sure to cook until very crisp and all the fat has been rendered.

Battuto
2 to 3 tablespoons extra-virgin
    olive oil
2 ounces pancetta, cut into small
    dice (about $1/2$ cup)
2 garlic cloves, peeled and left whole

Minced Together
1 medium red onion
1 small celery rib
$1/4$ teaspoon crushed chili pepper

Brodo
$4^1/2$ cups light Classic Meat Broth
    (page 36) (3 cups broth and
    $1^1/2$ cups water) or 1 cube beef
    or chicken stock dissolved in
    $4^1/2$ cups water

Sapori
12 ounces finely chopped pumpkin
    or butternut squash flesh
    (about 3 cups)
1 14-ounce can cannellini beans,
    drained, or $2/3$ cup dried, cooked
Salt

Condimenti
4 slices country bread, cut into
    $1/2$-inch slices
Reserved pancetta
3 to 4 tablespoons shredded basil
    leaves

1. Combine the oil, pancetta, and garlic in a heavy-bottomed soup pot and sauté over medium-low heat until the pancetta is crisp, 8 to 10 minutes. Remove the pancetta, place on paper towels, and set aside. When the garlic turns golden, press lightly with the back of a fork to release its juices, then discard.

Stir in the minced *battuto,* adding a little oil if needed, and sauté until soft.

2. Add the *brodo* and pumpkin and bring to a boil. Lower the heat and simmer, covered, until the pumpkin disintegrates into the broth, 30 to 40 minutes. Stir in the cannellini beans and continue to cook for 15 minutes more. Keeping in mind the saltiness of the pancetta, lightly add the salt to taste.

3. Toast the bread on both sides, place in each soup bowl, and ladle over with the soup. Garnish with the pancetta and basil and serve.

Crema di Zucchine e Basilico

Pureed Zucchini and Basil Soup

serves: 4

cooking time:
45 minutes

This refreshing soup from the Veneto is one of my springtime favorites. Its character and lovely bright green color come from using only the zucchini skins; be sure they are firm and unblemished. When Fulvia Sesani, a noted Venetian cooking teacher, prepared this soup, she added a touch of cream with the basil, the perfect final touch. Serve this lovely soup unadorned or with crostini and Parmesan cheese.

London's River Café serves its zucchini soup with slices of toasted ciabatta spread with chopped black olives mixed with chili and olive oil, providing a wonderful contrast to this delicate soup.

continued

Battuto

3 tablespoons unsalted butter

1 teaspoon olive oil

Minced Together

$^1/_2$ small celery rib

1 small onion

$^1/_2$ garlic clove (optional)

Brodo

$^3/_4$ cup finely chopped floury potato
   (6 ounces)

$4^1/_4$ cups Chicken Broth (page 39) or
   $1^1/_2$ cube chicken stock
   dissolved in $4^1/_4$ cups water

2 tablespoons chopped parsley

Sapori

$1^1/_4$ pounds zucchini, washed and
   scrubbed

Salt and freshly ground pepper

Condimenti

4 to 5 large fresh basil leaves, finely
   shredded

$^1/_4$ cup heavy cream (optional)

1. Over medium-low heat, combine the butter and oil in a heavy-bottomed soup pot. When the butter melts, stir in the minced *battuto* and gently sauté for about 5 minutes.

2. Stir the potato into the *battuto* and add the rest of the *brodo,* bring to a simmer, and cook, covered, for 15 to 20 minutes.

3. Meanwhile, using a vegetable peeler, peel the zucchini skins. Add the skins to the soup and cook, uncovered, for about 15 minutes more. Coarsely puree the soup using an immersion blender or food processor. Reheat and add the salt and pepper to taste.

4. Take the soup off the heat and add the *condimenti,* stirring well to combine, and serve hot or cold.

Variante: Another version from the Veneto replaces the potato with risotto rice. Sauté the zucchini skins with the *battuto* and add $^1/_2$ cup rice to $5^1/_2$ cups simmering broth. Coarsely puree the cooked soup and serve with freshly grated Parmesan cheese.

Minestra di Zucchine, Cacio, e Uova

Summer Zucchini Soup

serves: 4

cooking time:
45 minutes

*E*very region of southern Italy has its version of this summer soup and they all depend on the freshest young zucchini with glossy skins. In Naples, a sauce of eggs, fresh herbs, and pecorino cheese livens up this mellow soup. I came across this refreshing version, which adds young spinach greens and lemon zest.

If small young spinach leaves are unavailable, blanch the larger-leafed variety in salted water, or omit and increase the amount of zucchini. This soup can be prepared ahead of time up to the point of adding the egg mixture.

Sapori
4 tablespoons extra-virgin olive oil
1 pound zucchini, scrubbed, ends
  trimmed, and thinly sliced

Brodo
5 cups water
Coarse salt and freshly ground
  pepper to taste

Condimenti
2 cups (about 6 ounces) coarsely
  chopped spinach
2 to 3 eggs
2 tablespoons finely shredded fresh
  basil
2 tablespoons finely chopped Italian
  parsley
Zest from $1/2$ small lemon (optional)
3 tablespoons freshly grated pecorino
  cheese

1. Over moderate heat, warm the oil in a heavy, wide saucepan or frying pan. Add the zucchini and sauté, turning often, for about 5 minutes (if using a frying pan, transfer the contents to a soup pot).

continued

2. Add the *brodo,* cover, and cook at a slow but steady simmer for about 30 minutes.

3. Stir in the spinach and cook, uncovered, for a few minutes.

Meanwhile, in a bowl, beat together the eggs, herbs, lemon zest, and cheese. Pour into the soup while stirring vigorously with a wooden spoon.

Take the soup off the heat and allow to sit for a few minutes before serving. If you prefer, garnish with a few shavings of pecorino cheese placed in the center of each serving.

Variante: For a *zuppa di zucchine,* reduce the oil to 2 tablespoons and add 2 tablespoons butter or pancetta fat and coarsely chop the zucchini. Omit the spinach and lemon zest, replace the pecorino with Parmesan cheese, and serve with thin slices of toasted *crostoni.*

Funghi/Mushroom Soups

Since the time of ancient Rome, when special silver vessels called *boletaria* were designed for cooking mushrooms, to this day, *funghi* hold a special place in the Italian culinary hierarchy. From the prized *porcino* and *ovolo* to the common field mushroom, every region of Italy creates soups that make the most of their delicious woodsy taste and fragrance.

> **Cèpe** (*porcino*): These highly prized, wild mushrooms of the *Boletus edulis* family are widely used, both fresh and dried (page 44).
> **Caesar's** (*ovolo*): These rare and prized mushrooms are characterized by their egg (*uovo*) shape and beautiful bright orange caps.
> **Girolle** (*gallinaccio or finferlo*): From the same family of mushroom as the chanterelle, these wild mushrooms are characterized by their trumpet shape and yellow color.
> **Field Mushroom** (*prataiolo*): These are the wild version of the cultivated mushroom, but their fuller flavor and aroma distinguish them.

Buying and Storing Whether your mushrooms were picked in the fields or purchased in the supermarket, select young, fresh specimens without discoloration or bruising. Most varieties will keep refrigerated for a few days but will not freeze well. Mushrooms need to breathe and should never be placed in plastic bags. Keep in the bottom vegetable bin of your refrigerator.

Preparing Cut off and discard the earthy bases, keeping as much of the stem as possible. Wipe the dirt off with a soft brush or scrape with a sharp knife if needed. If possible, avoid washing mushrooms; too much water can dilute their flavor.

Cacciucco di Funghi

Mixed Mushroom Soup

Every October in the small town of Bagnolo, right outside of Grosetto, Italian mushrooms are celebrated at *la Sagra del Fungo,* "the Festival of the Mushroom." No dish shows them off better than this soup, which shares much in common with the well-known Tuscan fish soup *cacciucco,* also noted for its rich variety. Similarly, this sumptuous soup is flavored with tomatoes, wine, and chili pepper. The addition of cannellini beans or slices of toasted bread lends just the right amount of body.

The mushrooms range from the grand porcini to the humble field mushroom. Use any combination of fresh mushrooms, mixing the intensely flavored mushrooms such as shiitake with milder ones; for a deeper flavor, add a few dried porcini.

Battuto

3 to 4 tablespoons extra-virgin olive oil

Finely Chopped Together

¼ teaspoon crushed chili peppers

1 garlic clove

1 small red onion or shallots

¼ cup parsley leaves

Sapori

1¾ pounds mixed mushrooms, wild and cultivated, woody ends removed (page 189) and cleaned

⅔ cup dry red or white wine

½ cup pureed, peeled, and seeded tomatoes

Brodo

5 cups Classic Meat Broth (page 36) or Chicken Broth (page 39) or substitute

Condimenti

2 cups cooked cannellini beans (if canned, rinse and drain) or 4 to 6 slices of country bread, preferably stale

2 to 3 garlic cloves, peeled

1. In a heavy-bottomed soup pot, sauté the *battuto* over medium-low heat, stirring occasionally, for 5 to 7 minutes.

2. Meanwhile, coarsely chop the mushroom caps and finely chop their stems. Over medium heat, stir the mushrooms into the *battuto* and cook until the mushroom liquid has reduced, about 15 minutes. Add the wine and simmer until almost evaporated. Stir in the tomatoes and cook for 10 minutes more, stirring occasionally.

3. Bring the *brodo* to a lively simmer and add to the mushrooms. Lower the heat and gently simmer for about 45 minutes.

4. Add the cannellini beans and cook for 10 minutes. Or toast the bread on both sides under the grill, rub with garlic, place in each soup bowl, and ladle over with the soup.

Crema di Castagne con Porcini

Chestnut Soup with Porcini Mushrooms

*P*airing the sweetness of chestnuts with the earthy taste of mushrooms creates a deliciously rich soup. Using canned chestnut puree and any combination of wild and cultivated mushrooms yields wonderful results. A perfect beginning to a holiday dinner, this soup can be garnished with crostini or sliced sautéed mushrooms.

3/4 ounce dried porcini, soaked in
2 cups lukewarm water for
30 minutes

Battuto
2 tablespoons olive oil
2 tablespoons butter
3 to 4 finely chopped shallots
(about 1/3 cup)

Sapori
12 ounces fresh wild and cultivated
mushrooms, coarsely chopped
3/4 cup red wine or marsala
1 pound unsweetened chestnut puree

Brodo
4 cups Classic Meat Broth (page 36)
or substitute
2 cups reserved porcini liquid
Salt
1 1/2 teaspoons corn or potato flour
2/3 cup heavy cream

Condimenti
3 to 4 tablespoons chopped parsley
Crostini (page 42) or 3 to 4
mushrooms, thinly sliced and
sautéed in butter

1. Strain the porcini through a filter, reserving its soaking liquid; rinse and coarsely chop.

2. Combine the oil and butter in a heavy casserole and place over medium-low heat. When the butter melts, add the shallots and sauté until translucent, 4 to 5 minutes.

3. Stir in the porcini and fresh mushrooms and cook until softened, about 5 minutes. Turn the heat to medium-high, add the wine, and cook until almost evaporated. Add the chestnut puree, stirring well to combine with the shallots and mushrooms.

4. Add the broth and reserved porcini liquid and simmer for 20 minutes, stirring occasionally. Add the salt to taste.

In a separate bowl, beat the flour into the cream until dissolved. Then adding a little at a time, whisk in 2 ladlefuls of hot soup broth. Take the soup off the heat. Using a wooden spoon, add the cream mixture and stir well to combine.

5. Garnish with the parsley and crostini or the sautéed mushrooms and serve.

Nota: If preparing ahead of time, add the cream just before serving.

Zuppa di Funghi alla Scappi

Wild Mushroom Soup

serves: 4

cooking time:
30 minutes

 his sixteenth-century recipe is named after Bartolomeo Scappi, a celebrated cook who served this soup to cardinals, popes, and kings. Fittingly it was made with a combination of the most noble of mushrooms—porcini, the king of mushrooms, and *ovoli,* known as Caesar's mushrooms, to denote its being worthy of an emperor. Its simple preparation was designed to show off these delectable *funghi.* Any combination of fresh, flavorful wild mushrooms works well in this recipe.

continued

Battuto

3 tablespoons extra-virgin olive oil

Minced Together

2 ounces pancetta or prosciutto

$^{1}/_{3}$ cup parsley leaves

1 large garlic clove

Sapori

1 pound fresh wild mushrooms, such
 as Caesar, porcini, shiitake,
 chanterelle, or girolle, earthy
 bases cut off and cleaned

$^{1}/_{2}$ teaspoon dried oregano

Brodo

4$^{1}/_{4}$ cups Chicken Broth (page 39)
 or Vegetable Broth (page 40) or
 substitute

Condimenti

Freshly grated Parmesan cheese

1. In a heavy-bottomed soup pot, sauté the *battuto* over low heat, stirring occasionally, for 5 to 7 minutes.

2. Meanwhile, coarsely chop the mushroom caps and mince their tougher stems. Turn the heat to medium and stir the mushrooms into the *battuto*. Season with the oregano and cook until the mushrooms have reduced and much of their liquid has evaporated, about 10 minutes.

3. In a separate pot, bring the *brodo* to a boil, then add to the mushrooms. Simmer, covered, 15 to 20 minutes.

4. Serve with Parmesan cheese.

Variante: For a more delicate *minestra,* reduce the fresh mushrooms to 12 ounces and add 8 ounces fresh egg *tagliolini,* cut into short pieces, or 5 ounces *capelli d'angelo,* broken up. For a vegetarian soup, replace the pancetta with $^{1}/_{3}$ cup minced shallots.

Minestra di Funghi con Maccheroni

Mushroom and Sausage Soup with Pasta

serves: 4

cooking time:
45 minutes

*P*orcini mushrooms and rosemary are favorite ingredients in Liguria. This enticing soup combines them with sausage and pasta with great effect. Rigatoni, which takes the same amount of time to cook as the sausage, is the pasta of choice. For a wonderful main dish I simply increase the amount of mushrooms and sausage.

This recipe calls for using flavorful fresh mushrooms, or it can be prepared as more of a broth soup, using dried porcini as a predominant flavoring (see *Variante*). If using cultivated mushrooms, add about ¼ ounce dried porcini.

Battuto
2 to 3 tablespoons extra-virgin
    olive oil

Finely Chopped
1 medium celery rib
1 medium carrot
1 tablespoon fresh rosemary

Sapori
12 ounces brown mushrooms, such
    as porcini, coarsely chopped

Brodo
5½ cups Classic Meat Broth
    (page 36) or substitute
1 tablespoon tomato paste

Condimenti
4 ounces mild fresh sausage
Salt
6 ounces rigatoni (about 2 cups)
Freshly grated Parmesan cheese,
    preferably Parmigiano-Reggiano

1. In a heavy-bottomed soup pot, sauté the *battuto* over medium-low heat, stirring occasionally, for 3 to 4 minutes.

2. Add the *sapori* and stir to coat well for 2 to 3 minutes. Meanwhile, bring the *brodo* to a boil.

continued

3. Add the *brodo* and simmer, covered, for about 20 minutes.

4. In a separate pot, add the sausage to boiling water and cook for about 2 minutes. Remove and cut into 1-inch pieces.

Bring the soup to a lively simmer and add the salt to taste. Add the sausage and pasta and cook, stirring occasionally, until the pasta is *al dente,* about 10 minutes. Serve with the Parmesan cheese.

Variante: Substitute dried porcini for fresh. Soak ½ ounce dried porcini, reserving its soaking liquid, as directed on page 44. Add the soaking liquid to the broth to equal 5½ cups and add the porcini, finely chopped, with the *brodo.*

serves: 4 to 6

cooking time:
1½ hours

Zuppa di Funghi e Fagioli

Mushroom and Bean Soup

Served either on its own or with toasted bread, this hearty soup from the Marche is guaranteed to warm any winter night. Partial pureeing gives it a delectable creamy texture. This recipe can be made with all cultivated mushrooms, but is best with the addition of wild mushrooms or dried porcini for a deeper flavor.

Battuto

2 to 3 tablespoons extra-virgin
    olive oil

3 ounces (about $1/2$ cup) finely diced
    pancetta or prosciutto

2 whole garlic cloves, peeled

Sapori

$1^1/2$ pounds mixed mushrooms, caps
    roughly chopped and tougher
    stems finely chopped

2 medium boiling potatoes, peeled
    and diced

1 14-ounce can cannellini beans,
    drained

Brodo

$5^1/2$ cups Classic Meat Broth
    (page 36) or substitute

2 tablespoons tomato paste

1 small bay leaf (optional)

Condimenti

4 to 6 slices of white or whole wheat
    country bread

$1/3$ cup chopped fresh parsley

Freshly grated Parmesan cheese

1. In a heavy-bottomed soup pot, sauté the *battuto* over medium-low heat until the garlic is golden, about 5 minutes. Press the garlic with the back of a fork to extract its juices, then discard.

2. Add the mushrooms and stir well to combine. Cover the pot and sweat for 15 minutes. Stir in the potatoes and cannellini beans. Meanwhile, bring the *brodo* to a boil.

3. Add the *brodo,* adjust the heat, and gently simmer, covered, for about 1 hour. Remove the bay leaf. Puree half the soup and readd, stirring well to combine. Maintain over low heat while preparing the *condimenti.*

4. Toast the bread on both sides under the grill and place in each soup bowl. Stir the parsley into the soup and ladle over the bread. Serve with the grated Parmesan cheese.

Variante: In Basilicata the bread is replaced by the addition of $1^1/2$ cups cooked rice. Omit the potatoes and puree all of the cannellini beans before adding to the mushrooms. Serve with freshly grated pecorino cheese.

Zuppa di Funghi, Porcini, e Ceci

Porcini Mushroom and Chickpea Soup

Known for reinterpreting classic Tuscan dishes, Luciano Momini, well-known chef of Grosseto's La Buca San Lorenzo, created this soup. In this recipe, fresh porcini are substituted with a combination of wild and/or cultivated mushrooms and supplemented by dried porcini and their soaking liquid. Or use 1 pound of full-flavored mushrooms such as shiitake, omitting the dried porcini and increasing the *brodo* by about 1 cup.

Battuto
3 to 4 tablespoons extra-virgin
   olive oil

Minced Together
1 small onion
2 garlic cloves
1 small celery rib
1/2 cup parsley leaves
3/4 ounce dried porcini, soaked in
   1 cup warm water with the soaking liquid reserved (page 44)

Sapori
8 ounces fresh cultivated and wild
   mushrooms, stems coarsely
   chopped and caps very thinly
   sliced

2/3 cup dry white wine
3/4 cup peeled, seeded, and chopped
   ripe tomatoes
1 14-ounce can chickpeas, drained
   and rinsed

Brodo
3 1/2 cups Classic Meat Broth
   (page 36) or substitute
Reserved porcini soaking liquid

Condimenti
Salt and freshly ground pepper
Garlic crostini (page 43)
1 teaspoon minced fresh marjoram
   or 1 tablespoon minced fresh
   parsley
Extra-virgin olive oil, preferably
   estate Tuscan

1. In a heavy-bottomed soup pot, gently sauté the *battuto* over low heat, stirring occasionally, for 8 to 10 minutes.

2. Coarsely chop the porcini and the fresh mushrooms, then add to the *battuto* and stir well to combine for 2 to 3 minutes. Turn the heat to medium, add the wine, and cook until almost evaporated, about 5 minutes. Add the tomatoes and chickpeas and stir to combine.

3. Meanwhile, bring the *brodo* to a boil, then add to the soup pot. Lower the heat and simmer, covered, for 20 minutes. Add the salt and pepper to taste.

4. Serve the soup garnished with the crostini, fresh marjoram, and a thread of oil.

Ortaggi a Foglia/Soups of Leafy Greens

Cabbage, chicory, lettuce, and spinach, once considered to be poor man's food, create some of Italy's most popular soups. From the hardy winter soups of Tuscany and Valle d'Aosta to the delicate lettuce and chicory soups of Liguria, Abruzzi, and Campania, every region uses seasonal leafy greens to create soups of great simplicity and character.

The varieties of leafy greens, both wild and cultivated, are numerous. Round or conical, tightly packed or loose-leafed, each type imparts its unique character when made into a soup. Depending on the tartness of the greens, different types can be substituted for one another and several types can often be combined with great effect. The following list is a guide to the Italian names and their family of leafy greens.

Bitter Greens—*arugula, watercress,* and *dandelion greens (rucola, cressione, tarassaco)* A few ounces of these tender small-leafed greens go a long way. They have a singular peppery taste and are best cooked very quickly.

Cabbage/Kale (cavolo, cavolo nero) The cabbage most widely used in Italian soup cookery is the crinkly-leafed *verza* (Savoy cabbage), also known as *cavolo di milano.* Its milder and less musky flavor is considered superior to other cabbages. The long, elegant, finely crimped leaves of *cavolo nero* (black cabbage) are used extensively in Tuscan soups. Also known as *cavolo toscano,* this palm-tree cabbage has a stronger taste more akin to kale than to other cabbages.

Chicory (cicoria, radicchio, scarola) The two main varieties of Italian chicory are the green-leafed *indivia* (escarole and curly endive) and *scarola* (Batavian endive), and the red-leafed variety known as *radicchio rosso.* Characterized by their mildly bitter taste, they are best combined with unassertive ingredients. Blanching is often recommended.

Lettuce (lattuga) The two most common types of lettuce used in Italian soups are the soft leaves of the round-headed *cappuccia* (Boston lettuce) and the elongated crunchy leaves of *lattuga romana* (Roman lettuce).

Swiss Chard/Spinach (bietole, spinace) Best when they are young, the leaves of spinach and chard can be used interchangeably. The taste of chard is slightly stronger and its texture firmer than spinach. If using chard in place of spinach, cut out the white mid ribs, which are stronger in taste and take longer to cook; depending on the size of their stalks, you may have to purchase twice the amount.

Buying and Storing Leafy Greens Whichever type of greens you purchase, the leaves should appear fresh, brightly colored, and blemish-free. When choosing any round cabbage, look for a tight firm head. Loose-leafed greens, such as kale or chard, should be dark green, with no limp or yellowed leaves.

Refrigerate greens; they quickly turn limp. The firm red and shiny light green cabbages will keep up to 2 weeks in the refrigerator, while the looser-leafed Savoy cabbage will keep for only about 1 week. Spinach, lettuce, and chard will keep refrigerated in a perforated plastic bag for 2 to 4 days.

Yield:

2 pounds round cabbage or lettuce = 1½ pounds trimmed = 9 to 10 cups shredded leaves
1 pound kale or chard = 6 to 8 ounces trimmed = 5 to 6 cups shredded leaves

Preparation All greens need a thorough washing. Cabbage, lettuce, and soft greens are best washed in cold water. The crinkly leaves of kale, chard, and spinach trap soil and are best first soaked in lukewarm water before rinsing them under cold running water.

1. Peel off and discard the tough outermost leaves. Cut off the root end and blemished parts of the leaves. As long as they are unblemished, wilted leaves are fine to include. Keeping in mind that cooking easily tenderizes leafy greens, it is only necessary to remove the very tough parts close to the root.
2. Using a chef's knife, coarsely chop into strips or pieces. Cabbage is best cut lengthwise into quarters to easily remove its hard core. Slice into thin ribbons about ¼ inch wide.
3. Wash or soak in water.
4. All leafy greens cook quickly. Simmer, never boil greens; avoid aluminum pots, as they alter the flavor of the greens.

Crema di Foglie di Ravanelli

Cream of Radish Greens

While staying at my friend Antonia's country home in Lucca, she characterized the cooking of her fellow *Lucchesi* as being very parsimonious; absolutely nothing is wasted. She confirmed this by turning the greens from her crop of radishes into a deliciously fragrant soup. Radish leaves tenaciously hold the soil and require much soaking and rinsing with warm water to get them thoroughly clean. When made into soup, their raw bitter leaves become surprisingly sweet and mellow.

Brodo
3 cups Vegetable Broth (page 40)
   and 2 cups water

Battuto
1 to 2 tablespoons extra-virgin
   olive oil
³/₄ cup coarsely chopped spring
   onions or leeks, white and light
   green parts

Sapori
3 medium potatoes, peeled and finely
   chopped (about 1 pound)

6 radish bulbs, chopped
3 bunches of radish greens, roots cut
   off and leaves coarsely chopped
   and well washed

Condimenti
3 radish bulbs, sliced paper-thin
1 tablespoon unsalted butter
2 tablespoons grated Parmesan
   cheese
Salt and freshly ground pepper
Crostini, optional (page 42)

1. Bring the *brodo* to a simmer.

2. In a separate heavy-bottomed soup pot, sauté the *battuto* over medium heat, stirring often, for 1 to 2 minutes. Add a few tablespoons of the simmering *brodo* and cook until the onions are tender without coloring, about 3 to 4 minutes.

3. Add the potatoes and chopped radishes to the *battuto* and stir well to combine for 1 to 2 minutes. Add the *brodo* and simmer for 15 to 20 minutes. Add the radish leaves and cook, uncovered, for 10 minutes more.

4. Meanwhile, blanch the *condimenti* radishes in boiling salted water for 1 minute; drain and reserve.

Strain the soup, readding its cooking liquid to the pot. Add the vegetables with 1 to 2 ladlefuls of the cooking liquid to a food processor and, using short pulses, break down the ingredients without pureeing them. Readd to the pot and stir; bring back to a simmer.

5. Take off the heat and stir in the butter and Parmesan cheese. Add the salt and pepper to taste. Garnish with the sliced radishes and serve with crostini and Parmesan cheese.

Crema Fredda di Rucola e Pere

Cold Cream Soup of Arugula and Pear

*E*ven though Italy is not known for its cold soups, this luscious soup may indicate otherwise. The tart arugula is perfectly balanced by the sweet taste of the pears, and a small addition of cream beautifully binds all the ingredients. Choose pears that are very ripe and very sweet and if arugula is unavailable, substitute watercress.

Battuto

2 tablespoons unsalted butter

Minced Together
1 small red onion
1 medium celery rib

Brodo

1/2 cup white wine
4 cups light Chicken Broth (page 39)
  (3 cups chicken broth and 1 cup
  water) or 1 1/2 cubes chicken
  stock dissolved in 4 cups water

Sapori

2 large baking potatoes, peeled and cut
  into cubes
2 ripe pears, cored and chopped
2 cups chopped arugula, stems
  removed (3 to 4 ounces)

Condimenti

1/3 to 1/2 cup heavy cream
Salt and freshly ground pepper
2 to 3 tablespoons coarsely chopped
  arugula

1. Over medium-low heat, melt the butter in a heavy-bottomed soup pot. Add the minced *battuto* and sauté until softened, 3 to 4 minutes.

2. Turn the heat to medium and add the wine. Simmer until the wine has reduced by about half. Add the broth and potatoes and simmer, partially covered, for about 20 minutes. Add the pears and arugula and cook for another 5 minutes.

3. Take the soup off the heat and allow to cool. Stir in the cream and lightly puree in a food processor or blender. Add the salt and pepper to taste.

Serve chilled, garnished with the chopped arugula.

Minestra di Verdure alla Pugliese

Vegetable Soup with Leafy Greens

serves: 4

cooking time:
1 hour

*T*his vegetable soup, composed of basic vegetables and leafy greens, is enlivened by adding a savory *battuto* in the final stage of cooking. *Cime di rape* (broccoli de rabe), widely used in Puglia, are the greens of choice. If unavailable, substitute another medium sharply flavored green, such as beet greens or collards. This delicious soup is made even better when served with abundant grated pecorino Romano cheese.

Sapori

2½ cups new potatoes, scrubbed,
    unpeeled, and cut into bite-sized
    pieces (12 to 14 ounces)
3 cups shredded Savoy cabbage
    (about 8 ounces)
3 cups shredded greens
    (about 8 ounces)
1 celery rib, diced (about ¼ cup)
1 large carrot, diced (about 1 cup)

Brodo

5½ cups cold water
1 teaspoon coarse salt

Battuto

2 to 3 tablespoons extra-virgin
    olive oil
2 ounces pancetta, cut into small
    cubes (about ½ cup)

Finely Chopped Together

2 garlic cloves
½ cup fresh parsley leaves

Condimenti

Salt
¾ cup (4 ounces) short pasta
Freshly grated pecorino Romano
    cheese

1. Combine the *sapori* and *brodo* in a soup pot and bring to a boil. Lower the heat and gently simmer, uncovered, for about 30 minutes.

continued

2. Meanwhile, prepare the *battuto.* Combine the oil and pancetta in a heavy-bottomed saucepan and sauté over low heat until the pancetta renders its fat, 8 to 10 minutes. Add the garlic and parsley and sauté, stirring, for 2 to 3 minutes more.

3. Bring the soup to a lively simmer and add the sautéed *battuto.* Add the salt to taste, then add the pasta and cook, stirring from time to time, until *al dente.*
Serve with abundant pecorino cheese.

Verzata alla Veneziana

Cabbage Soup, Venetian Style

serves: 4

cooking time:
1³/₄ hours

There are many versions of this simple cabbage soup ladled over slices of toasted bread. They all depend on the slow, gentle cooking of the cabbage, which renders its taste sweet and its texture meltingly soft. I like this version from the Veneto, which uses pancetta, parsley, and ample amounts of garlic in the *battuto.*

Battuto
2 tablespoons extra-virgin olive oil

Minced Together
2 to 3 garlic cloves
¹/₃ cup parsley leaves
2 to 3 ounces lean pancetta

Brodo
4¹/₂ cups Classic Meat Broth
(page 36) or substitute

Sapori
1 to 1¹/₄ pounds Savoy or green
cabbage, shredded into thin strips
Salt and freshly ground pepper

Condimenti
4 slices white or whole wheat
country bread
Freshly grated Parmesan cheese
Salt and freshly ground pepper

1. In a heavy-bottomed soup pot, sauté the *battuto* over low heat, stirring occasionally, until the pancetta is lightly colored, 8 to 10 minutes.

2. Add the *brodo* and bring to a boil.

3. Stir in the cabbage, adjust the heat to low, and gently simmer, covered, for about 1½ hours. Add some more boiling water if needed and salt and pepper to taste.

4. Lightly toast both sides of the bread under the grill and place a slice in each bowl.

Stir 2 heaping tablespoons of the Parmesan cheese into the soup and add the salt and pepper to taste. Ladle over the bread and serve with the grated Parmesan cheese.

Variante: In Calabria, the *brodo* is a rich lamb broth and the cheese a pecorino.

Zuppa di Cavolo e Mele

Cabbage and Apple Soup

serves: 4

cooking time:
35 minutes

This unusual soup balances the savory sweetness of cabbage and apples with smoked pancetta. Made with a touch of cinnamon and garnished with sautéed crostini, this soup is the perfect opener before grilled or roasted pork or lamb.

This soup is best made using the inner light green leaves of the cabbage. For an even milder flavor, blanch the cabbage in boiling salted water before adding to the soup.

continued

Sapori

2 tablespoons unsalted butter

3 to 4 ounces ($^2/_3$ cup) chopped
 smoked pancetta

1 medium head of Savoy cabbage,
 outer leaves removed, cored and
 thinly shredded (about 5 cups)

1 cup thinly sliced leeks, white and
 light green parts

3 cooking apples, peeled and cut into
 small, thin slices (see Nota)

Spice Mixture

Scant $^1/_4$ teaspoon ground cinnamon

Scant $^1/_4$ teaspoon freshly ground
 pepper

$^1/_2$ teaspoon salt

Brodo

5 cups light Classic Meat Broth
 (page 36) or substitute

1 bay leaf

Condimenti

Salt and freshly ground pepper

Crostini, sautéed in butter or oil
 (page 42)

1. Over medium heat, melt the butter in a heavy-bottomed soup pot. Add the pancetta, cabbage, and leeks. Cover the pot and sweat until the vegetables soften, about 10 minutes.

Add the apples and sprinkle with the spice mixture.

2. Add the *brodo* and gently simmer, uncovered, for 20 minutes. Remove the bay leaf and add the salt and pepper to taste.

3. Serve with the crostini either sprinkled on top and/or at the table.

Nota: Sweeter eating apples can be substituted, but add only 2.

Minestra Maritata alla Dauna

Layered Chicory Soup

serves: 4 to 6

cooking time:
1 hour

Originating from the province of Foggia, once known by its ancient Greek name Dauna, this rustic soup has become part of the lexicon of Pugliese cuisine. Chicory, fennel, and celery are *maritata*—married—with a savory broth and grated pecorino and then baked in the oven to meld all the flavors.

Brodo

5 cups Classic Meat Broth (page 36)
  or substitute (see Nota)

3 ounces fatty pancetta, cut into
  small cubes

Sapori

2 medium fennel bulbs, trimmed,
  cored, and thinly sliced

3 celery ribs, preferably white, cut
  into about 1-inch pieces

1 pound curly endive (chicory),
  trimmed and washed

1 pound Batavian endive, trimmed
  and washed

Condimenti

3 ounces freshly grated pecorino
  Romano cheese
Freshly ground pepper

1. Preheat the oven to 350°F.
Over medium-high heat, simmer the *brodo,* covered, for about 20 minutes.

2. Meanwhile, prepare the *sapori.* Add the fennel and celery to a pot of lightly salted boiling water and cook until just tender but not soft, about 10 minutes. Drain.

Meanwhile, in a separate pot, blanch the leafy greens in lightly salted boiling water for 2 to 3 minutes. Drain well and coarsely chop.

Mix all the vegetables and leafy greens together.

3. In an ovenproof casserole, preferably earthenware, place a layer of the vegetables and generously sprinkle with pecorino and a twist of pepper. Ladle over with enough boiling *brodo* to cover. Repeat the layering and adding the broth until all the ingredients are used up. Sprinkle the top with the pecorino and place in the center of the hot oven. Bake for 20 minutes and serve from the casserole.

Nota: Pancetta and abundant Romano cheese are added, so be sure your broth is either unsalted or very lightly salted.

Variante: In neighboring Basilicata, sausage is added. Replace 1 fennel bulb with 3 cups coarsely shredded cabbage leaves and the broth with 6 cups water. Cook the leafy green and vegetables together for 10 minutes, then add 8 ounces of grilled, sliced sausage (fresh or smoked) to the vegetables and cook, uncovered, for 20 minutes more. Stir in grated pecorino cheese to taste and serve garnished with slivered pieces of the pecorino.

serves: 4

Cooking time:
15 minutes

Minestra di Spinaci e Pasta con Pesto

Pasta and Spinach Soup with Pesto

In this simple country soup from Liguria, just a touch of pesto is added. Its flavor is almost imperceptible, that is, unless you omit it—in which case this soup will lack its special character. If fresh basil is unavailable, prepare spinach soup as they do in Modena (see *Variante*) and replace the pesto with a *condimento* of egg and Parmesan cheese, perfect for the colder weather.

Sapori
1 pound fresh spinach, stems removed,
    well rinsed, or 10 ounces defrosted
    frozen
Coarse salt

Brodo
5 cups Classic Meat Broth (page 36)
    or Chicken Broth (page 39) or
    substitute

Condimenti
4 ounces (1 cup) small pasta, such as
    farfalle or shells, or ¹/₃ cup long-
    grain rice
2 tablespoons Pesto, ¹/₂ recipe
    (page 45)
Freshly grated pecorino Romano or
    Parmesan cheese

1. Place the spinach in a large saucepan and sprinkle with a little salt. Cook over moderate heat until just wilted, stirring, 2 to 3 minutes. Drain the spinach, pressing out its liquid, and chop finely; reserve.

2. Bring the *brodo* to a boil and add the pasta. When the pasta is almost *al dente*, stir in the chopped spinach and cook for 1 to 2 minutes.

Take the soup off the heat and stir in the pesto, adding about 2 tablespoons of the grated cheese to taste. Serve with the Parmesan cheese.

Variante: For *zuppa di spinaci alla modenese,* omit the pasta and pesto. Sauté the chopped spinach in 3 tablespoons butter, beat together 2 eggs, ¼ cup grated Parmesan cheese, and a pinch each of grated nutmeg and freshly ground pepper. Stir into the soup at the end of cooking and serve with crostini.

Paparot

Spinach and Polenta Soup

*T*his traditional winter soup comes from Friuli, where polenta is part of the agricultural heritage. Yellow cornmeal gives this soup its dense texture as well as its lovely maize flavor. The flavor of spinach is the essence of this soup and choosing absolutely fresh greens, then eliminating their bitter juices, is the key to its success.

Sapori

2 pounds fresh spinach, tough stems
   removed

Battuto

3 tablespoons unsalted butter
1 tablespoon olive oil
2 garlic cloves, peeled and flattened

Brodo

7¹/₂ cups Classic Meat Broth
   (page 36) or substitute
³/₄ cup (4 ounces) coarse yellow
   cornmeal
¹/₃ cup unbleached flour, sifted
Salt and freshly ground pepper

1. Wash the spinach several times in tepid water. Over moderate heat, place the spinach in a large pot and cook it with the water that still clings to its leaves. Cook, rotating the leaves, until the spinach wilts, 3 to 4 minutes. Drain in a colander and press out its liquid with a wooden spoon. Finely chop in a food processor, pulsing for just a few seconds, and reserve.

2. In a heavy-bottomed soup pot, sauté the *battuto* over medium-low heat. When the garlic is golden, remove. Add the spinach and stir for about 1 minute.

3. Add 6 cups of broth to the spinach and simmer, uncovered.

4. In a small bowl, mix together the cornmeal and flour. Whisk in about 1 cup broth, mixing vigorously for a smooth consistency. Slowly pour the cornmeal mixture into the soup, stirring constantly with a wooden spoon to mix well. Gently simmer for about 20 minutes, stirring frequently. Add the salt and pepper to taste and serve very hot.

Zuppa di Lattuga

Lettuce Soup

serves: 4

cooking time:
30 minutes

*P*orcini mushrooms flavor the broth in this light and satisfying soup from Liguria. For a greater depth of flavor, the lettuce is supplemented by parsley and Swiss chard. This refined soup calls for the less strong taste of *grana padano* and cutting the greens and mushrooms *a striscioline,* "into thin strips." If substituting spinach for the chard, add at the end of cooking.

Battuto
2 tablespoons extra-virgin olive oil
1 medium onion, finely chopped
¾ ounce dried porcini mushrooms,
    soaked in 2 cups warm water
    (page 44) and cut into thin strips

Sapori
2 heads soft green lettuce, cut into
    thin strips (about 10 cups)
3 to 4 ounces Swiss chard, cut into
    thin strips (about 2 cups)

¼ cup chopped parsley

Brodo
3½ cups water
1 teaspoon coarse salt

Condimenti
Freshly ground pepper
Leaves from 2 fresh marjoram
    sprigs, finely chopped (optional)
Freshly grated grana padano cheese
4 slices toasted country bread

1. In a heavy-bottomed soup pot, sauté the *battuto* over medium-low heat, until the onion becomes soft without coloring.

2. Over medium heat, add the sliced porcini and *sapori* and stir with a wooden spoon until the greens are well mixed and wilted, 4 to 5 minutes.

3. Add the *brodo* and cook at a lively simmer, uncovered, for 20 minutes.

4. Season with a few twists of pepper and the marjoram. Serve accompanied with the grated cheese and toasted bread.

Minestre e Zuppe di Grani

Grain and Bread Soups

*G*rains or grani *are one of the oldest foods known to mankind, tracing their origin back to Roman times. Easy to store and inexpensive to grow in poor soil, grains combine all of the necessary properties for* la cucina povera, *"the poor kitchen," and their soups represent some of the oldest recipes. The most widely used grains in Italian soup are wheat, rice, and barley. Left whole or ground into flour and made into bread, grains provide a nutritious and comforting base to a vast variety of Italian soups.*

Perhaps the best known of Italy's grain soups are those prepared with bread. Going by the names of l'acquacotta, pancotto, *or* pappa, *these soups are part of Tuscany's oldest and most traditional first courses. For centuries, bread soups were the mainstay of the* peasant diet, when few people could afford to waste anything. Their fundamental ingredients were and still are water, vegetables, and stale bread. Eggs, cheese, and oil, when available, enriched these humble soups. Their possible combinations were endless. It took the imagination of the individual cook to turn these basic ingredients into soups that were both nourishing and delicious.

Soups prepared with whole grains such as barley, rice, and *farro* (spelt) are staples of the Italian winter meal. The great rice-producing areas of the north use rice as the basis for their rich soups, many of which are more akin to risotto. In the hands of the Genovesi, rice becomes delicately perfumed with herbs. The northernmost regions of Piedmont, Valle d'Aosta, and the Alto Adige are known for their winter-warming barley soups, while Umbria and Tuscany are known for what has now become their very fashionable soups prepared with their oldest and much-loved wheat grain, *farro*.

It may be an anomaly to still think of grain and bread soups as a "poor dish," when we consider that many of their ingredients are now some our most prized foods: wild greens, mushrooms, fresh herbs, *farro,* and the finest olive oils. Once only the provenance of the home and trattoria, their goodness and simplicity have come to be appreciated by all, and these "humble" soups are increasingly found on the menus of some of Italy's best restaurants.

Grani/Barley, Farro, and Rice Soups

Barley, farro, and rice are the main ingredients of these soups. These mellow grains easily take on the character of the other ingredients, yielding soups of supreme delicacy, as well as those that are hearty and filling.

Gerstsuppe

Barley and Ham Soup

serves: 4

cooking time:
2 hours

The German word for soup—*suppe*—recalls the strong Germanic culinary tradition found in Trentino–Alto Adige, where pork and barley are prominently featured. From the Alps to the Dolomites, barley and ham soups are popular fare, with the main difference being the local preference of meat. In Valle d'Aosta, sausage is added and in Piedmont, fresh pork is preferred. This recipe comes from Trentino–Alto Adige, where *speck,* "smoked prosciutto," is the meat of choice. Slow and gentle cooking gives these soups their rich and mellow character.

continued

Brodo

9 cups water

Battuto

Coarsely Chopped Together

1 medium carrot

2 medium celery ribs

1 garlic clove

1/3 cup Italian parsley leaves

1 leek, white and light green parts

Sapori

1 1/8 cups (8 ounces) pearl barley,
  rinsed well (see Nota)

3 ounces speck or fatty prosciutto
  slice, cut into small cubes

1 large onion, cut in half and very
  thinly sliced (about 8 ounces)

6 to 7 ounces boiling potatoes, peeled
  and cut into 1/4-inch slices
  (about 1 cup)

1 cube beef stock, diluted in a little
  hot water

Salt and freshly ground pepper

1. In a heavy-bottomed soup pot, bring the *brodo* to a boil.

2. Add the *battuto,* barley, prosciutto, and onion. After it returns to a boil, lower the heat and cook at a very gentle simmer with the lid slightly ajar, for about 1 hour. Stir occasionally with a wooden spoon.

Add the potatoes and stock cube and cook for about 45 minutes more. Stir occasionally and add a little boiling water if needed.

Add the salt and pepper to taste and serve this soup very hot.

Nota: Rinse the barley in several changes of water until the water runs clear.

Minestra d'Orzo e Ortaggi

Barley and Garden Vegetable Soup

serves: 4

cooking time:
1¾ hours

*B*arley is usually associated with winter-warming soups. In this Piemontese soup, it is combined with celery, leeks, and leafy greens and takes on an entirely light and fresh quality, perfect for the year round.

¾ cup (4½ ounces) pearl barley,
(see Nota)

Sapori
2 celery ribs, cut into diagonal
⅓-inch slices (about ⅔ cup)
2 large leeks, white and green parts,
thinly sliced (about ¾ cup)
1 medium onion, halved and thinly
sliced
1 garlic clove, finely chopped

Brodo
6¼ cups cold water
1 bay leaf
1 teaspoon coarse salt
2 tablespoons extra-virgin olive oil

Condimenti
Salt
4 cups (7 ounces) finely shredded
spinach
1 cup (1 to 1½ ounces) shredded sorrel
or ⅓ cup chopped cilantro
Freshly grated Parmigiano-
Reggiano cheese

1. Combine the *sapori* and *brodo* in a soup pot and bring to a boil. Lower the heat and simmer, covered, for about 30 minutes.

2. Drain the barley and rinse well. Add to the soup and simmer, covered, for 1 hour more, stirring occasionally with a wooden spoon. Remove the bay leaf.

3. Add the salt to taste. Add the spinach and sorrel and cook, uncovered, for about 3 minutes. Serve with the Parmesan cheese.

continued

Nota: For the best results, soak the barley for 2 to 4 hours; if time does not permit, soak in a bowl of cold water until ready to add.

Variante: Replace the spinach and sorrel with shredded Swiss chard leaves and parsley and cook for 8 to 10 minutes.

serves: 4

cooking time:
50 minutes

Zuppa d'Orzo

Barley Soup

While watching Fulvia Sesani prepare this soup, I learned an invaluable technique. First, the oil is intensely flavored by gently sweating it with the *battuto;* then, similar to how a risotto is prepared, the barley is sautéed in the flavored oil. This seals in the flavors and elevates this humble soup to new heights. In the Veneto this soup is served with a generous sprinkling of Parmigiano-Reggiano. For a more delicate soup, prepare it as they do in neighboring Venezia Giulia and replace the Parmesan cheese with peas and parsley.

Battuto
2 to 3 tablespoons extra-virgin
    olive oil
2 ounces pancetta, cut into small
    dice (about 1/2 cup)
3 tablespoons minced shallot or
    onion

Sapori
1 cup (6 ounces) pearl barley, rinsed
    and drained (see Nota)

Brodo
6 1/2 cups Chicken Broth (page 39)
    or substitute
Salt and freshly ground pepper

Condimenti
Freshly grated Parmigiano-
    Reggiano cheese or 3/4 cup fresh
    or defrosted frozen peas
1 tablespoon chopped fresh parsley

1. Place the *battuto* in a heavy-bottomed soup pot. Cover and sweat over low heat, stirring occasionally, for about 10 minutes.

2. Turn the heat to medium, add the barley, and using a wooden spoon, stir to coat well with the *battuto* for 2 to 3 minutes.

3. Meanwhile, bring the broth to a simmer, then add. Cover and cook until the barley is tender, stirring occasionally, for about 35 minutes. If needed, add a little broth or boiling water. Add the salt and pepper to taste.

4. Serve sprinkled with Parmesan cheese. Or add the peas just before the soup has finished cooking and sprinkle with the parsley.

Nota: The washed barley should be as dry as possible before sautéing. Rinse it before you start the recipe and leave to dry in a sieve.

Variante: In Trentino, a similar soup known as *orzetto* adds any number of vegetables, such as carrots, potatoes, celery, leeks, zucchini, green beans, spinach, and peas. Add the vegetables of choice to the simmering soup according to their cooking time. Omit the Parmesan cheese and serve, sprinkled with fresh parsley.

Minestra di Farro con Pollo

Farro Soup with Chicken

serves: 4

cooking time:
50 minutes

I prepare this lovely soup often, either as a hearty first course or, by simply increasing the amount of chicken, as a main course. The nutty grains of *farro* are equally delicious when combined with turkey. For an even heartier dish, serve over slices of bread that have been fried in oil.

continued

Battuto

2 tablespoons extra-virgin olive oil

Finely Chopped Together

3 ounces pancetta

1 small onion

1 garlic clove

Sapori

8 ounces chicken breast, cut into
   small cubes

1¹/₈ cups farro or spelt (7 ounces),
   soaked 4 hours or overnight

Brodo

6¹/₄ cups Classic Meat Broth
   (page 36) or Chicken Broth
   (page 39) or substitute

Salt and freshly ground pepper

Condimenti

2 tablespoons finely chopped parsley

Freshly grated Parmigiano-
   Reggiano cheese

1. In a heavy-bottomed soup pot, sauté the *battuto* over medium-low heat, stirring occasionally, for about 5 minutes.

2. Turn the heat to medium-high, add the *sapori*, and stir well to combine for 3 to 4 minutes. Rinse and drain the *farro* and, using a wooden spoon, stir into the sautéed chicken.

3. Add the broth, cover, and cook at a slow but steady simmer until the *farro* is tender, about 40 minutes. Add the salt and pepper to taste.

4. Take the soup off the heat and stir in the parsley. Serve with the cheese.

Minestra di Farro col Radicchio

Farro and Radicchio Soup

serves: 4

cooking time:
1¼ hours

When Italians use the adjective *raffinato,* they express it with definitiveness, never indifference. This word signifies an elegance, a stylishness, a fineness. A perfect combination of mellow, nutty-tasting grains of *farro* with the slightly tart taste of radicchio, this soup is, in a word, *raffinato.* When cooked, the magenta leaves of radicchio turn a brownish color. The addition of red wine not only lends sweetness, but gives it a lovely pink hue.

1 cup (7 ounces) farro or spelt,
   soaked for 1 to 3 hours and rinsed

Battuto
3 to 4 tablespoons extra-virgin olive oil
⅔ cup finely chopped red onion

Sapori
1 cup (2 to 3 ounces) finely shredded
   radicchio

Brodo
½ cup dry red wine
5 cups Vegetable Broth (page 40) or
   Chicken Broth (page 39) or substitute
Coarse salt

Condimenti
Freshly grated Parmesan cheese

1. In a heavy-bottomed soup pot, sauté the *battuto* over medium-low heat until softened, 2 to 3 minutes.

2. Add the radicchio and continue to sauté, stirring often, for 3 to 4 minutes. Using a wooden spoon, add the *farro* and stir 2 to 3 minutes more.

3. Turn the heat to medium-high, add the wine, and stir often, until nearly evaporated. Add the broth, cover, and cook at a slow but steady simmer for about 1 hour. Stir occasionally and add the salt to taste. If too much liquid has evaporated, add a little boiling water. Remove from the heat and allow to sit for a few minutes.

4. Serve with the Parmesan cheese.

Zuppa di Gran Farro

Farro Soup of Lucca

For centuries *farro* (emmer wheat or spelt) was a staple of the poor *Lucchesi*. Today, food lovers well outside Tuscan borders have come to appreciate its firm, nutty-flavored grains, and *zuppa di gran farro* is found in Italy's most fashionable restaurants.

The *farro* is cooked in an aromatic bean broth, perfectly flavored with tomatoes and a touch of cinnamon. A food mill is essential for removing the borlotti skins to create this soup's delicate broth.

1 cup (6 ounces) dried borlotti
    beans, soaked and rinsed
    (page 47), or 2½ cups canned,
    drained (see Nota)
1 cup (6 ounces) farro or spelt,
    soaked for 4 hours or overnight
    and drained (see Nota)

Brodo
6½ cups cold water
Prosciutto end
2 garlic cloves, chopped
1 sage branch or 2 to 3 leaves
1 teaspoon coarse salt

Battuto
3 tablespoons extra-virgin olive oil
Minced Together
1 medium onion
1½ medium carrots
1½ medium celery ribs

Sapori
½ cup peeled, seeded, and chopped
    tomatoes
Generous pinch of cinnamon
    and salt

Condimenti
Salt and freshly ground pepper
Estate olive oil, preferably from
    Lucca

1. Except for the salt, combine the borlotti beans and *brodo* in a heavy-bottomed soup pot, cover, and place over medium heat. When it reaches a boil, lower the heat and gently simmer with the lid just slightly ajar, until the beans are tender, about 1¼ hours. Add the salt toward the end of cooking. Remove the sage and prosciutto.

2. In a small heavy saucepan, sauté the *battuto* over medium-low heat until softened, 3 to 4 minutes. Add the *sapori* and stir well to combine for 4 to 5 minutes. Stir into the cooked beans and puree through the small-holed disc of a food mill. Add back to the soup pot and bring to a boil over medium heat. Add the *farro,* lower the heat, and cook, covered, at a gentle but steady simmer until tender, about 40 minutes. Stir occasionally with a wooden spoon and add boiling water if needed.

3. Add the salt and pepper to taste. Ladle into each serving bowl and pour *un filo,* a thread of oil, on each serving. Serve with the oil at the table.

Nota: If using canned borlotti beans, add 3 ounces prosciutto, 1 garlic clove, and a few sage leaves to the *battuto.* Simmer the beans in 4½ cups water for about 15 minutes before pureeing.

If time does not permit soaking the *farro,* rinse well and increase its cooking time to about 1 hour.

Variante: In Lazio, the beans are omitted. Increase the *farro* to 1⅓ cups and the tomatoes to 1½ cups. Omit the *battuto* and sauté 2 garlic cloves in the oil before adding the tomatoes, replacing the sage and cinnamon with minced parsley, basil, and marjoram. Simmer for 15 minutes before adding the *farro.* Serve, sprinkled with freshly grated Romano cheese.

Brodolese di Riso

Rice and Chestnut Soup

*T*he use of chestnuts in soup dates back to antiquity when their abundance made them a staple ingredient of *la cucina povera*. Chestnuts cooked with rice and milk still remains a favorite winter-warming dish. This soup comes from the Casentino, the upper valley of the Arno, where the sweetness is offset by the pancetta and pecorino.

Sapori
8 ounces fresh chestnuts or 7 ounces
    cooked, peeled, and chopped

Brodo
6 cups water
1 teaspoon coarse salt
2 to 3 cups milk

Battuto
2 tablespoons olive oil
Fresh rosemary branch
3 ounces pancetta, cut into small cubes
    (about ¾ cup)

Condimenti
1 cup (7 ounces) risotto rice
Freshly grated pecorino Romano cheese

1. Preheat the oven to 450°F. Rinse the chestnuts and, using a small sharp knife, cut a cross on both sides of each chestnut, being careful not to dig into the chestnut meat. Place on a wide pan, sprinkle over with some water, and bake until the shells open, about 20 minutes. Taking a few out at a time, peel the outer shell and the inner skin while still hot (I start peeling the chestnuts wearing oven mitts; after the outer shell comes off, rubbing will peel off any remaining inner skins). Throw away any that have an unpleasant smell.

2. In a heavy saucepan, combine the chestnuts, water, and salt and bring to a boil. Skim off any surface scum. Adjust the heat and simmer, uncovered, until soft, about 1 hour. Reserving the cooking liquid, drain the chestnuts. There should be 2 to 3 cups of chestnut broth. Add enough milk to equal 5 cups, keeping the proportion of broth and milk about equal. Bring to a simmer.

3. Meanwhile, in a heavy-bottomed soup pot, sauté the *battuto* over medium-low heat until the pancetta colors, 8 to 10 minutes. Discard the rosemary.

4. Add the rice and chestnuts and stir to coat well with the flavored oil. Add the hot broth and cook until the rice is tender, stirring to prevent sticking. If needed, add a little milk or water, and serve with the cheese.

Variante: For **minestrone alla lunigiana,** replace half the chestnuts with ⅔ cup borlotti beans, dried and soaked. Add 1 small onion, celery, and carrot to the *battuto* and sauté. Add the beans and chestnuts, replace the milk with water, and cook until tender. Add ¾ cup rice and then add ⅓ cup white wine when the rice is half cooked. Serve with grated Parmesan cheese.

Minestra di Riso e Porri

Rice and Leek Soup

Every rice-producing area of northern Italy has its version of this comforting soup. In the Veneto this soup is thickened with flour and is dense with leeks and rice. In Lombardy *erbette,* young spinach or beet leaves, replace half the leeks for a lighter soup. This recipe combines the qualities I like most—abundant leeks with just enough greens to provide more interest.

Sapori

2 tablespoons olive oil

2 tablespoons unsalted butter

2 pounds leeks, white and light
   green parts, washed and thinly
   sliced (about 4¹/₂ cups, trimmed
   weight about 12 ounces)

Coarse salt

1 tablespoon and 2 teaspoons
   all-purpose flour

1¹/₂ cups shredded spinach or ¹/₃ cup
   coarsely chopped Italian parsley

Brodo

5 cups Classic Meat Broth (page 36)
   or Vegetable Broth (page 40) or
   substitute

Condimenti

³/₄ cup (6 ounces) risotto rice
   (see Nota)

1 to 2 tablespoons unsalted butter,
   cut into small pieces (optional)

Pinch of nutmeg, preferably freshly
   grated

Freshly ground pepper

Freshly grated Parmigiano-
   Reggiano cheese

1. Combine the oil and butter in a heavy-bottomed soup pot and place over medium heat. As soon as the butter melts, stir in the leeks and sprinkle with a few pinches of salt. Sauté, stirring often with a wooden spoon, until the leeks are very soft, about 10 minutes. Don't allow the leeks to brown; lower the heat or add a little water if needed.

2. Add the flour to the leeks, continuing to stir for a few minutes until the flour becomes amalgamated and lightly colored. Add the spinach or parsley and stir to combine well.

3. Add the *brodo,* bring to a lively simmer, and cook for 5 minutes.

4. Add the rice and continue to cook until *al dente,* stirring occasionally, for about 15 minutes. If needed, add a little boiling water. Take the soup off the heat and stir in the butter, nutmeg, pepper, and 2 tablespoons of the cheese. Serve with the Parmesan cheese.

Nota: The favorite rice of the Veneto is Vialone Nano, which is recommended for this soup. If you use the more glutinous Arborio, omit the flour.

Variante: For a spinach and rice soup omitting the leeks, sauté 1 small onion in 3 tablespoons butter, omit the salt and flour, and add 1 pound spinach, blanched and root ends removed.

Minestra di Riso e Rape alla Milanese

Rice and Turnip Soup, Milanese Style

A staple of northern Italy, this comforting recipe is dense with rice and closely resembles a risotto. This recipe adds pancetta, but outside of Milan sausage or smoked pancetta is preferred; its simplest interpretation comes from the rugged mountain cooking of Valle d'Aosta where no meat is added (see *Variante*). This soup is best when prepared with new spring turnips; buy those with bright green tops, which can be used for making a springtime *ribollita*.

Battuto
3 tablespoons unsalted butter
2 ounces ($^1/_3$ cup) minced pancetta
1 small garlic clove, minced

Sapori
12 ounces (about 2 cups) peeled and
    thinly sliced turnips

Brodo
5 cups turnip cooking liquid or
    1 cube chicken stock dissolved in
    5 cups water

Condimenti
Salt
1 cup (7 ounces) risotto, such as
    Carnaroli or Vialone Nano
2 tablespoons chopped fresh parsley
Freshly grated Parmigiano-
    Reggiano cheese

1. Combine the butter and pancetta in a heavy-bottomed soup pot. Gently sauté over low heat, stirring occasionally, for 8 to 10 minutes. Add the garlic and stir for 1 to 2 minutes more.

2. Meanwhile, blanch the turnips in boiling salted water for about 2 minutes. Drain, reserving its cooking liquid (see *Nota*). Add the turnips to the sautéed *battuto* and stir to coat well.

3. Bring the *brodo* to a boil and add to the turnips. Lightly season with salt to taste; add the rice and simmer until *al dente,* stirring occasionally, for about 15 minutes. Stir in more *brodo* or boiling water if the soup becomes too dense.

4. Take off the heat and stir in the parsley and 2 to 3 tablespoons of the Parmesan cheese to taste. Serve with cheese.

Nota: Turnips, which are 90 percent water, easily dehydrate and develop a spongy texture and bitter taste. After slicing, blanch them and then taste their cooking liquid. Depending on its flavor, use all or part for the *brodo*. If too bitter, use a light chicken broth in its place.

Variante: For a vegetarian soup, omit the *battuto,* sauté the blanched turnips in 4 tablespoons butter, and use water or vegetable broth. If replacing the pancetta with sausage, boil 6 to 8 ounces mild sausage for a few minutes and cut into thin slices before adding to the *battuto*.

Preboggion

Genovese Rice Soup

*Y*ou will not find the word *preboggion* in any Italian dictionary but in the markets of Genoa and the surrounding area. It describes assortments of the seasonal local wild herbs and greens, which might include *borragine* (borage), *cerfoglio* (cilantro), *pimpinella* (parsley), wild chicory, young spinach, and beet greens. In this springtime soup, a *pesto battuto* completes this rich bouquet of flavors.

Choose any combination of very fresh greens and herbs, balancing out the mild and sharp greens. As a general guideline, half should be mild greens, such as beet, spinach, and/or turnip leaves; a quarter should be herbs, such as coriander, borage, and/or flat-leaf parsley; and the remaining quarter, the more intense greens, such as sorrel, watercress, dandelion greens, and/or arugula. This soup depends on the aromatic intensity of the greens. If your greens are somewhat lackluster, you may want to add a chicken stock cube to the *brodo*.

Brodo

6^1/$_2$ *cups water*
1 cube chicken stock or about
    1 teaspoon coarse salt

Sapori

1 pound mixed herbs and greens, stems
    removed, washed and coarsely
    chopped (12 ounces trimmed)
    (see Nota)

Battuto

1 cup packed fresh basil leaves,
    washed well and spun dry
2 garlic cloves
^{1}/$_4$ teaspoon coarse salt
^{1}/$_4$ cup grated Parmesan or pecorino
    cheese

Condimenti

^{2}/$_3$ cup (6 ounces) long-grain rice
3 tablespoons extra-virgin olive oil,
    preferably estate Ligurian
Freshly grated Parmesan cheese

1. In a soup pot, bring the *brodo* to a boil. Stir in the *sapori* and simmer, uncovered, for about 20 minutes.

2. Meanwhile, prepare the pesto. Combine the basil and garlic in a food processor, sprinkle with a pinch of salt, and pulse until well blended. Add the grated cheese and about 2 tablespoons of the soup cooking liquid and process until well blended. Reserve.

3. Bring the soup to a lively simmer, add the rice, and cook until tender, stirring often, about 15 minutes. Stir in the pesto and olive oil.

Sprinkle each serving with Parmesan, serving the remaining cheese at the table.

Nota: A food processor can be used to chop the washed, well-drained greens. Add in small batches so the bottom half doesn't puree as the upper leaves shred.

Risi e Bisi

Rice and Fresh Pea Soup

serves: 4

Cooking time:
1¼ hours

A soup of great Venetian tradition, *risi e bisi* was the first dish served to the Doge on St. Mark's Day, April 25. It also marked the arrival of the first small peas of spring, to which the Doge always had first claim. Over the centuries, all Venetians have laid claim to *risi e bisi,* but not without some controversy. For some it is a very thick soup; for others, a thin risotto to be served with a fork. Depending on the amount of broth, it could be either. This recipe prepares this classic dish in its original form, when it was known as *minestra di risi e bisi* and served with a spoon.

The best *risi e bisi* is made by cooking the pods separately to create a broth that heightens the sweet taste of the peas. Unless the pods are young and not stringy, they must be rid of their fibers. I prefer to use *mange-tout;* every part of their tender skins can be added for the sweetest and fullest flavor. While the broth is cooking, you can shell the peas and prepare the *battuto.* If you decide not to make a broth using the pods, substitute a good homemade chicken or vegetable broth.

continued

Minestre e Zuppe di Grani / Grain and Bread Soups   233

Brodo

8 ounces mange-tout, root ends
removed

8 cups cold water

1 teaspoon coarse salt

Battuto

4 tablespoons unsalted butter

1 tablespoon olive oil

Minced Together

2 ounces prosciutto (optional)

1 small onion or equivalent amount
of shallots

1 medium celery rib

Sapori

2 pounds fresh peas
(unpeeled weight)

1 cup (7 ounces) risotto rice,
preferably Vialone Nano

Condimenti

4 tablespoons freshly grated
Parmesan cheese

2 tablespoons chopped flat-leaf
parsley

2 tablespoons chopped parsley
(optional)

Salt and freshly ground pepper

1. Cook the *brodo,* uncovered, at a lively simmer for about 45 minutes. Reserving its cooking liquid, drain the pods. There should be about 5 cups of broth; if not, add some water and return to the pot. Puree the pods with a little of its liquid until completely smooth, then readd to the pot. Stir to combine well and bring to a simmer.

2. Over medium-low heat, combine the butter and oil in a heavy-bottomed soup pot. When the butter melts, add the minced *battuto* and sauté until softened, 2 to 3 minutes.

3. Add the shelled peas to the *battuto* and stir to combine well for 1 to 2 minutes. Add the rice and stir to coat well. Reserving ½ cup, add the simmering broth. Cover and cook until the rice is tender, stirring occasionally with a wooden spoon for about 15 minutes. If needed, add the reserved broth.

4. Remove from the heat and stir in the Parmesan cheese and parsley. Add the salt and pepper to taste and serve.

Pane/Bread Soups

Once only a means of survival, the most ancient bread soups are known as
l'acquacotta. *The name, from the words* acqua cotta, *"cooked water," describes a*
simple preparation of seasonal herbs and vegetables cooked in water and poured over
stale bread. True to its name, pancotto, *the bread is cooked as part of the soup. In*
these popular soups, depending on how long the bread cooks, it may remain a distinct
element or become completely amalgamated into the broth.

The line that divides a bread soup from a zuppa, *which is ladled over bread, can*
be subtle, at times almost indistinguishable. The very essence of a bread soup conjures
up a dish prepared from a few basic ingredients, added to stale bread, and turned into
a soup that satisfies both taste and hunger. Their thoroughly rustic taste and texture
leave little doubt as to why bread soups are considered in a class by themselves.

Preparing Bread Soups The key to preparing a bread soup lies in using *pane raf-*
fermo—a good country bread that is slightly stale. Fortunately, you don't have to wait
for bread to become stale. Placing it in the oven to dry out yields the same result. The
other essential element is adding the right amount of liquid. With the bread absorb-
ing much of the cooking liquid, these rustic soups are less brothy than a *zuppa*.

Brodo Most recipes call for adding just water and salt, the way the earliest bread
soups were made. Today, it is just as common to find bread soups made with a more
flavorful prepared broth. Depending on the intensity of the ingredients, you may
decide to use water, broth, or a combination of the two. Much of the *brodo* will be
absorbed by the bread.

Battuto Often omitted, the *battuto* usually consists of a few sautéed aromatic
ingredients such as garlic, peperoncino, and herbs. Oil often acts as one of the flavor-

ings and slightly more than usual is added. For this reason, always use a good-quality extra-virgin oil.

Sapori The few vegetables that are added should be very fresh. The one exception is the excellent plum tomatoes imported from Italy.

Condimenti Many of these soups are embellished with cheese, oil, or eggs. Raw eggs are always added after the soup has been taken off the heat. If the recipe calls for a generous amount of Parmesan cheese, make sure the *brodo* is not overly salted. Whenever possible, if oil is called for in the *condimenti,* use estate oil (page 26).

Bread for Zuppe di Pane

In Italy, homemade or country bread refers to a firm, coarse-textured bread with a hard crust; airy French baguettes will not do. The range of choice is wide: whole wheat, sourdough, or seedless rye. The more delicate the ingredients, the more delicate tasting the bread should be. When liquid is added to slightly stale country bread, it plumps up to a beautiful soft texture; or if called for, it can be totally amalgamated into the soup.

Preparation It is essential that the bread be stale or dried out, otherwise it will not absorb or break down properly. The best consistency is achieved after the bread is a few days old, still retaining some malleability. It is best to keep your bread in a paper, not a plastic, bag. If your bread is not stale, dry out the slices in a 325°F. oven for 7 to 10 minutes, being careful not to let it brown.

Amount and Yield As a general rule, about 1 ounce of bread is added per serving. The amount of bread or *brodo* can always be adjusted for the consistency you prefer. One ounce of bread cut into ½-inch cubes equals about 1 cup; 4 ounces cut into 1-inch cubes equals about 3 cups.

Acquacotta alla Grossetana

Yellow Pepper Bread Soup

serves: 4

cooking time:
40 minutes

*A*cquacotta traces its origins to the Maremma, the once poor and barren land that surrounds Grosseto. Although, when a soup tastes as rich as this one, it may be difficult to recall its heritage as a typical poor dish. The original recipe calls for eggs, which binds the soup and softens its flavors. For a lighter soup, I omit the eggs and add fresh basil. Red instead of yellow peppers can be used, but then this soup will lack its beautiful contrast of colors.

Battuto
4 to 5 tablespoons extra-virgin olive oil
2 cups chopped red onion

Brodo
4½ cups cold water
Salt and freshly ground pepper

Sapori
2 medium yellow peppers, chopped
  into bite-sized pieces
1 large celery rib, coarsely chopped
  (about 1 cup)
4 ripe tomatoes with a little of their
  juice, peeled, seeded, and chopped
  (about 1 cup) or 1 14-ounce can,
  lightly drained

Condimenti
6 thin slices of country bread,
  preferably stale
2 eggs or 3 to 4 chopped basil leaves

1. In a heavy-bottomed soup pot, sauté the *battuto* over moderate heat until the onion softens, stirring often, for 3 to 4 minutes.

2. Add the *sapori* and stir to coat well for 1 to 2 minutes. Slightly lower the heat, cover, and sweat, stirring occasionally, for about 10 minutes. If needed, add a little hot water.

continued

3. Add the water and bring to a boil, then lower the heat and simmer, covered, for about 20 minutes. Add the salt and pepper to taste.

4. Meanwhile, toast the bread and break into bite-sized pieces. If adding eggs, mix together in a small bowl, then slowly whisk in 1 to 2 ladles of hot soup broth. Take the soup off the heat and briskly stir in the egg mixture or add the basil.

Distribute the bread in each bowl, ladle over with the soup, and allow to sit for a minute or two before serving.

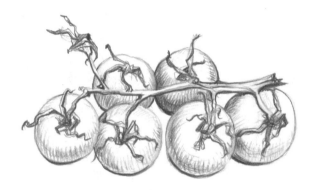

serves: 4

cooking time:
35 minutes

Acquacotta alla Senese

Mushroom, Tomato, and Egg Soup

Aromatic mushrooms dominate this ancient recipe from Siena. Wild mushrooms, such as porcini, are combined with eggs and Parmesan cheese; for more sustenance, fresh sausage is added (see *Variante*). Any combination of wild and cultivated mushrooms can be used. For a deeper flavor, add a few dried porcini and use their soaking liquid as part of the broth (page 44).

Sapori

4 tablespoons extra-virgin olive oil

2 garlic cloves, thinly sliced

1 pound fresh mushrooms, wild and
   cultivated, thinly sliced

Coarse salt

$^1/_2$ cup peeled, seeded, and chopped
   ripe tomatoes or 1 9-ounce can

Condimenti

4 $^1/_2$-inch-thick slices of stale country
   white or whole wheat bread

3 eggs

3 tablespoons freshly grated
   Parmesan cheese

2 tablespoons chopped fresh parsley

Brodo

4 $^1/_2$ cups boiling water

Coarse salt

1. Combine the oil and garlic in a heavy-bottomed soup pot. Sauté over low heat until the garlic becomes lightly colored, being careful not to let it brown.

Stir in the mushrooms, season with a few pinches of salt, and sauté over medium heat, stirring occasionally, for about 15 minutes. Stir in the tomatoes and cook for 2 to 3 minutes more.

2. Add the *brodo,* cover, and simmer for 10 minutes. Add the salt to taste.

3. Meanwhile, toast the bread in the oven until crisp and place in the bottom of each soup bowl.

Beat the eggs with the cheese until well amalgamated. While continuing to beat, slowly pour in a ladle of the hot soup broth. Take the soup off the heat and stir in the cheese and egg mixture. Ladle the soup over the bread, sprinkle with the parsley, and allow to sit for 1 to 2 minutes before serving.

Variante: Partially cook 2 sausages, skins pricked, in boiling water until almost done. Slice into $^3/_4$-inch rounds and add toward the end of cooking.

Pancotto Calabrese con Cicoria

Bread and Chicory Soup

*I*n this Calabrian *pancotto,* chicory and bread are cooked in a flavorful tomato broth. The traditional way to serve this soup is to lift out the bread and chicory and serve them with only the broth that still clings to them. I prefer serving this soup with all its delicious broth. For a milder soup, first blanch the leafy greens before adding.

Brodo

5 cups cold water

1 cup parsley leaves and stems

1 cup chopped celery rib and/or leaves

2 garlic cloves, flattened

1¼ cups chopped ripe tomatoes or 1 14-ounce can, drained

1 bay leaf

4 tablespoons extra-virgin olive oil

4 ounces fresh sausage, removed from its casing, or chopped pancetta

1 teaspoon coarse salt

Sapori

10 ounces chicory or escarole, trimmed and coarsely shredded (about 4 cups)

4 slices stale country bread, thickly sliced and broken into large pieces (8 to 10 ounces)

Condimenti

Freshly grated black pepper

Freshly grated pecorino Romano cheese

1. In a soup pot, bring the *brodo* to a boil. Adjust the heat and simmer, partially covered, for about 30 minutes. Strain the broth, adding only the cooking liquid back to the pot.

2. Bring the broth back to a boil, stir in the chicory, and cook for 3 to 4 minutes. Add the bread and cook just long enough for it to soften, 1 to 2 minutes.

3. Serve either by lifting out the bread and chicory and placing in the individual soup plates or serve with the broth. Season with a robust twist of pepper and a generous sprinkling of pecorino cheese.

Variante: To turn this *pancotto* into a wonderfully rustic meal, top with poached eggs or grilled sausage, cut into slices.

Pancotto alla Foggiana
Bread and Vegetable Soup

serves: 4

cooking time: 1½ hours

*P*uglia is known for the excellence of its vast quantity of vegetables, which take center stage in its cooking. This recipe, from the town of Foggia, can be made with any number of combinations, or its simple preparation can be used to turn your leftover vegetable soup into a rustic *pancotto*. In the winter, a garnish of sautéed pancetta replaces the Pugliese olive oil, whose slightly tart taste seems the perfect complement to its fine vegetables.

The vegetables are added raw and simmered in water for about an hour before the bread is added. Add or substitute any fresh vegetable, such as carrot, eggplant, peas, or sweet red and yellow peppers.

continued

Sapori

2½ to 3 pounds mixed vegetables:

2 cups finely diced baking potatoes

1 cup peeled, seeded, and chopped tomatoes

1 cup chopped green beans

2 cups sliced zucchini

1 cup sliced celery

2 cups chopped onion or leek

1 cup chopped fennel

Brodo

6½ cups water

1 teaspoon coarse salt

1 red chili pepper or pinch of peperoncino flakes

2 garlic cloves, peeled and flattened

Condimenti

Stale coarse bread, broken into small pieces (4 to 5 cups)

3 cups mixed shredded greens, such as arugula, curly endive, water-cress, or soft lettuce, or ½ cup chopped flat-leaf parsley

Extra-virgin olive oil, preferably estate Pugliese or Ligurian, or ½ cup diced pancetta, sautéed

1. Combine the *sapori* and *brodo* in a soup pot. Cover with the lid slightly ajar, and simmer over moderate heat for about 1¼ hours.

2. Add the bread and cook, uncovered, stirring occasionally, for about 10 minutes. Stir in the greens just a few minutes before the end of cooking.

Drizzle with the olive oil or garnish with the sautéed pancetta and serve.

Pancotto con Rucola e Patate

Bread Soup with Arugula and Potatoes

serves: 4

cooking time:
30 minutes

*A*rugula grows abundantly in the fields of southern Italy. This recipe calls for almost one pound. A specialty of Apulia, this simple soup contrasts the mellowness of potatoes and bread with the pungency of arugula and a spicy oil flavored with garlic and chili. Other peppery greens such as watercress or dandelion can be substituted; for a milder soup, lightly blanch the greens.

Brodo
5³/4 cups cold water

1 teaspoon coarse salt

Sapori
1¹/4 pounds potatoes, such as King Edward, peeled, cut in half lengthwise, and then into ¹/4-inch-thick slices

4 to 5 cups cubed stale Italian bread

14 ounces arugula, stems removed, coarsely shredded

Condimenti
¹/3 cup fruity extra-virgin olive oil, preferably from Liguria

1 dried chili pepper or ¹/4 teaspoon crushed flakes

2 garlic cloves, lightly crushed

1. Over medium-high heat, combine the *brodo* and potatoes in a soup pot. When it reaches a boil, adjust the heat and simmer, uncovered, until the potatoes are tender, about 15 minutes.

Stir in the bread and arugula and cook for a few minutes more.

2. Meanwhile, in a small heavy saucepan, sauté the *condimenti* over low heat for 8 to 10 minutes. When the garlic is deep golden, press with the back of a fork to release its juices, then discard. If using whole pepper, remove; if using crushed flakes, strain the oil.

continued

Ladle the soup into the bowls, drizzle with a thread of the flavored oil, and serve.

Nota: The soup and flavored oil require approximately the same amount of time to cook; cook simultaneously so the oil is ready to be added when the soup is done.

Pappa al Pomodoro

Tomato and Bread Soup

serves 6 to 8

cooking time:
1 hour

Prepared with very ripe tomatoes, either fresh or canned, *pappa al pomodoro* is a Tuscan staple. In Florence, Cibreo is thought to make an exceptional one. Fabio Picchi's secret is adding a light broth, not just water, and always adding the basil after the soup has been taken off the heat. This classic soup can be served hot or at room temperature.

Pappa refers to the consistency of this soup, a pap or mush. This may sound heavy, but the combination of tomatoes and basil makes this a surprisingly refreshing soup. As a guideline, the proportion of tomatoes to bread is about 2½ to 1.

Sapori

1/3 cup extra-virgin olive oil

3 to 4 garlic cloves, finely chopped

1 28-ounce can Italian imported
* plum tomatoes or 2¹/₂ pounds*
* very ripe fresh (see Nota)*

Pinch of crushed chili flakes
* (optional)*

Brodo

6 cups light Classic Meat Broth
* (page 36) or Chicken Broth*
* (page 39) or substitute*

Condimenti

1 pound very stale white or whole
* wheat country bread, cut into*
* 1-inch cubes*

Salt and freshly ground pepper

6 to 8 large basil leaves, finely
* shredded*

Extra-virgin olive oil, preferably
* estate Tuscan*

1. Combine the oil and garlic in a heavy-bottomed soup pot. Sauté over low heat until the garlic is golden, 3 to 4 minutes.

Add the tomatoes and chili flakes and cook over medium heat for about 10 minutes, breaking up the tomatoes with a wooden spoon.

2. Reserving a ladleful of the *brodo*, add about 5 cups to the tomatoes. Cover and simmer for about 30 minutes.

3. In a large bowl, add the bread with just enough of the reserved *brodo* to soften it. Mash the bread, pounding it with the bottom of a whisk. Add to the soup, stir well to combine, and gently simmer for about 10 minutes. If the soup appears too thick, add a little broth or water. Add the salt and pepper to taste.

Take the soup off the heat, stir in the basil, and serve, or allow to sit, covered, to come to room temperature. Serve with a generous drizzle of oil.

Nota: If using fresh tomatoes it is essential they be very ripe, otherwise the taste will be too acidic. Pass through the fine-holed disc of a food mill into the pot, or peel and seed before adding. If using canned, choose only Italian plum tomatoes; seeding them is unnecessary; add the entire contents.

Variante: In Umbria and Lazio, it is customary to stir in a few tablespoons of grated Parmesan cheese at the end of cooking.

Zuppa Valpellinense

Layered Cabbage Soup with Fontina

serves: 4 to 6

cooking time:
1¼ hours

*T*he beautiful region of Valle d'Aosta is not only known for its Alpine slopes, but for one of Italy's finest cheeses, fontina Val d'Aosta, unrivaled for its superb melting quality. In this winter dish, which is halfway between a soup and a casserole, layers of bread, cabbage, and fontina are layered and baked in the oven. Many variations exist, from a vegetarian soup to adding the leftover meat pan drippings. This recipe adds layers of prosciutto, which can easily be omitted if you prefer. The more flavorful breads, such as whole wheat, seedless rye, or sourdough, best complement this soup's rugged tastes.

Sapori
1 small Savoy cabbage (about
    1 pound), cored, ribs removed
3 tablespoons unsalted butter
Spice mixture: ¼ teaspoon nutmeg,
    ½ teaspoon coarse salt, pinch of
    cinnamon, and a twist of pepper

Brodo
5 to 6 cups Classic Meat Broth
    (page 36) or substitute

4 to 8 slices stale country bread, cut
    into ½-inch slices or broken into
    small pieces
3 to 4 ounces thinly sliced prosciutto,
    cut into thin slivers
5 to 6 ounces Italian fontina cheese,
    rind removed, cut into slivers
    (see Nota)
Unsalted butter

1. Preheat the oven to 325°F.

Blanch the cabbage in a pot of lightly salted boiling water for 2 to 3 minutes. Drain, rinse with cold water, and shred. Drain or pat with paper towels to remove excess moisture.

Over medium-low heat, melt the butter in a heavy-bottomed soup pot. Add the cabbage, sprinkle with the spice mix, and stir to coat well. Add a couple of ladlefuls of *brodo* and gently simmer until the cabbage is very tender, stirring occasionally, for about 20 minutes.

2. Meanwhile, lightly toast the bread in the oven. Butter an ovenproof dish, preferably terra-cotta, and place a layer of bread on the bottom. Cover with a layer of cabbage, then prosciutto, and top with fontina. Repeat the layers, ending with the fontina on top.

3. Bring the remaining *brodo* to a boil and add enough to cover the layers. Wait a few minutes until it has been absorbed, then add enough to barely cover the top. Dot with butter and bake for about 45 minutes. Serve while still very hot or reheat the next day.

Nota: Produced nearby, Fontal has a milder taste and can be substituted. However, if this is unavailable, bypass the non-Italian cheeses that may call themselves fontina; they will yield disappointing results. A taleggio or a French Morbier are better substitutes.

Variante: In Lombardy, onions replace the cabbage. Thinly slice 2¼ pounds mild onions and sauté in 6 tablespoons butter until softened, then gently simmer, uncovered, with 2 cups broth for 1 hour. Coarsely puree and cook with the remaining broth for 15 minutes. Make a layer of bread, fontina, and onion puree, topping the final layer of onions with grated Parmesan cheese.

Minestre e Zuppe di Pesce

Fish Soups

*I*n a country that is surrounded by water on three sides and that has over *1,500 miles of coastline, it is no surprise that fish soups have a long and important tradition in Italian gastronomy. Born from the tradition of the* pescatori, *fishermen, making use of their daily unsold catch, fish soups range from light first courses to substantial main dishes. Although once considered a "poor" dish, these less prized fish, when combined with the ingenuity of the cook and a few simple ingredients, were transformed into dishes of uncompromising taste.*

More akin to a stew than a soup, the most well known of the fish soups are the regional zuppe di pesce, *which to this day display their roots in Italy's numerous fishing villages. Every stretch of the Italian coastline has its own variations with local* names to claim superiority for its own special preparation. The Marche alone, with its seven port towns, has at least as many recipes and names. Although a *zuppa di pesce* is called a *brodetto* along the Adriatic coast, *ciuppin* in Liguria, *cacciucco* in Tuscany, and *cassola* in Sardinia, there are but a few basic preparations for all these hearty soups.

Often there is a fine line between what constitutes an Italian fish soup and what we more commonly think of as a fish or seafood dish. Many *zuppe* simply refer to the fact that the fish or seafood is served in the same liquid in which it has cooked, no matter how minimal it may seem. When you order a *zuppa di cozze* in an Italian restaurant, more often than not you will receive a plate with unshelled mussels in a thin layer of broth. Order a *zuppa di pesce* and you may be surprised when it arrives at your table in a large pot with its various elements cut into large pieces or left whole, ready to be transferred to a dish. Eaten with a fork, not a spoon, bread becomes the implement for enjoying its broth.

With the increased cost of fish in Italy, fish soups are no longer the frugal dishes they once were. Refined and elaborated on, *zuppe di pesce* now are some of the most sophisticated and expensive dishes on restaurant menus. Today, fish soups derive as much from the masterly touch of the chef as from the humble fisherman.

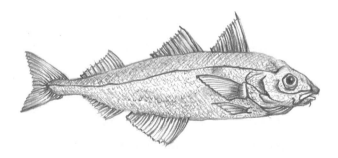

Brodo di Pesce/Fish Broth

When cooked, fish and seafood readily yield their juices and flavors, often making the addition of a prepared fish broth unnecessary. But at the base of many fish soups is brodo di pesce, *"fish broth," added both for a richness of taste and texture. Either used as the primary ingredient or for a deeper flavor,* brodo di pesce *may vary from a light broth to a creamy* passato *or "puree."*

Fumetto di Pesce

Basic Fish Broth

yield: About 8 to 10 cups

cooking time: 45 minutes

Making fish broth is straightforward; fish trimmings from lean, nonoily white fish are cooked with a few basic ingredients and strained. The most flavorful fish broth is known as a *fumetto,* a basic broth reduced to concentrate its flavors.

The key is not to overcook the fish, preventing any bitterness. If possible, try to include at least one fish head, the most flavorful part. Just be sure the gills have been removed. Fish gives off its own salt as it cooks, so none is added to this broth.

3 to 4 pounds bones and trimmings of any lean white fish such as sole, halibut, sea bass, red mullet, or whiting, scaled and gutted

1 large celery rib with leafy top, cut into chunks

5 to 6 fresh parsley sprigs

1 large onion, cut into chunks

2 fresh bay leaves or 1 dried

2 to 3 ripe plum tomatoes (optional)

Some fennel tops or a pinch of fennel seeds (optional)

14 cups cold water

12 black peppercorns

2 cups dry white wine

continued

1. Wash the fish well under cold water. Combine all the ingredients except the peppercorns and wine in a stockpot and place over medium heat. As soon as it reaches a boil, lower the heat and simmer, uncovered, for 15 minutes, skimming the surface from time to time. Add the peppercorns and wine and simmer for 15 minutes more.

2. Strain through a large, fine sieve, returning the liquid to a clean pot. Over high heat, boil until reduced by about half.

3. If not using immediately, pour into a wide glass or ceramic bowl and allow to cool to room temperature. Store in a closed container, refrigerated, for up to 2 days or freeze for up to 2 months. Boil before using.

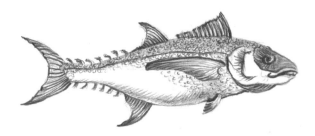

Passato di Pesce

Pureed Fish Broth

This richer fish broth cooks whole fish or chunks of fish, whose meat is then boned and pureed and added back to the broth. To the above recipe add 1 to 2 pounds of whole fish or chunks. If possible, include some fish heads (gills removed).

1. After the trimmings and fish have simmered for about 30 minutes (see preceding recipe), ladle the broth and fish into a strainer set over a bowl. Press the fish (using a large pestle works well) to extract its juices.

2. Place the fish on a plate and allow to cool slightly. Detach all the meat you can find attached to the larger bones. Discard the fins and the larger, harder bones. Strain, adding any liquid back to the broth.

3. There are several ways to puree the fish. Pass the picked-over fish and vegetables through the medium disc of a food mill; if using heads, use the coarse disc, then pass through the fine disc or sieve through a strainer.

Or, if you have carefully removed all the bones (feeling with your hands works best), add the picked-over fish and the vegetables to a food processor and process to a coarse puree. If you think there still may be bones, use a wooden spoon and push through a fine sieve. Readd to the broth and stir well to combine.

Preparing Fish Soups

Preparing fish soups is foremost knowing how to choose and cook the various types of fish and seafood. The differences in their texture and bone structure, and whether they are added whole, cut into large chunks, or filleted, determine how they are cooked.

Battuto Most of these soups call for the more delicate taste of a lighter olive oil. When the flavor of the oil is integral to the soup, the recipe specifies extra-virgin.

Sapori If you intend to sauté the fish, pat it dry to remove surface moisture, ensuring that the fish sears instead of steams. A well-sautéed *sapori* will give your soup a better flavor and texture. If you are adding fish and seafood to a simmering broth, add in stages so the soup stays at a constant simmer.

Brodo Though some recipes call for the deeper flavor of a prepared fish broth, most often the broth is obtained from the fish as it cooks and releases its juices. As might be expected, fish has a high water content and often very little other liquid needs to be added.

Wine is a natural complement to fish; it should be dry, never sweet.

Condimenti Usually just parsley is added, as its taste is considered the best herb to complement fish. Its leaves can be added chopped or whole.

The Recipes

Fish soups may be delicate first courses or substantial main dishes. This chapter divides the recipes to reflect these differences.

Zuppe di Pesce These main-course soups are usually made with several types of fish and require more planning and preparation. The recipes are written to serve 4 as a main course or 6 as a first or light main course.

Minestre e Zuppe di Pesce These lighter soups are usually prepared with only one type of fish. They are brothier and often have other main elements, such as vegetables or legumes.

Pesce/Fish Stews

These substantial zuppe di pesce *are considered* uno piatto unico, *a single dish that becomes both the first and second course. The recipes may vary according to local traditions and tastes, but they all derive from the humble fisherman using the remains of his daily catch; accordingly, the combinations of fish are never the same. The recipes in this chapter reflect some of the different ways of preparing* zuppe di pesce, *allowing you to add your own selection of the freshest fish.*

Fish and Seafood for Zuppe di Pesce The Adriatic Sea on Italy's eastern coastline and the waters surrounding Sicily are two of the richest parts of the Mediterranean. Their blue-green waters provide Italy with a myriad of fish and seafood. Most of these species, or similar ones, can be found in American markets. The types of fish, mollusks, and crustaceans found in Italian markets and on restaurant menus are not only numerous, but may be known by many different names depending on the region. And to further complicate matters, the English names can not only be numerous as well but often misleading.

Many fish soups call for the addition of several types of seafood and fish. This requires respecting how quickly each type cooks, with the firmest fish added first and the most delicate last. For the purposes of preparing a *zuppa di pesce,* this list is categorized by their types and cooking qualities. Where there is an equivalent Mediterranean fish, the Italian name is given. Substitutions include other names the fish may go by as well as varieties that may not be found in the Mediterranean, but their availability and similar characteristics make them fine choices.

Zuppe di pesce are best cooked in wide, heavy pots with sides that are not too high, which allows for easier handling. It is customary to serve the soup from the pot.

Pesce/Fish The fish used for *zuppe di pesce* are nonoily white-fleshed fish, preferably with firm flesh. Most of the fish that will go into the soup will come from the category called Firm White Fish. The more delicate Flaky White Fish break down more easily when cooked, but they can make fine additions.

The following is a list of the most commonly used fish and their respective families:

Bony "Broth" Fish These fish offer less in the way of meat, but their prominent bones and large heads make them the best choice when you want a flavorful broth.

> *Scorpion fish, gurnard (scorfano, capone)* *Scorfano rosso,* red rascasse or scorpion fish, is the principal ingredient in many Italian *zuppe di pesce* and is considered indispensable for French bouillabaisse. Unfortunately, it is rarely available. A good second choice is the family of fish known as the gurnards.
> **Substitute: sea robin, sculpin, bluemouth, weever, wrasse, John Dory, skate**

Firm White Fish These are the fish that will be most widely used. Fish from each and every group can be combined.

> *Dogfish* and *smooth hounds (gattopardo, palombo)* These small sharks may have flesh that looks like cod, but it is much firmer. Like all sharks, they lack a bony skeleton, so their bone-free meat is easy to cut up.
> **Substitute: sand or nurse shark, rock salmon, skate, grayfish, flake**

> *Grouper (cernia)* The many kinds of fish that go under the name of grouper offer excellent taste and a firm texture, making them excellent all-purpose fish.
> **Substitute: sand perch, coney, red snapper, orange roughy**

> *Halibut* Of all the more delicate flatfish, halibut is the most well suited for soups. With its texture firmer than sole or cod it makes a fine substitution. It is usually sold in steaks with the skin on, and its cooking time will vary with the thickness. To maintain the shape of the fish, leave its edible skin on.

Monkfish (rane pescatrice or coda di rospo) Often described as "poor man's lobster," monkfish has firm and tasty meat that holds up well in cooking.
Substitute: angler or lotte, tilefish

Rockfish Including an enormously large number of fish, rockfish have firm sweet fillets. Like grouper, they should be considered excellent all-around fish.
Substitute: ocean perch, Pacific red snapper, rock cod

Sea bass, red mullet (spigola, triglia) These fine-textured fish are purported to be the best tasting of the white fish, with sea bass claiming highest honors. The red mullet found in the Mediterranean is very similar to the North American goatfish. Depending on size, they are cut into chunks or added whole.
Substitute: weakfish, croaker, drum, redfish

Flaky White Fish These less firm fish tend to break up when cooked and are best used in combination with firmer fish. However, when firmer varieties are unavailable, they can still be fine substitutes. Always add after the firm-fleshed variety.

Cod, hake (merluzzo, nasello) These tender fish can be fine additions, with the flesh of cod and haddock being somewhat firmer than hake and whiting.
Substitute: haddock, pollack, scrod, coley, whiting

Sole (sogliola) This group encompasses a wide variety of fish renowned for their fine texture and delicate taste. Sole is usually sold already filleted and skinned; it needs to be cooked quickly, usually in under 5 minutes.

Whole Fish These 1- to 2-pound mild white-fleshed fish contain many small bones and are best added whole.

Porgy and sea bream (orata, dentice) These have a mild and sweet flavor. Make sure to have them gutted and scaled.
Substitute: scup, bream, and pink, white, or silver snapper

Crostaci/Crustaceans Technically these are animals with external skeletons and include the shrimp and lobster.

Crayfish (*arogosta*) These can be used for any recipe calling for lobster or shrimp. Unless they are very large, only the tail contains meat. To clean, twist the tail off the head and peel; if you prefer, devein the tail.

Lobster (*astice, aragosta*) The largest of the Mediterranean crustaceans is the spiny lobster. They have no claws; all of their meat is in the tail, which are generally marketed as frozen tails.
Substitute: rock lobster, Florida lobster, crayfish

Shrimp (*gambero, gamberetto, mazzancolla*) Most of the time, shrimp are frozen. If possible, substitute fresh crawfish, whose meat is similar. Frozen shrimp are better purchased unthawed, and if possible, unpeeled. Buy the largest shrimp you can and defrost in the refrigerator or in cold water.

Molluschi/Mollusks This classification includes such widely used bivalves as clams, mussels, and scallops as well as the family known as cephalopods, which includes cuttlefish, squid, and octopus. It is particularly important in soup cookery that the bivalves be well washed so that any grit doesn't find its way into the broth.

Mussels (*datteri di mare, mitili, cozze*) These require thorough cleaning. Start by leaving them to soak for 1 to 2 hours, changing the water several times, or sitting in a pot under slowly running water. Scrub the shells, pulling or scraping off the beards and any attached barnacles. Discard any with broken shells or ones whose shells remain open after being tapped. Also, discard any that feel unusually heavy; this probably indicates mud inside. Rinse thoroughly.

Clams (*vongole, telline, arselle*) The nearest equivalent to the Mediterranean *vongole veraci* (baby clams) are our carpet shell or bean clams. Alternatively, purchase the smallest littleneck clams. These require a good soaking and scrubbing under cold running water. Store live clams in a bowl in the refrigerator, never in a plastic bag or under water.

Octopus (polpo, moscardino) Most come frozen and already cleaned; defrost in the refrigerator or in cold water. To clean fresh octopus, turn the head inside out and cut away the eyes and innards. Push the "beak" through the other side and cut away. Fresh octopus need to be tenderized; beat with a mallet on each side for a couple of minutes. Peel the skin off, parboiling if necessary.

Scallops (canestrelli) The best are the sea, bay, and pink scallops. The smaller calico scallops, the ones usually sold in supermarkets, can be good if not over-cooked. In Italy, the coral-colored roe is eaten along with the white muscle.

Squid (calamari) and **cuttlefish** *(seppie)* These can be used interchangeably. They have a slightly chewy texture and become tough if overcooked. They are best cooked slowly over gentle heat or quickly over a higher heat. Buried within their flesh lies a vestige of skeleton that needs removing; cut off the head with the tentacles attached, then grasp the remainder of the head and pull it away from the body. Clean out the innards, pulling out the transparent quill. Pop the small hard beak out of the tentacles. Wash well under cold running water, pulling or scraping off the purple skin.

Buying and Storing The optimum taste and texture of fish only last a short time. Choosing top-quality fish and storing it properly is paramount to making any fish soup. Without a doubt, top-quality fresh fish is superior to its frozen counterpart. However, a top-quality frozen product is preferable to fish that is fresh in name only.

Fish purchased already cut into fillets or steaks are the easiest to deal with; however, many soups benefit from the more intense flavor created by the addition of bones, shells, or skin. If using whole fish, cut into pieces; it should be thoroughly cleaned with all the innards, gills, and fins and any trace of blood removed. With the exception of very thin-skinned fish, the scales almost always need to be scraped off.

Fresh The best way to buy fresh fish is to shop at a trustworthy and discerning fish store. Genuinely fresh fish looks fresh and has a clean, salty mild odor, never strong or "fishy." The skin should glisten and not be dull or what Italians refer to as *appassiti* (faded). Look for shiny eyes and gills that are moist and red colored. The body should be firm and the scales appear slippery. When choosing steaks or fillets, the flesh should be firm, unmarred, and have a moist but not watery appearance. Octopus and calamari should have a wet appearance. Shellfish should be alive and closed.

Very fresh fish can keep up to four days. Shellfish deteriorates much more rapidly and will keep for no more than a day. Store in the coldest part of your refrigerator. If you don't plan to cook it that day, place it wrapped in a dish with ice and refill the ice once or twice.

Frozen Fortunately, much of the fish called for in Italian soup cookery, the firmer-fleshed fish and mollusks, freeze the best. Avoid any that show signs of freezer burn or ice crystals. Defrost slowly in the refrigerator for 24 to 48 hours, never at room temperature or in the microwave. If you must speed up the process, use very cold water, never warm. Once the fish has defrosted it should be cooked promptly.

Brodetto alla Pescarese

Fish Soup of Pescara

serves: 4 to 6

cooking time:
35 minutes

$\mathcal{A}$bruzzi is well known for its fine saffron and liberal use of *peperoncino* (chili pepper). This easy-to-prepare fish soup uses both with great effect. Prepared with vinegar and tomatoes, this zesty *zuppa* is ladled over or accompanied with slices of toasted bread rubbed with garlic. Any seafood of your choice, such as squid or mussels, can be added to this basic recipe.

Battuto

6 tablespoons extra-virgin olive oil

Minced Together

1 large onion
2 garlic cloves
1 celery rib
1/3 cup fresh parsley leaves

Brodo

3/4 cup dry white wine
1 14-ounce can plum tomatoes,
    chopped with their juices
1/2 teaspoon crushed chili pepper
1/4 teaspoon ground saffron
1/2 cup red wine vinegar

1 cup hot water
Coarse salt

Sapori

2 1/2 to 3 pounds mixed fish fillets or
    steaks, such as sea bass, halibut,
    monkfish, sea bream, or cod,
    cleaned and cut into large pieces

Condimenti

4 to 6 slices of country bread
Extra-virgin olive oil
2 to 3 garlic cloves, peeled and left
    whole
1/3 cup chopped fresh Italian parsley

1. In a large heavy casserole, sauté the *battuto* over low heat until softened, stirring occasionally, for about 5 minutes.

continued

Minestre e Zuppe di Pesce / Fish Soups

2. Turn the heat to medium, add the wine, and cook until almost evaporated. Stir in the tomatoes, chili, and saffron and bring to a simmer. Add the vinegar, water, and a few pinches of salt and simmer, uncovered, for about 15 minutes more.

3. Add the fish, placing in a single layer, and enough hot water to just barely cover. Adjust the heat and gently simmer, covered, until the fish is tender, about 10 minutes.

4. In the meantime, drizzle the bread with oil and place under a broiler or fry until lightly colored on both sides. Rub one side with garlic.

Sprinkle the soup with abundant parsley and serve with the bread.

Variante: In neighboring Marche, a similar *brodetto* is prepared—*in bianco*—without tomatoes. Lightly coat the fish in flour before adding.

Brodetto di Pesce alla Veneta

Venetian Fish Soup

serves: 4 to 6

cooking time:
20 minutes

Venetian cooking is often described as being refined, the perfect description for this fish soup. Its preparation is done in several phases: a flavorful pureed fish broth is prepared, then choice fish are lightly simmered and sautéed with garlic and parsley before being added. This recipe comes from Fulvia Sesani, who adds her own unique touch by including sparkling white wine at the very end, giving this soup a wonderful freshness.

Sapori

$2^{1}/_{2}$ to 3 pounds fish chunks or
  fillets, monkfish, sea bass, or
  red mullet

Battuto

4 to 6 tablespoons olive oil

3 tablespoons unsalted butter

2 garlic cloves, left whole

$^{1}/_{4}$ cup chopped parsley

Brodo

3 to $4^{1}/_{2}$ cups Pureed Fish Broth
  (page 253) (see *Variante*)

Salt and freshly ground pepper

Condimenti

$^{1}/_{4}$ to $^{1}/_{2}$ cup sparkling white wine
  to taste (optional)

Crostini, fried in oil (page 42)

1. Bring a pot of lightly salted water to a boil. Add the fish a little at a time to maintain the water at a constant simmer. Cook until the fish is slightly undercooked. Lift out the fish and reserve. If there are any bones, remove them.

2. In a heavy casserole, combine the oil and butter over low heat. When the butter melts, add the garlic and parsley. Sauté until the garlic turns deep golden, then remove.

Turn the heat to medium, add the boned fish, and coat with the *battuto*. Sauté for 3 to 4 minutes.

3. Meanwhile, in a separate pot, bring the *brodo* to a simmer over moderate heat. Pour over the fish and simmer together for about 5 minutes. Add the salt and pepper to taste.

4. Take the soup off the heat. Add the wine to taste and serve with the crostini.

Variante: For a particularly delicate soup suitable for a first course or a light main course, add a light fish broth instead of the *passato*.

Burrida

Ligurian Fish Stew with Porcini

The cooking of Liguria is known for its expert pairing of *mare e monte,* tastes of the sea and land. In this splendid soup, mushrooms and pine nuts exquisitely combine with anchovy and fish. Traditionally, *burrida* is prepared using either several varieties of fish or only one very flavorful type. I like using monkfish whose taste and texture hold up so well, but any tasty firm white fish can be used with great results. Ligurians are said to be famous for being *parsimoniosi* and their leftover *burrida,* after being reduced by boiling, becomes a much appreciated pasta sauce.

A savory anchovy-porcini pesto is combined with white wine, making the addition of a fish broth unnecessary. Walnuts are commonly used in place of pine nuts, and though equally delicious, they require blanching to enable their bitter skins to be peeled. A Sardinian rendition of *burrida* adds capers to the pesto, which I think makes this soup even better.

1 ounce dried porcini mushrooms,
soaked in 1¹/₂ cups warm water
for 20 to 30 minutes

Brodo

2 tablespoons pine nuts
3 anchovy fillets, cut into small
pieces
1 cup dry white wine
6 capers

Battuto

3 to 4 tablespoons extra-virgin
olive oil
2 garlic cloves, peeled and left whole

Minced Together
1 medium onion
¹/₄ cup parsley leaves

3 ripe plum tomatoes, peeled, seeded,
and chopped (about ³/₄ cup)

Sapori

2¹/₂ *pounds (boned and trimmed*
weight) monkfish or mixed firm
fish (page 257), cut into medi-
um-sized chunks

Condimenti

4 to 6 slices of country bread

1. Lift out the mushrooms, rinse, and pat dry. Add to the bowl of a food processor and puree with the pine nuts, anchovy, a little wine, and capers until a paste is formed. Transfer to a small bowl and dilute with the remaining wine. Stir to combine well and reserve.

Strain the porcini soaking liquid through a filter and reserve.

2. In a large heavy casserole, combine the oil and garlic over medium-low heat. Sauté until the garlic is deep golden, lightly pressing down with the back of a fork to release its juices, then discard. Add the minced onion and parsley and sauté for 4 to 5 minutes. Add the tomatoes and continue to sauté, stirring, for 1 to 2 minutes.

3. Stir in the reserved anchovy pesto. When it reaches a simmer, add the fish (if using several varieties, add in order of their cooking time). Cover with the lid slightly ajar, and gently simmer until the fish is tender, about 15 minutes (see *Nota*). If more liquid is needed, add a little of the reserved porcini liquid.

4. Meanwhile, place the bread under the broiler and lightly toast. Distribute the fish in the individual bowls, ladle over with the broth, and serve with the bread.

Nota: If using a less firm fish, once it is added to the *battuto* leave it to cook without stirring and serve from the casserole dish.

Variante: In Genoa, a small amount of pancetta (1 ounce) and basil may be added to the *battuto*. Add cooked mussels, squid, and/or large shrimp to the monkfish.

Cacciucco

Tuscan Fish Stew

From the coastal strip known as La Versiglia comes Tuscany's most well-known fish soup, *cacciucco.* Its name comes the Turkish word *kucuk,* which means "a mixing together of various elements." And indeed it is; this substantial soup is brimming with mollusks, crustaceans, and several types of fish. Its broth is flavored with tomatoes, wine, and *zenzero,* the Tuscan name for chili pepper. This full-bodied recipe comes from the celebrated restaurant Romano in Viareggio where it is prepared with red wine and abundant chopped tomatoes.

When you are preparing this classic soup, the broth can be the simple addition of water; or for a richer-tasting soup a *passato di pesce,* "pureed fish broth," can be added. When using only water, I add onion, celery, carrot, and the juice of ½ lemon to the *battuto.*

Battuto
5 to 6 tablespoons extra-virgin olive oil
3 garlic cloves, chopped
1 small dried red chili pepper, seeded
    and crushed, or ½ teaspoon chili
    flakes

Sapori
1 pound (trimmed weight) mollusks,
    such as squid or small octopus,
    cleaned and cut into large pieces
¾ cup dry red wine
1½ cups peeled, seeded, and
    chopped ripe tomatoes
Coarse salt

2 to 2½ pounds mixed firm white fish
    (page 256), such as dogfish, rock
    fish, grouper, and red snapper, heads
    removed and cut into large chunks
4 crayfish or 8 ounces cooked lobster
    meat or shrimp or 1 pound mussels

Brodo
2 to 3 cups fish broth, water, or Passato
    di Pesce (page 253)

Condimenti
⅓ cup coarsely chopped parsley
4 to 6 slices of country bread
2 garlic cloves, peeled

1. In a heavy casserole (see *Nota*), sauté the *battuto* over low heat until the garlic lightly colors.

2. Add the mollusks and stir to coat well with the *battuto*. Splash with the wine and gently simmer for about 5 minutes. Add the chopped tomatoes, a few pinches of salt, and a ladleful of broth and gently simmer for 10 minutes.

3. After the fish has been thoroughly washed, pat dry with paper towels to remove excess moisture. Place the mixed fish chunks side by side on top of the mollusks and tomatoes. Place the crayfish on top and ladle over with 2 cups of *brodo*. Cover and cook, without stirring, until the fish is cooked through, about 15 minutes. If needed, add more *brodo*.

Lightly shake the pot to ensure the fish does not stick. If adding shrimp or cooked lobster, add at this point. If using mussels, cook separately (see page 258), drain well, and add without disturbing the fish. If more broth is needed, add some of the strained mussel broth.

4. Take the soup off the heat and sprinkle with the parsley. Allow to rest with the cover on while preparing the bread.

Lightly toast the bread under the broiler on both sides and rub one side with garlic. Place the bread in each soup bowl, distribute the fish and seafood on top, and ladle over with the soup broth.

Nota: Be sure to use a casserole that is wide enough to comfortably hold the fish in one layer. Traditionally, *cacciucco* is cooked in an earthenware pot over low heat and served in the pot it cooks in. Using a Flame Tamer helps to maintain a gentle heat.

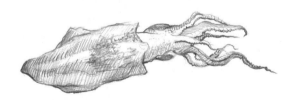

Ciuppin

Pureed Genovese Fish Stew

*U*ntil the turn of the century, along the Italian coast that borders the Côte d'Azur, *zuppa di pesce* was known as *bujabesca,* taking its name and character from the French bouillabaisse. The Genovese bestowed their own name, *ciuppin,* and fashioned their own distinct preparation, *una passato di pesce,* "a puree of fish." Both Gallic and Ligurian renditions are characterized by a rich broth made from a variety of rockfish, notably the red scorpion fish, known as *scorfano rosso* in Italy and *rascasse* in France.

Ciuppin has many interpretations, from the pureed *genovese* version to that of Ventimiligia, where a portion of the fish is left whole, making it more akin to bouillabaisse. Whatever its preparation, the basic recipe always includes a vegetable *battuto,* white wine, and a small amount of tomatoes; that is, unless you come from La Spezia, where it's claimed the best *ciuppin* is made without tomatoes and using only *scorfano.* All *ciuppin* are served over bread, browned in the local full and fruity olive oil.

Battuto

4 to 6 tablespoons olive oil

Minced Together
1 medium onion
1 medium carrot
1 medium celery rib
$^{1}/_{3}$ cup parsley leaves
2 garlic cloves

Brodo

$^{3}/_{4}$ cup dry white wine
1 cup peeled, seeded, and chopped
   ripe tomatoes
$6^{1}/_{2}$ cups boiling water

Sapori

3 to $3^{1}/_{2}$ pounds assorted fish, bony
   and firm white (page 256),
   cleaned and cut into chunks or
   see Nota
Coarse salt and freshly ground pepper

Condimenti

4 to 6 slices of crusty country bread,
   preferably slightly stale
Extra-virgin olive oil, preferably
   from Liguria
2 to 3 tablespoons chopped fresh
   parsley

1. In a wide heavy casserole, sauté the *battuto* over low heat until softened, about 5 minutes.

2. Raise the heat to medium, add the wine, and allow it to evaporate. Add the tomatoes and water and simmer, uncovered, for about 20 minutes.

3. Add the fish and season with salt and pepper. Cook at a slow but steady simmer for about 30 minutes. Strain the soup, adding its broth back to the pot and pressing the fish to extract its juices. Puree the fish as described on page 253 and add with its liquid back to the soup. Add the salt and pepper to taste and bring to a simmer.

4. Meanwhile, fry the bread slices in the oil or drizzle with oil and place under the broiler. Place a slice of bread in each soup plate and ladle over with the soup.
Sprinkle with the parsley and serve.

Nota: For a simpler preparation, use all boned fish (about 2 to 2½ pounds), which purees easily, and add a fish broth in place of water.

Variante: In Sardinia, a similar soup known as *cassola* is prepared. Replace the carrot and celery with 1 chopped chili pepper and 4 to 5 basil leaves. The fish can either be pureed or its boned flesh added back to the broth.

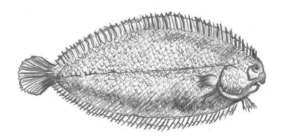

Zuppa di Cozze alla Napoletana

Mussel Soup with Tomatoes

Everything about this mussel soup is Neapolitan—plenty of tomatoes and garlic. Were this dish not preceded by the name *zuppa*, it might easily be mistaken for a big hearty bowl of mussels—which in fact it is. However, serving the mussels with all their cooking liquid and bread to soak up every last delicious bit earns this dish its namesake.

In Italy, the raw mussels are cooked in the tomato sauce (see *Nota*). To avoid the possibility of any sand in the broth, this recipe cooks the mussels separately, then adds them with their filtered juices. To save time, scrub and debeard the mussels while the tomato sauce is cooking.

Sapori

2 to 3 garlic cloves, chopped

4 tablespoons extra-virgin olive oil

*1¹/₂ cups peeled, seeded, and
    chopped tomatoes*

1 small dried red chili pepper

Juice of 1 lemon

*3 to 3¹/₂ pounds mussels, washed
    (page 258)*

Condimenti

4 to 6 slices of toasted country bread

2 garlic cloves, peeled

¹/₄ cup chopped parsley

1. Over low heat, sauté the garlic in the oil in a heavy-bottomed soup pot until pale golden, 3 to 4 minutes.

Add the tomatoes, chili pepper, and lemon juice and simmer for 25 to 30 minutes.

2. Shortly before the tomato sauce has finished cooking, cook the mussels separately or add to the sauce (see *Nota*). Place the washed mussels in a large pot, cover tightly, and cook over high heat until the shells open, 3 to 5 minutes. To ensure the mussels cook evenly, occasionally shake the pot to rotate. Drain the mussels, reserving the cooking liquid. Discard any unopened shells and strain the mussel juices and cooking liquid through a filter into the tomato sauce. Stir the mussels into the tomato broth and maintain over low heat while preparing the bread.

3. Toast the bread under the broiler on both sides and rub with the garlic. Sprinkle with the parsley and serve with the bread.

Nota: Place the cooked tomato sauce in a large pot, turn the heat to high, and add the mussels. Cover and cook until their shells open, 3 to 5 minutes.

Variante: In Liguria, *zuppa di cozze* is cooked without tomatoes. Sauté 1 small chopped onion with the garlic and replace the chili pepper with 2 to 3 tablespoons chopped parsley. Serve with plain toasted bread.

For a lighter *minestra*, sauté 1 medium chopped onion with 1 small diced green pepper and add to the tomato sauce. Shell the mussels and add to the sauce along with their strained juices. Garnish each serving with parsley and a few unshelled mussels.

Zuppa di Pesce all'Amalfitana
Fish Soup with Tomatoes

serves: 4 to 6

cooking time:
30 minutes

As I watched this soup being prepared I was struck by its sheer simplicity. Owner and chef Riccardo Rocchi proudly informed me that his restaurant, Da Gemma, is known for having the best *zuppa di pesce* on the Amalfi coast. He prepared it using the succulent sweet cherry tomatoes that are one of the many culinary delights of this region. At the end of cooking, the parsley leaves were added whole, in perfect tandem with the tomatoes. Serve with a good crusty bread to soak up its delicious broth.

continued

When you are making this soup, keep the broth at a very lively simmer so the oil and water emulsify. A wonderful tip that I once observed and use whenever I can is to use pasta cooking liquid as the *brodo;* it helps to bind the soup. Adding a pinch of pasta flour to the sautéed *battuto* will achieve similar results.

Battuto

1/2 cup olive oil

Chopped Together
2 to 3 garlic cloves
1/2 cup parsley leaves
Pinch of durum wheat pasta flour

Sapori

2 to 2 1/2 pounds assorted firm fish (page 256), such as dogfish or grouper, cut into large chunks, and small whole fish, such as porgy (page 257)
1 1/2 to 2 pounds cherry tomatoes or 2 1/2 cups peeled, seeded, and coarsely chopped tomatoes

1/4 teaspoon dried chili flakes

Brodo

3/4 cup dry white wine
2 to 3 cups lightly salted boiling water

Condimenti

1 1/2 pounds mussels, washed (page 258)
12 large shrimp, preferably uncooked, with shells
1/2 cup whole parsley leaves
4 to 6 slices of fresh crusty bread

1. In a heavy wide pot, combine the oil and chopped *battuto* and sauté over low heat until the garlic is golden. Add the flour and stir well to combine.

2. Add the *sapori.* Raise the heat to medium-high and ladle the wine and a little *brodo* over it. Simmer until the fish turns tender, 10 to 15 minutes. From time to time, ladle over with the water to keep the fish moist.

3. Turn the heat to high and add the mussels, shrimp and half the parsley. Cover the pot and cook until the mussels open, about 3 to 4 minutes (see *Nota*).
Sprinkle with the remaining parsley, and serve with the bread.

Nota: The mussels are cooked in the soup pot, with their juices becoming part of the broth. To avoid the possibility of sand in your final soup, they can be cooked separately and added with their strained cooking liquid (page 258).

Variante: In neighboring Capri, the fish of choice is tuna, cut into thin steaks. Sauté a thinly sliced onion in the oil before adding the chopped *battuto.* Season the fish with a little oregano and serve with slices of fried bread.

Zuppa di Pesce alla Maniera di Ustica

Fish Soup with Saffron and Fennel

serves: 4 to 6

cooking time:
1 hour

This splendid soup of mixed fish and seafood, scented with fennel, saffron, and a touch of brandy, shows the lingering French influence found in Sicilian cooking. This recipe adapts a similar soup prepared at London's River Cafe, where they added fresh fennel and potatoes.

continued

Battuto

5 to 6 tablespoons olive oil

Finely Chopped Together

1 medium onion

1 large leek, white and light green
    parts

3 garlic cloves

Sapori

2 fennel bulbs, quartered and cut
    into thin slices (about 2½ cups)

2 teaspoons fennel seeds

12 ounces small new potatoes,
    scrubbed

1½ cups pureed tomatoes

¼ teaspoon crushed saffron

2 fresh bay leaves or 1 dried

1 pound boneless fish fillets or thin
    steaks, such as red mullet,
    halibut, bass, or monkfish

Salt and freshly ground pepper

12 ounces large shelled shrimp,
    mussels, scallops, or lobster meat,
    coarsely chopped

Brodo

¼ cup brandy

2 to 3 cups water

Condimenti

¼ cup chopped fresh Italian parsley

4 to 6 slices of toasted country bread

1. In a large heavy casserole, sauté the *battuto* over low heat until the garlic is pale golden, 3 to 4 minutes.

2. Add the fennel and fennel seeds and stir to coat well for 2 to 3 minutes. Add the potatoes, tomatoes, saffron, and bay leaves. Cover and gently simmer until the fennel is tender, 20 to 30 minutes, stirring occasionally. Remove the bay leaves.

3. Add the fish and season with a few pinches of salt and pepper. Turn the heat to medium-high and add the brandy and enough water to barely cover the fish. Simmer, uncovered, until the fish just turns tender, 5 to 10 minutes. Add the shrimp or mussels, cover, and cook until done, 4 to 5 minutes more.

4. Sprinkle with abundant parsley and serve with the toasted bread.

Zuppa di Vongole Veraci

Clam Soup

serves: 6

cooking time:
10 minutes

*I*talian clams come in many sizes and shapes, but the finest are the small *vongole veraci,* known for their tender and succulent meat. Cooked in white wine, this simple preparation is designed to show off these preferred clams. Although you are most likely to find this soup prepared around Naples, this recipe comes from Tuscany where chili pepper is added and the bread is rubbed with garlic.

Sapori	*Condimenti*
3¹/₂ pounds small clams	*6 slices of country bread, preferably*
	slightly stale
Brodo	*2 garlic cloves, peeled*
4 to 6 tablespoons olive oil	*3 to 4 tablespoons chopped fresh*
2 garlic cloves, crushed	*Italian parsley*
2 small dried chili peppers	
2 cups dry white wine	

1. Soak the clams for 5 minutes in salted cold water. Drain and readd the clams to cold water. Scrub each clam under running water to make sure all the sand comes out and readd to the water. Change the water until no more sand appears. Discard any clams that stay open.

2. Over moderate heat, combine the oil, garlic, and chili pepper in a large heavy pot. Sauté until the garlic turns golden, then remove both the garlic and pepper. Turn the heat to high and add the wine. When the wine starts to reduce, after about 2 minutes, add the clams and stir to coat well. Cover the pot and cook, stirring occasionally to rotate the clams. As the clams open, remove and place in a bowl.

continued

Drain the remaining clams and strain the cooking liquid through a dampened piece of cheesecloth or paper towel. Over low heat, add the liquid to a clean pot and add the clams just long enough to heat through.

3. Meanwhile, toast the bread on both sides and rub with garlic. Place a slice in each soup bowl and cover with the clams and their liquid. Sprinkle with the parsley and serve.

Variante: In Rome, clams known as *telline* are used. Finely chop 1 anchovy fillet and ½ cup parsley leaves with the garlic, then add ½ cup pureed tomatoes. Add the clams, cooked in water, with their strained liquid and cook over very low heat for about 10 minutes. Serve with a garnish of crostini.

Pesce/Fish Soups

These lighter minestre *and* zuppe *are usually prepared using only one type of fish, often complemented by the addition of vegetables. The recipes range from the traditional regional soups to the artistry of the Italian chef, using his imagination to create soups of great originality and taste. Though generally served as a first course, these fish soups often make wonderful light main dishes or, with the addition of more fish, can easily be made into more substantial main-course soups.*

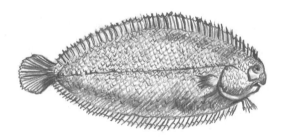

Crema di Farro con Gamberi

Pureed Farro Soup with Shrimp

This elegant soup was created by Giampiero Gemignani. Lucca's grain of choice, *farro,* "spelt," is cooked in cannellini broth and pureed to form a velvety back-drop for the shrimp. If possible, add the shrimp raw so as it cooks it flavors the broth. If fresh marjoram is unavailable, its dried form will not do; substitute fresh basil or flat-leaf parsley. If you have no cannellini broth at hand, I have used canned beans to create the broth.

1 cup (7 ounce) farro or spelt,
   soaked 4 hours or overnight and
   drained

Brodo
1 14-ounce can cannellini beans,
   undrained
5½ cups water
1 cube vegetable stock
1 teaspoon tomato paste

Battuto

Minced Together
1 small carrot

1 small celery rib
2 teaspoons minced fresh rosemary
   or 1 teaspoon dried

Sapori
Salt
8 to 12 ounces fresh or frozen uncooked
   shrimp (shelled weight), deveined
   and cut in half lengthwise

Condimenti
Crostini, sautéed in butter (page 42)
2 teaspoons minced fresh marjoram

1. To prepare the cannellini broth, combine the *brodo* and *battuto* in a soup pot and simmer over medium heat, covered, for about 30 minutes. Strain, returning the liquid to the soup pot.

2. Bring the bean broth to a lively simmer, then add the *farro.* Lower the heat and simmer, covered, until the grains are very tender, about 40 minutes. Remove from the heat. Strain the *farro* and readd its liquid back to the soup pot. Reserve about one quarter of the *farro* and pass the remainder through a vegetable mill or puree in a food processor until smooth. Add the pureed *farro* back to the broth and stir to combine well.

3. Bring the soup to a gentle simmer. It should have the density of heavy cream; if it's needed, add a little hot water. Add the salt to taste and the reserved *farro.* Add the shrimp and gently simmer until cooked, 5 to 10 minutes.

In the meantime, fry the crostini in butter, preferably in a nonstick pan. Stir the marjoram into the soup and serve with the crostini.

Variante: Substitute ⅔ cup pearled barley for the *farro* or use only cannellini beans to create the creamy broth. Pass all of the beans (3 cups) through a food mill.

Minestra di Lenticchie con Gamberi

Lentil and Shrimp Soup

"*T*astes of the land and tastes of the sea"—*sapori di terra* and *sapori di mare*—are commonly used in Italian cooking. In this delicious soup, pureed lentils are the perfect foil for shrimp sautéed in garlic-flavored oil.

Battuto

2 tablespoons extra-virgin olive oil

Finely Chopped Together

1 small onion

1 medium celery rib

1 medium carrot

Sapori

1⅛ cups (7 ounce) brown lentils, rinsed well

1 medium potato, peeled and chopped

½ cup peeled, seeded, and chopped tomatoes

Brodo

3 cups fish broth and 2½ cups water

3 to 4 fresh sage leaves or 2 dried

Salt and freshly ground pepper

Condimenti

4 tablespoons extra-virgin olive oil

1 garlic clove, peeled and lightly crushed

12 ounces shrimp (trimmed weight), cleaned and chopped if large

½ cup coarsely chopped parsley

1. In a heavy-bottomed soup pot, sauté the *battuto* over medium-low heat for 5 minutes.

2. Add the *sapori* and stir to coat well.

3. Add the *brodo* and simmer, covered, for 1 hour. Reserving about ½ cup of the lentils, coarsely puree the rest of the soup. Readd to the pot along with the whole lentils. Add the salt and pepper to taste and maintain over low heat while preparing the *condimenti*.

4. Combine the oil and garlic in a frying pan, preferably nonstick. Sauté over medium heat until the garlic turns golden, then press with the back of a fork to extract its juices and remove. Turn the heat to high, add the shrimp and parsley, and fry for 3 to 4 minutes.

Serve the soup garnished with the shrimp and parsley.

Variante: Replace the shrimp with squid cut into rings or short pieces.

Pasta con Broccoli in Brodo d'Arzilla

Pasta and Broccoli Soup in Skate Broth

serves: 4

cooking time:
2 hours

Skate has a mild but insistent flavor that combines beautifully with broccoli in this centuries-old popular Roman soup. Sold as wings, skate is part of the shark family and has no bones; when cooked, its meat easily separates from the cartilage. Traditionally, the whole skate is first simmered, lending its flavor to the broth, and then removed and served separately (see *Variante*). Untraditionally, I cook the skate until it falls apart and then add its flesh back to the soup. This soup can be prepared using a fish stock instead of skate, but then it will be missing its special glutinous texture and lovely taste.

continued

Brodo

2 pounds skate, scrubbed with salt
    and water to remove any slime
1 garlic clove, peeled and left whole
1 small onion, peeled and left whole
1 celery rib, left whole
6 cups cold water
Pinch of coarse salt

Battuto

3 tablespoons extra-virgin olive oil

Minced Together
2 garlic cloves
$1/2$ cup parsley leaves
Pinch of chili pepper flakes
1 anchovy fillet

Sapori

4 ripe plum tomatoes, peeled, seeded,
    and chopped (about $3/4$ cup)
$1/2$ cup dry white wine
Salt and freshly ground pepper
8 to 10 ounces small broccoli florets
    (about $2^1/2$ cups) (see Nota)

Condimenti

1 cup (5 to 6 ounces) short pasta,
    preferably conchiglie (small
    shells)
Freshly grated Parmesan cheese
    (optional)

1. Over moderate heat, bring the *brodo* to a boil. Lower the heat and simmer, covered, for about 1½ hours. Strain, reserving the cooking liquid and the skate separately.

2. In a heavy-bottomed soup pot, sauté the *battuto* over very low heat, stirring often, for 5 to 7 minutes.

3. Raise the heat to medium, add the tomatoes and wine, and cook until about half evaporated. Add the reserved cooking liquid plus enough water to equal about 4 cups and simmer for about 15 minutes.

Meanwhile, pull the cooked skate flesh from the cartilage and push through a sieve into the soup; if you prefer a thinner soup, omit this step.

Season with salt and pepper to taste and add the broccoli.

4. Bring the soup to a boil, add the pasta, and simmer until *al dente,* adding some boiling water if needed. Serve with the Parmesan cheese.

Nota: Cavolbroccolo is the "broccoli" of choice. Its taste is reminiscent of both broccoli and cauliflower. If you prefer, prepare this soup with all or part cauliflower.

Variante: Cook the skate in half water and half fish broth and lift out after about 20 minutes. Serve the skate as a second course, drizzled with oil and lemon and garnished with a *battuto* of minced parsley and garlic.

Zuppa di Pesce Spada

Swordfish Soup

On Sicily's eastern shore, swordfish is prepared in numerous ways, with capers being a favorite accompaniment. Distinctive in its taste, this soup is served with crusty bread to enjoy all its broth. Other steaklike fish such as halibut or tuna make fine alternatives.

Battuto
4 tablespoons extra-virgin olive oil

Finely Chopped Together
1 small celery rib
1 small onion
2 garlic cloves
1 tablespoon capers, drained

Sapori
1 cup chopped ripe tomatoes
Juice of 1/2 lemon

1 1/2 to 2 pounds swordfish, cut into
   large chunks
1/2 teaspoon thyme
2 teaspoons chopped fresh oregano or
   rosemary or 1 teaspoon dried
Coarse salt and freshly ground
   pepper

Brodo
1 cup dry white wine
1 to 2 cups water

1. In a heavy casserole, sauté the *battuto* over low heat, stirring occasionally, for 4 to 5 minutes.

2. Add the tomatoes and lemon juice and cook for about 10 minutes. Add the swordfish and sprinkle with the herbs, a pinch of salt, and a grinding of pepper.

3. Over moderate heat, cover the fish with the *brodo* and simmer until the fish is tender, 10 to 15 minutes. Add more water if needed and salt and pepper to taste.
   Arrange the fish in each plate and ladle over with the broth.

Zuppa di Porri e Cozze Gratinate
Leek and Mussel Soup au Gratin

serves: 4

cooking time:
45 minutes

*T*he Gran Ristorante Quadri, which has the enviable position of overlooking Venice's Piazza San Marco, was the perfect setting to enjoy this elegant soup. Its recipe was created by chef Graziano Bettiol, who aptly expressed, "I wanted something different." A perfect orchestration of leeks and mussels topped with fresh tomatoes and a gratiné of Emmentaler and Parmesan cheese, its combination of tastes is irresistible.

Battuto
1 tablespoon olive oil
3 tablespoons butter, unsalted
1 1/2 pounds leeks, thinly sliced
   (about 6 cups) (see Nota)
Coarse salt

Brodo
4 1/2 cups light Classic Meat Broth
   (page 36) or substitute

Sapori
3 tablespoons olive oil
2 garlic cloves, peeled and flattened

1/4 cup Cognac or Armagnac
2 pounds fresh mussels, washed
   (page 258)

Condimenti
1/4 cup grated Parmesan cheese
1/4 cup grated Emmentaler cheese
Ciabatta or French bread, cut into
   1/3-inch slices
2 ripe fresh tomatoes, peeled, seeded,
   and diced
2 teaspoons chopped fresh chives or
   1 teaspoon dried

1. Over medium heat, combine the oil and butter in a heavy-bottomed soup pot. When the butter melts, add the leeks, sprinkle with a few pinches of salt, and sauté, stirring often, until wilted, about 5 minutes. Add a little broth, cover, and sweat for 10 to 15 minutes, stirring occasionally.

continued

2. Bring the *brodo* to a boil and add to the leeks. Lower the heat and simmer, partially covered, for about 30 minutes.

3. Meanwhile, prepare the mussels. Over medium heat, add the oil and garlic to a large pot. When the garlic is golden, add the Cognac and cook until reduced by half. Over high heat, add the mussels, cover the pot, and cook until the mussels open, 3 to 4 minutes, shaking the pot to rotate the mussels. Drain, discarding any mussels that have not opened. Remove the mussels from their shells, pulling off any remaining beards, and reserve.

4. Mix the grated cheeses together. Cover the bread slices with ample cheese and place under the broiler until they bubble, without browning.

To serve, ladle the soup into each bowl, add the mussels, garnish with the tomatoes and chives, and top with the slices of grilled bread.

Nota: The entire leek is used except for the very end where the stalk turns dark green and its leaves start to splay. I find it easiest to slice the leeks in a food processor, using the thinnest slicing blade; then using a salad spinner, wash the leeks in several changes of water and spin until well drained.

serves: 4

cooking time:
40 minutes

Zuppa di Tonno Fresco con Peperoni

Soup of Fresh Tuna and Peppers

This colorful soup of tuna, tomatoes, sweet peppers, and potatoes was created by Franco Colombani of Del Sole in Piacenza. A hot pepper oil heightens the tastes of this elegant soup, which is equally delicious made with any meaty, firm fish such as swordfish or mako shark.

Condimenti

2 tablespoons olive oil

2 tablespoons water

1 teaspoon crushed chili pepper

Battuto

4 to 6 tablespoons extra-virgin
  olive oil

1/2 cup finely chopped onion or shallot

Sapori

12 ounces fresh tuna (trimmed
  weight), cut into about 1-inch
  chunks

1 cup dry white wine

2 medium waxy potatoes, cut into
  small dice (about 1 1/4 cups)

4 plum tomatoes, peeled, seeded, and
  chopped (about 1 scant cup)

Coarse sea salt

1 small sweet red pepper, cut into
  short, very thin strips
  (about 3/4 cup)

1 small sweet green pepper, cut into
  short, thin strips

Brodo

2 to 3 cups boiling water

Salt and freshly ground pepper

1. Over moderate heat, simmer the *condimenti* in a small saucepan for about 10 minutes. Strain and reserve.

2. Over medium-low heat, sauté the *battuto* in a heavy-bottomed soup pot until the onion is golden, 3 to 4 minutes.

3. Pat the tuna with paper towels to remove excess moisture. Add to the *battuto* and sauté until the tuna lightly colors on all sides.

Turn the heat to medium-high and add the wine. After about 5 minutes, when its alcohol has evaporated, add the potatoes, tomatoes, and a pinch of salt. Add enough boiling water to cover and cook, partially covered, at a gentle but steady simmer for about 20 minutes.

4. Add the sweet peppers and 1 teaspoon of the hot oil. Cook until the peppers are tender, about 10 to 15 minutes, adding enough water to keep the vegetables just barely covered. Season to taste with salt, pepper, and the hot oil and serve.

Minestre di Carne

Meat Soups

Unlike other types of soup there is no great tradition of meat soups. After all, meat was hardly the typical foodstuff of the peasant. Perhaps these soups were created by the more prosperous borghesia, "middle class," who stretched their more costly ingredients into soups that were both nourishing and satisfying. Most probably these soups simply display the Italian know-how of taking scraps of leftover meat and turning them into delicious soups.

What we do know is that many of these soups were created from the broth obtained from slowly simmering the less tender cuts of meat served as the second course. And as with other types of food, meats display their regionality. Tuscany is known for its fine beef, Emilia-Romagna for its pork, and Rome for its tender lamb.

Similarly as with *zuppe di pesce,* many of these soups are easily adapted to a main dish. Others, such as the *brodetto alla romana,* not only make wonderful broth soups, but the meat that creates the broth becomes the second course.

serves: 4

cooking time:
30 minutes

Minestra di Pollo

Chicken Soup

*P*repared as a way of using leftover bits of chicken, *zuppe* and *minestre di pollo* are simple combinations of broth, chicken, and a few flavorings. This recipe comes from the Veneto where rice and fresh sage are added.

Battuto

2 tablespoons olive oil

1 tablespoon unsalted butter

Minced Together

1 small onion, or 2 to 3 shallots

1/4 cup parsley leaves

1 to 2 fresh sage leaves

Sapori

1 chicken breast (about 8 ounces),
   cut into small pieces

2 to 3 chicken livers, cut into small
   pieces

Brodo

1 teaspoon tomato paste

5 1/2 cups Chicken Broth (page 39)

Coarse salt and freshly ground
   pepper

Condimenti

3/4 cup long-grain or risotto rice

1 tablespoon unsalted butter

Freshly grated Parmesan cheese

1. Over moderate heat, combine the oil and butter in a heavy saucepan. When the butter melts, add the minced *battuto* and sauté for 3 to 4 minutes.

2. Add the *sapori,* stir well to coat, and sauté for a few minutes.

3. Dilute the tomato paste in 1 cup hot chicken broth and add. Season with a generous pinch of salt and a twist of pepper and simmer for about 30 minutes.

4. Meanwhile, in a separate soup pot, bring the remaining chicken broth to a boil. Add the rice and cook, covered, until *al dente*, about 15 minutes. Add more boiling broth or water if needed. Stir in the cooked *sapori,* butter, and 1 tablespoon Parmesan cheese.

Serve with the Parmesan.

Variante: For a *zuppa*, add 2 ounces minced pancetta to the *battuto* and replace the sage with 2 teaspoons of rosemary. Add a splash of white wine to the chicken, omit the rice, and serve over toasted bread.

Zuppa di Mais e Pollo con Peperoni

Corn and Chicken Soup with Roasted Peppers

serves: 4

cooking time:
40 minutes

When living in Verona during the eighties, I was delighted when I saw fresh corn make its first appearance in Piazza dell'Erbe. My enthusiasm was short-lived when I learned it was grown predominantly for cattle feed. In fact, it wasn't sweet corn but a variety known as dent corn. Its higher starch and lower sugar content may have required longer cooking, but it yielded a splendid soup. I make this soup often using fresh or frozen corn. It becomes a wonderful main dish simply by increasing the amount of chicken.

continued

Battuto

3 to 4 tablespoons unsalted butter

²/₃ cup sliced leeks, white and light
green parts

Sapori

4 ears of corn, kernels removed
(about 4 cups fresh or frozen)

Brodo

4¹/₂ cups light Chicken Broth
(page 40) or water and
1¹/₂ chicken stock cubes

Condimenti

Salt

1 pound chicken breast, cut into
slivers

¹/₄ cup mascarpone or ¹/₃ cup heavy
cream

2 sweet peppers, red and yellow,
roasted and cut into slivers
(see Nota)

Freshly ground pepper

1. Over low heat, melt the butter in a heavy-bottomed soup pot. Add the leeks and sauté until softened, stirring often, for 5 to 7 minutes.

2. Add the corn and stir to coat well with the *battuto* for 2 to 3 minutes.

3. Meanwhile, bring the *brodo* to a boil, then add. Cook the soup at a lively simmer, partially covered, for about 15 minutes.

Using an immersion blender or food processor, coarsely puree the soup.

4. Add the salt to taste and return the soup to a lively simmer. Add the chicken and cook until done for about 8 minutes. Take off the heat, add the mascarpone, and stir well to combine.

Add the roasted peppers and serve hot or at room temperature with a twist of pepper.

Nota: Roast the peppers at the beginning to allow enough time to steam and cool them before removing their skins (page 180).

Zuppa di Anatra

Duck Soup

A final touch of a fine balsamic vinegar, though imperceptible in its taste, is indispensable to this elegant soup. The original recipe from Del Sole in Piacenza makes the broth from the duck carcass; however, I find that using lean duck breast and classic broth, even stock cubes, yields excellent results. Zucchini skins and cabbage are added at the end of cooking, so it's essential they be very finely shredded, not only to cook quickly, but for their refined appearance. This recipe calls for about one pound of duck breast and can be served as a light main-course soup; for a first course you may want to use slightly less meat.

Battuto
3 tablespoons extra-virgin olive oil
2 leeks, white and light green parts,
 thinly sliced (about $3/4$ cup)
$1^1/2$ medium onions, thinly sliced
 (about $3/4$ cup)

Minced Together
1 medium carrot
2 medium celery ribs

Brodo
$4^1/4$ cups Classic Meat Broth
 (page 36) or substitute

Sapori
1 to $1^1/4$ pounds trimmed duck
 breast, all fat removed, cut into
 small bite-sized pieces
$1/2$ cup dry white wine
5 to 6 Savoy cabbage leaves, white
 ribs removed, very finely
 shredded (about $2^1/2$ cups)
Skins from 2 medium zucchini
 (see Nota)
Salt and freshly ground pepper

Condimenti
Balsamic vinegar

1. Over moderate heat, combine the oil, leeks, and onion in a heavy-bottomed soup pot. Sauté until soft, stirring frequently, for about 5 minutes. Add the minced *battuto* and sauté for 5 minutes more, stirring often. Meanwhile, in a separate saucepan, bring the *brodo* to a simmer.

2. Add the duck and wine. Cook, stirring from time to time, until the wine evaporates, about 5 minutes. Add the simmering *brodo* and cook for 10 minutes. Add the cabbage and zucchini and cook for about 10 minutes more. Add the salt and pepper to taste.

3. Take the soup off the fire. Add the balsamic vinegar in ½-teaspoon increments, always tasting after each addition, and serve.

Nota: Only the skins of the zucchini are used, so they must be firm and unblemished. Use a vegetable peeler and, if need be, cut into finer strips with a knife.

Minestra di Gulasch
Goulash Soup from Trento

serves: 4

cooking time:
2 hours

Once part of the Austro-Hungarian empire, Trentino-Alto Adige displays its German heritage in this spiced winter soup of meat and potatoes. Made with either veal or beef, its simple preparation only requires a long and gentle cooking to prevent the meat from drying out. Increasing the amount of meat yields a fine main-course dish.

Soups of Italy

Battuto

1 tablespoon extra-virgin olive oil

2 tablespoons unsalted butter

Finely Chopped Together

1 medium-large onion

2 garlic cloves

2 ounces pancetta

Sapori

12 ounces lean stewing veal or beef,
  cut into $1/2$-inch cubes

$1/4$ teaspoon ground cumin

1 teaspoon chopped fresh marjoram
  or $1/2$ teaspoon dried

$1/2$ teaspoon sweet paprika

Pinch of hot paprika (optional)

Grated rind of $1/2$ lemon

$3/4$ cup dry white wine or marsala

12 ounces potatoes, peeled and cubed

Brodo

6 cups hot water

2 tablespoons tomato paste

1 teaspoon coarse salt

1 bay leaf

Condimenti

Crostini (page 42) or 1 to 2
  tablespoons chopped fresh parsley

1. Over medium-low heat, combine the oil and butter in a heavy-bottomed soup pot. When the butter melts, add the chopped *battuto* and sauté until soft, 3 to 4 minutes.

2. Add the meat, season with the cumin, marjoram, paprikas, and lemon rind, and stir to combine well. Sauté, stirring often, for about 10 minutes. Raise the heat to medium, splash over with the wine, and cook until nearly evaporated.

3. Add the *brodo,* adjust the heat, and cook at a slow simmer, covered, for about 45 minutes. Taste from time to time and add more spices to taste. Add the potatoes and gently simmer, covered, for 45 minutes more.

4. Serve with the crostini or garnished with the parsley.

Pasta in Brodo con Polpettine

Pasta in Broth with Meatballs

*T*his Silician recipe combines delicate veal meatballs and pasta in an egg and cheese-thickened meat broth. The pasta of choice is a large macaroni that cooks in the same amount of time as the *polpettine*. I add a touch of fresh lemon juice to sharpen the flavors.

Sapori

2 slices of white bread, crusts
   removed

1/2 cup milk

8 ounces lean ground veal

1 egg

2 tablespoons grated Parmesan
   cheese

1 tablespoon grated pecorino
   Romano cheese

1/3 cup chopped parsley

Brodo

6 cups Classic Meat Broth (page 36)
   or Chicken Broth (page 39) or
   substitute

Salt

5 to 6 ounces large tubular pasta,
   such as large macaroni or
   rigatoni

Condimenti

2 eggs

2 tablespoons grated Parmesan
   cheese

2 tablespoons grated pecorino cheese

Juice of 1/2 lemon

Twist of freshly ground pepper

1. In a bowl, soak the bread in the milk until soft. Drain and squeeze the bread and readd to the bowl. Add the remainder of the *sapori* and mix well. Form into small round balls and place on a plate (if the mixture is too soft, add some bread crumbs).

2. Add the broth to a soup pot and bring to a lively simmer. Season with salt to taste and add the pasta and meatballs. Cook over moderate heat, gently stirring with a wooden spoon from time to time, until the pasta is *al dente,* 10 to 12 minutes. Take the pot off the heat.

3. Meanwhile, combine the *condimenti* in a bowl and whisk until well amalgamated. Adding a little at a time, whisk in about 1 cup of hot broth.

Stir the egg mixture into the soup, being careful not to break up the meatballs, and serve.

Brodetto di Verza e Carne

Pork and Cabbage Soup

serves: 4

cooking time:
1½ hours

Friuli-Venezia Giulia, the easternmost part of Italy, may be considered one region but gastronomically it remains two. Friuli is characterized by its homey cooking, while Venezia Giulia displays a more cosmopolitan cooking closely linked to its historical ties with central Europe. Flavored with herbs, wine, and vinegar, this rustic soup of cabbage and fresh pork combines the best of both worlds.

Lunch or dinner *alla friulana* is almost inconceivable without a *minestra,* and often it is the sole dish. The word *brodetto* is usually reserved for this region's hearty fish stews. Here it indicates a dish substantial enough to merit that name.

continued

Brodo

6 cups water

1 teaspoon coarse salt

1 bay leaf

Sapori

1 medium-large Savoy cabbage,
  outer leaves removed, cored and
  shredded (about 8 cups or 12
  ounces trimmed weight)

8 ounces pork loin, cut into small
  bite-sized pieces

2 ounces pancetta, cubed

1/2 cup dry white wine

1 tablespoon white wine vinegar

Battuto

2 tablespoons extra-virgin olive oil

2 tablespoons unsalted butter

Finely Chopped Together

1 medium onion

1 medium carrot

1 medium celery rib

1 garlic clove

2 to 3 fresh sage leaves

1 tablespoon fresh rosemary or
  1 teaspoon dried

1. In a soup pot, bring the *brodo* to a boil. Add the cabbage and simmer for about 15 minutes.

2. Meanwhile, in a heavy saucepan, sauté the *battuto* over medium-low heat. Add the pork and pancetta and sauté until lightly colored. Add the wine and vinegar and cook until evaporated, 10 to 15 minutes. Stir into the cabbage and gently simmer, covered, for 1 hour.

Minestra di Verza e Luganighe con Riso
Savoy Cabbage and Sausage Soup with Rice

serves: 4

cooking time:
1 hour

Sausage is the perfect complement to cabbage, a combination that makes a wonderful main-course soup. This recipe comes from the Veneto where the cabbage of choice is Savoy and the sausage *luganega,* a coarsely ground mild pork sausage.

Battuto
2 tablespoons extra-virgin olive oil
2 tablespoons butter

Minced Together
1 medium onion
1 small carrot
1 medium celery rib
2 garlic cloves
1/3 cup parsley leaves

Sapori
1 small Savoy cabbage, cored and
    thinly shredded (4 to 5 cups)

Coarse salt
Freshly ground pepper
8 to 10 ounces fresh mild pork
    sausage

Brodo
5 1/2 cups Classic Meat Broth
    (page 36) or substitute

Condimenti
2/3 cup (5 ounces) long-grain rice
Freshly grated Parmesan cheese

1. Over medium-low heat, combine the oil and butter in a heavy-bottomed soup pot. When the butter melts, add the minced *battuto* and gently sauté, stirring occasionally, until the vegetables are soft, about 5 minutes.

2. Add the cabbage and stir until it starts to wilts, 2 to 3 minutes. Season with salt and pepper and add one ladle of *brodo.* Adjust the heat and simmer, covered, for about 45 minutes.

continued

3. In the meantime, prepare the sausages. Prick the skins with a fork and cook in boiling water for about 5 minutes. Allow to cool, then cut into about ¾-inch-long pieces. When the cabbage has finished cooking, place the sausages on top and cover with the remaining *brodo*.

4. Over moderate heat, bring to a lively simmer, then carefully add the rice so as not to disturb the sausage. Add a little boiling water if too much of the *brodo* has evaporated. Cook, covered, until the rice is tender, about 15 minutes.

Season with a grinding of pepper and 2 heaping tablespoons of Parmesan cheese. Serve with the Parmesan.

Variante: For *zuppa di verza alla milanese,* replace the oil with butter and the garlic and parsley with 6 sage leaves. Omit the rice and serve over slices of toasted or fried bread.

Index

D

duck soup, 293–294
dumplings in broth, 121–122
  mortadella, 130
  porcini, 124
  ricotta, 125
  spinach, 123

E

egg(s):
  and broth soup, 128
  in broth soup with omelet,
    126–127
  in dumplings in broth,
    121–122
  in little rice balls in broth, 120
  in mortadella dumplings in
    broth, 130
  and Parmesan strands in broth,
    129
  in pasta in broth with
    meatballs, 296–297
  in porcini dumplings in broth,
    124
  soup, mushroom, tomato and,
    238–239
  in summer zucchini soup,
    187–188
  in yellow pepper bread soup,
    237–238
eggplant:
  in minestrone napoletano,
    107–108
  and porcini minestrone,
    95–97
  soup with cannellini beans,
    141–142
  in springtime minestrone with
    pesto, 105–106
Emmentaler in leek and mussel
    soup au gratin, 285–286
endive:
  in layered chicory soup,
    209–210

  in springtime minestrone of
    legumes, 98–100

F

farro:
  minestrone of beans and,
    94–95
  and radicchio soup, 223
  soup, pureed, with shrimp,
    278–279
  soup of Lucca, 224–225
  soups, barley, rice and,
    217–234
  soup with chicken, 221–222
fava bean(s), *see* bean(s), fava
fennel, 166
  in bread and vegetable soup,
    241–242
  and chickpea soup, 68–69
  fish soup with saffron and,
    273–274
  in layered chicory soup,
    209–210
  and leek soup with sun-dried
    tomato pesto, 167–168
  pasta and bean soup with herbs
    and, 55–56
  Sardinian minestrone with,
    109–110
  and shallot soup with arugula,
    168–169
finocchio, 166; *see also* fennel
fish:
  broth, 251–253
  broth, basic, 251–252
  broth, pureed, 253
  soup, Venetian, 262–263
  soup of Pescara, 261–262
  soups, 249–287
  soup with saffron and fennel,
    273–274
  soup with tomatoes, 271–273
  stew, pureed Genovese, 268–269
  stew, Tuscan, 266–267
  stews, 255–276

  stew with porcini, Ligurian,
    264–265
  see also specific fish and shellfish
Florentine red onion soup,
    172–173
fontina, layered cabbage soup
    with, 246–247
frufella, 143–144
fumetto di pesce, 251–252
funghi, 189–199
  porcini secchi, 44

G

gardener's soup, 146–147
garlic:
  in fish soup of Pescara,
    261–262
  in fish soup with saffron and
    fennel, 273–274
  in fresh basil sauce, 45–46
  in lentil soup with red onions,
    84–85
  in mussel soup with tomatoes,
    270–271
  in pasta and chickpea soup,
    70–71
  in tomato and bread soup,
    244–245
  in Tuscan fish stew, 266–267
  in Tuscan pasta and bean soup,
    62–63
  in twice-cooked Tuscan
    minestrone and bread soup,
    102–104
  in vegetable broth, 40–41
garmugia, 144–146
Genovese:
  fish stew, pureed, 268–269
  rice soup, 232–233
  vegetable soup, 148–149
gerstsuppe, 217–218
giardiniera, 146–147
gnocchetti:
  in brodo ai funghi, 124
  di ricotta in brodo, 125

in layered chicory soup,
209–210
in lentil and chestnut soup,
82–83
lentil and pumpkin soup with,
81–82
in minestrone of beans and
farro, 94–95
in minestrone with rice,
100–102
in mushroom and bean soup,
196–197
in pasta and bean soup,
Lombardy style, 58–59
in pasta and bean soup, Veneto
style, 66–67
in pasta and bean soup with
cauliflower, 60–61
in pasta and bean soup with
tomatoes, 57–58
in pasta and chickpea soup,
70–71
in piquant cabbage and bean
soup, 143–144
in rice and chestnut soup,
226–227
pancotto:
calabrese con cicoria, 240–241
alla foggiana, 241–242
con rucola e patate, 243
pane, 235–247
paparot, 212
pappa al pomodoro, 244–245
Parmesan:
and egg strands in broth, 129
in fresh basil sauce, 45–46
in leek and mussel soup au
gratin, 285–286
in pasta in broth with
meatballs, 296–297
rind, 44
in stuffed lettuce soup in broth,
131–133
Parmigiano-Reggiano in
mortadella dumplings in
broth, 130

passato:
di peperone giallo, 178–179
di pesce, 253
pasta:
and artichoke soup, 156–157
broccoli soup with, 159–160
and broccoli soup in skate
broth, 281–283
in broth with meatballs,
296–297
in chickpea and fennel soup,
68–69
and chickpea soup, 70–71
and leek soup, 170–171
mushroom and sausage soup
with, 195–196
pea and prosciutto soup with,
176–177
and spinach soup with pesto,
210–211
in springtime minestrone of
legumes, 98–100
in springtime minestrone with
pesto, 105–106
pasta:
con broccoli in brodo d'arzilla,
281–283
in brodo col polpettine, 296–297
e ceci, 70–71
pasta and bean soups:
with cauliflower, 60–61
with fennel and herbs, 55–56
Lombardy style, 58–59
with tomatoes, 57–58
Trento style, 64–65
Tuscan, 62–63
Veneto style, 66–67
pasta e fagioli (pasta e fasoi),
54–67
alla erbe, 55–56
all'ischitana, 57–58
alla lombarda, 58–59
minestra di, alla siciliana, 60–61
alla toscana, 62–63
alla trentina, 64–65
alla veneta, 66–67

pea(s):
fresh, and rice soup, 233–234
in gardener's soup, 146–147
and lettuce soup with mint,
cream of, 175–176
in minestrone with rice,
100–102
and prosciutto soup with pasta,
176–177
in springtime minestrone of
legumes, 98–100
in springtime soup of Lucca,
144–146
in squash and herb
minestrone, 111–113
pear, cold cream soup of arugula
and, 204
pecorino Romano:
in fresh basil sauce, 45–46
in pasta in broth with
meatballs, 296–297
pepper, bell, pureed yellow, soup,
178–179
pepper(s), sweet:
corn and chicken soup with
roasted, 291–292
minestrone with roasted,
107–108
pureed cauliflower soup with
red, 163–164
roasted, soup with chicken,
179–180
soup, 138–139
soup of fresh tuna and,
286–287
pepper, yellow, bread soup,
237–238
pesto:
fennel and leek soup with sun-
dried tomato, 167–168
pasta and spinach soup with,
210–211
sauce, green minestrone with,
114–115
springtime minestrone with,
105–106

sausage:
  in bread and chicory soup, 240–241
  in chickpea and fennel soup, 68–69
  in minestrone of beans and farro, 94–95
  and mushroom soup with pasta, 195–196
  in Sardinian minestrone with fennel, 109–110
  and Savoy cabbage soup with rice, 299–300
  in Tuscan onion soup, 173–174
shallot and fennel soup with arugula, 168–169
shrimp:
  in fish soup with saffron and fennel, 273–274
  in fish soup with tomatoes, 271–272
  and lentil soup, 280–281
  pureed farro soup with, 278–279
skate broth, pasta and broccoli soup in, 281–283
sorrel in barley and garden vegetable soup, 219–220
spinach:
  in barley and garden vegetable soup, 219–220
  dumplings in broth, 123
  in green minestrone with pesto sauce, 114–115
  and pasta soup with pesto, 210–211
  and polenta soup, 212
  in rice and leek soup, 228–229
  in springtime minestrone of legumes, 98–100
  in summer zucchini soup, 187–188
springtime:
  minestrone of legumes, 98–100
  minestrone with pesto, 105–106

soup, 151–152
soup of Lucca, 144–146
squash and herb minestrone, 111–113
stew(s), fish, 255–276
  with porcini, Ligurian, 264–265
  pureed Genovese, 268–269
  Tuscan, 266–267
stock cube broth, 38
stracciatella alla romana, 128
summer zucchini soup, 187–188
Swiss chard in lettuce soup, 213
swordfish soup, 284

T

tomato(es):
  in artichoke and pasta soup, 156–157
  in bread and chicory soup, 240–241
  in bread and vegetable soup, 241–242
  in chickpea and fennel soup, 68–69
  in eggplant soup with cannellini beans, 141–142
  fish soup with, 271–273
  in fish soup with saffron and fennel, 273–274
  in leek and mussel soup au gratin, 285–286
  and leek soup, 181–182
  in minestrone with rice, 100–102
  mussel soup with, 270–271
  in porcini and eggplant minestrone, 95–97
  pureed Genovese fish stew, 268–269
  sauce, 46
  soup, mushroom, egg and, 238–239
  in springtime minestrone of legumes, 98–100

in swordfish soup, 284
in Tuscan fish stew, 26–267
in vegetable broth, 40–41
in yellow pepper bread soup, 237–238
tomato(es), plum:
  and bread soup, 244–245
  in fish soup of Pescara, 261–262
  in Ligurian fish stew with porcini, 264–265
  in minestrone napoletano, 107–108
  pasta and bean soup with, 57–58
  in pasta and broccoli soup in skate broth, 281–283
  in Sardinian minestrone with fennel, 109–110
  in soup of fresh tuna and peppers, 286–287
  in springtime minestrone with pesto, 105–106
tomato, sun-dried, pesto, fennel and leek soup with, 167–168
Trento:
  goulash soup from, 294–295
  style, pasta and bean soup, 64–65
tuna, soup of peppers and fresh, 286–287
turkey in dumplings in broth, 121–122
turnip(s):
  and carrot soup, cream of, 161
  in gardener's soup, 146–147
  and rice soup, Milanese style, 230–231
  in vegetable broth, 40–41
Tuscan:
  fish stew, 266–267
  minestrone and bread soup, twice-cooked, 102–104
  onion soup, 173–174
  pasta and bean soup, 62–63